Bootstrap 4 Cookbook

Over 75 recipes to help you build elegant and responsive web applications with Bootstrap 4

Ajdin Imsirovic

BIRMINGHAM - MUMBAI

Bootstrap 4 Cookbook

First published: June 2017

Production reference: 1290617

Published by Packt Publishing Ltd.
Livery Place
35 Livery Street
Birmingham
B3 2PB, UK.

ISBN 978-1-78588-929-5

www.packtpub.com

Credits

Author
Ajdin Imsirovic

Reviewer
Zlatko Alomerovic

Commissioning Editor
Ashwin Nair

Acquisition Editor
Siddharth Mandal

Content Development Editor
Arun Nadar

Technical Editor
Rashil Shah

Copy Editor
Dhanya Baburaj

Project Coordinator
Ritika Manoj

Proofreader
Safis Editing

Indexer
Francy Puthiry

Graphics
Jason Monteiro

Production Coordinator
Shantanu Zagade

About the Author

Ajdin Imsirovic has been working with frontend technologies, as well as web and print design, for almost 2 decades. He is an accomplished video course creator and an author of a wildly popular video course series on Bootstrap development. He is dedicated to making the learning of the practical use of HTML, CSS, and JavaScript technologies with Bootstrap easy and fruitful. In his *Bootstrap 4 Cookbook*, he brings together all his experience while teaching Bootstrap development to make a must-read guide to the newest version of Bootstrap.

> *I would like to thank my family for their selfless support. Without their help, I would not have achieved nearly as many of my goals as I have. Also, I would like to thank all my colleagues in the IT companies I have worked for who inspired me to learn and grow both as a person and as a developer. You know who you are.*

About the Reviewer

Zlatko Alomerovic is a full-stack web developer with a degree in electrical engineering and computer science. Zlatko likes solving problems with Ruby. He chooses Ruby on Rails, ReactJS, and EmberJS to get the job done. In his spare time, he gives lessons in Judo, teaches kids to code, explores Blockchain, Bitcoin, and Ethereum technologies. Check out his website at www.ingneer.com.

To my beautiful wife, thank you for your endless support and understanding.

www.PacktPub.com

For support files and downloads related to your book, please visit `www.PacktPub.com`.

Did you know that Packt offers eBook versions of every book published, with PDF and ePub files available? You can upgrade to the eBook version at `www.PacktPub.com` and as a print book customer, you are entitled to a discount on the eBook copy. Get in touch with us at `service@packtpub.com` for more details.

At `www.PacktPub.com`, you can also read a collection of free technical articles, sign up for a range of free newsletters and receive exclusive discounts and offers on Packt books and eBooks.

`https://www.packtpub.com/mapt`

Get the most in-demand software skills with Mapt. Mapt gives you full access to all Packt books and video courses, as well as industry-leading tools to help you plan your personal development and advance your career.

Why subscribe?

- Fully searchable across every book published by Packt
- Copy and paste, print, and bookmark content
- On demand and accessible via a web browser

Customer Feedback

Thanks for purchasing this Packt book. At Packt, quality is at the heart of our editorial process. To help us improve, please leave us an honest review on this book's Amazon page at `https://www.amazon.com/dp/178588929X`.

If you'd like to join our team of regular reviewers, you can e-mail us at `customerreviews@packtpub.com`. We award our regular reviewers with free eBooks and videos in exchange for their valuable feedback. Help us be relentless in improving our products!

Table of Contents

Preface   1

Chapter 1: Installing Bootstrap 4 and Comparing Its Versions   7

  Introduction   7
  Installing Bootstrap 4 to Cloud9 IDE using npm   8
    Getting ready   9
    How to do it...   10
  Installing Bootstrap 4 to Cloud9 IDE via Git   12
    Getting ready   13
    How to do it...   13
  Installing Bootstrap 4 Jekyll-powered docs   15
    Getting ready   15
    How to do it...   15
  Customizing the styles of Bootstrap 4 docs   17
    Getting ready   17
    How to do it...   17
  Making custom Grunt tasks in Bootstrap 4   20
    Getting ready   20
    How to do it...   21
    How it works...   24
  Comparing Bootstrap 4 versions with Bower   24
    Getting ready   24
    How to do it...   24
  Installing Bootstrap 4 to our Cloud9 IDE with Bower   27
    Getting ready   28
    How to do it...   28

Chapter 2: Layout Like a Boss with the Grid System   29

  Introduction   29
  Preparing a static server with Bootstrap 4, Harp, and Grunt   30
    Getting ready   30
    How to do it...   30
  Deploying your web project with Surge   41
    Getting ready   42
    How to do it...   42
  Splitting up our Harp project into partials   44

How to do it...	44
Using containers with margin and padding utility classes	46
Getting ready	46
How to do it...	46
How it works...	48
Explanation of the data-* HTML5 attributes	48
There's more...	49
Renaming main.scss	49
Adding columns in a row	51
Getting ready	51
How to do it...	51
Making col-* classes work	53
Getting ready	53
How to do it...	53
Building a simple page with the default grid	55
Getting ready	56
How to do it...	56
How it works...	60
Building a real-life web page example with the default grid	60
Getting ready	61
How to do it...	61
How it works...	66
Chapter 3: Power Up with the Media Object, Text, Images, and Tables	67
Introduction	67
Extending the text classes of .display-* and adding hover effects with Hover.css	69
Getting ready	69
How to do it...	70
How it works...	73
Creating comment sections using media objects	74
Getting ready	74
How to do it...	74
How it works...	77
Enriching text content with Bootstrap typography classes	78
Getting ready	79
How to do it...	79
How it works...	80
Customizing the blockquote element with CSS	81
Getting ready	81

How to do it...   81
How it works...   83
Extending the blockquote styles with Sass   84
Getting ready   84
How to do it...   84
How it works...   85
Aligning text around images   85
Getting ready   85
How to do it...   86
How it works...   87
Wrapping text around rounded images   88
Getting ready   89
How to do it...   89
How it works...   90
Styling a pricing section using Bootstrap's default table classes   91
Getting ready   91
How to do it...   92
How it works...   95

Chapter 4: Diving Deep into Bootstrap 4 Components   97
Creating custom alerts and positioning them in the viewport   97
Getting ready   98
How to do it...   98
How it works...   100
Making full-page modals   101
Getting ready   101
How to do it...   101
How it works...   104
Altering the behavior of popups using tether options   105
Getting ready   105
How to do it...   105
How it works...   107
Controlling the color and opacity of ToolTips using Sass variables   108
Getting ready   108
How to do it...   108
How it works...   110
Using Bootstrap's Sass mixins to create custom buttons   110
Getting ready   110
How to do it...   111
How it works...   113

Adjusting the rounding of corners on buttons and button groups	113
Getting ready	114
How to do it…	114
How it works…	116
Controlling the number of card columns on different breakpoints with SCSS	116
Getting ready	117
How to do it…	117
How it works…	119
Making cards responsive	120
Getting ready	120
How to do it…	120
How it works…	122
Easily positioning inline forms	122
Getting ready	122
How to do it…	123
How it works…	125
Chapter 5: Menus and Navigations	127
Adding Font Awesome to Bootstrap navbar	127
Getting ready	128
How to do it…	128
How it works…	130
Placing a single Bootstrap navbar dropdown to the right	131
Getting ready	131
How to do it…	131
How it works…	134
Centering navbar links	134
Getting ready	134
How to do it…	134
How it works…	137
Making a transparent navbar on a darker background	137
Getting ready	137
How to do it…	137
How it works…	141
Creating a Navbar with Icons and Flexbox	141
Getting ready	141
How to do it…	142
How it works…	146
Adding another row of links to the navbar	146

Getting ready	146
How to do it…	146
How it works…	151
Adding Yamm3 Megamenu images to a navbar dropdown	152
Getting ready	152
How to do it…	152
How it works…	157
Adding Yamm3 Megamenu list of links to a navbar dropdown	157
Getting ready	157
How to do it…	158
How it works…	162
Chapter 6: Extending Bootstrap 4	163
Introduction	164
Converting checkboxes into Toggles with Bootstrap Toggle plugin	164
Getting ready	164
How to do it…	165
How it works…	166
Onboarding users with Shepherd	167
Getting ready	167
How to do it…	167
Toggling visibility of password fields with custom jQuery code	170
Getting ready	170
How to do it…	170
How it works…	173
Extending the functionality of select elements with Bootstrap Select plugin	174
How to do it…	175
How it works…	176
Customizing select boxes with Select2 plugin	177
Getting ready	177
How to do it…	177
How it works…	179
Adding input sliders with Rangeslider.js	179
Getting ready	179
How to do it…	180
Allowing users to easily add dates to your input fields with jQuery UI Datepicker	182
How to do it…	182
Converting plain tables into sophisticated data tables with Bootgrid	186

Getting ready	186
How to do it…	187
How it works…	189
Navigating easily with simple-sidebar jQuery plugin	**189**
Getting ready	189
How to do it…	189
How it works…	193
Adding fully customizable notifications with Notify.js	**193**
Getting ready	194
How to do it…	194
How it works…	195
Integrating a fancy modal using animatedModal.js	**195**
Getting ready	196
How to do it…	196
How it works…	198
Making pagination dynamic with the jQuery Pagination plugin and simplePagination.js	**199**
Getting ready	199
How to do it…	199
How it works…	202
Validating forms with svalidate.js	**202**
Getting ready	202
How to do it…	202
How it works…	204
Adding a rating system using jQuery Bar Rating plugin	**204**
Getting ready	205
How to do it…	205
How it works…	206
Chapter 7: Make Your Own jQuery Plugins in Bootstrap 4	207
Introduction	**207**
Making the simplest possible jQuery plugin	**207**
Getting ready	208
How to do it…	208
How it works…	210
Making the plugin customizable with the extend() and each() methods	**211**
Getting ready	211
How to do it…	211
How it works…	213
Integrating a simple CSS Class Replacement plugin with Bootstrap 4	**216**

Getting ready	216
How to do it...	216
How it works...	218

Chapter 8: Bootstrap 4 Flexbox and Layouts | **219**

Introduction	219
Breakpoint-dependent switching of flex direction on card components	220
Getting ready	220
How to do it...	220
How it works...	221
Letting cards take up space with the .flex-wrap and .col classes	223
Getting ready	223
How to do it...	223
How it works...	225
Adding any number of columns with Flexbox	226
Getting ready	227
How to do it...	227
How it works...	228
Combining numbered .col classes with plain .col classes	230
Getting ready	230
How to do it...	230
How it works...	231
Working with card layouts and the Flexbox grid	232
Getting ready	232
How to do it...	232
How it works...	236
Center-aligning cards on wider viewports only	239
Getting ready	239
How to do it...	239
How it works...	242
Positioning nav-tabs with Flexbox	243
Getting ready	243
How to do it...	244
How it works...	248

Chapter 9: Workflow Boosters | **251**

Introduction	251
Customizing Bootstrap builds by cherry-picking Sass partials	251
Getting ready	252
How to do it...	252

How it works...	255
Cleaning up unused CSS with UnCSS and Grunt	256
Getting ready	256
How to do it...	257
How it works...	258
Removing CSS comments with the grunt-strip-CSS-comments plugin	259
Getting ready	259
How to do it...	259
How it works...	260

Chapter 10: Creating a Blog with Jekyll and Bootstrap 4 | 261 |

Making Jekyll work with Bootstrap 4	261
Getting ready	261
How to do it...	262
How it works...	265
Splitting Jekyll files into partials	266
Getting ready	266
How to do it...	267
How it works...	271
Making Jekyll blog-aware	271
Getting ready	272
How to do it...	272
How it works...	277
Deploying your blog to the web with GitHub	278
Getting ready	279
How to do it...	279
How it works...	281

Chapter 11: Bootstrap 4 with ASP.NET Core | 283 |

Starting a project in ASP.NET Core and Bootstrap 4 in Visual Studio 2017	283
Getting ready	283
How to do it...	284
How it works...	286
Migrating the default web page of a .NET Core project from Bootstrap 3 to Bootstrap 4	287
Getting ready	287
How to do it...	288
How it works...	291
Working with Bower, Sass, and Grunt in our .NET Core project	291

Getting ready	292
How to do it...	292
How it works...	296

Chapter 12: Integrating Bootstrap 4 with React and Angular 297

Introduction	297
Integrating Bootstrap 4 with React	298
Getting ready	298
How to do it...	299
How it works...	303
Replacing the Default Styles in Angular 2 QuickStart with Bootstrap 4 CDN CSS	303
Getting ready	303
How to do it...	304
How it works...	307
Integrating Angular 4 and Bootstrap 4 with the help of ng-bootstrap	308
Getting ready	308
How to do it...	308
How it works...	310
Conclusion	311
Next Steps	311

Index 313

Preface

Bootstrap is the most popular frontend framework today. One of its advantages is that it is easy to start working with. In fact, it is possible to simply get the links for Bootstrap's CSS and JS files over a **Content Delivery Network (CDN)**, and you are good to go!

However, under this low barrier to entry lies a whole world of possibilities to put together websites in Bootstrap 4.

For example, there are additional ways to install Bootstrap, such as cloning it via Git or installing it via NPM or Bower.

There are also several ways to work with it, with increasing levels of complexity. For example, you can simply use its CSS as is. You can also use its SCSS files, which come with the default installation in Bootstrap 4. By tweaking SCSS files, using includes, variables, and mixins (Sass functions), you can create highly customized layouts.

Bootstrap 4 also includes the amazing Flexbox grid, which gives us a whole new way of working with layouts.

When working with any frontend technology, there are always a lot of repetitive tasks, such as minification and Sass-to-CSS compilation. These tasks are performed using task runners, and in this book, the focus is on Grunt. Although working with task runners does add an extra layer of complexity to our development with Bootstrap 4, it also increases our efficiency as frontend developers.

Bootstrap 4 is powered by Sass and jQuery, so due care was given to covering the use of both technologies in this book's recipes.

In the last few chapters, we are looking into integrating Bootstrap with Jekyll, GitHub's serverless blog system, and deploying it onto GitHub pages. We also take a look at using GitHub with .NET Core, Angular, and React.

One of the more ambitious goals of this book was to truly build on the available Bootstrap 4 documentation, rather than just reiterate the existing concepts. If some of the recipes seem a bit too advanced, understanding Bootstrap's official documentation might be a prerequisite for better understanding. Also, each recipe was built to be as straightforward and beginner-friendly as possible, while remaining self-contained.

The world of the frontend web development is changing fast, and it is becoming increasingly complex. In the recipes of this book, emphasis was given to catering for this complexity in a manner that would suit developers of various levels of expertise.

What this book covers

Chapter 1, *Installing Bootstrap 4 and Comparing Its Versions*, covers various ways of installing Bootstrap 4 and using it with an online IDE, Cloud9, or on your local machine. It also explains the workings of Grunt, Sass, and Jekyll, which are all used in the full local installation of Bootstrap 4.

Chapter 2, *Layout Like a Boss with the Grid System*, deals with the basics of using containers, rows, and columns, as well as building a couple of real web page examples. All these are done with the help of Harp and Grunt.

Chapter 3, *Power Up with the Media Object, Text, Images, and Tables*, helps you to create a comments section, customize the blockquote element, align text and images, and work with tables.

Chapter 4, *Diving Deep into Bootstrap 4 Components*, explores customizing alerts, modals, popups, and tooltips. It also looks into using Bootstrap's Sass mixins to customize components such as cards and buttons.

Chapter 5, *Menus and Navigations*, explains various ways of working with navbars.

Chapter 6, *Extending Bootstrap 4*, teaches you a number of ways to extend Bootstrap 4 with the help of jQuery plugins. Some of the recipes in this chapter extend the functionality of the existing components, such as the pagination component. Others deal with integrating nonexisting components, such as the datepicker on input fields.

Chapter 7, *Make Your Own jQuery Plugins in Bootstrap 4*, covers the foundations of making your own jQuery plugins. Since jQuery is such an integral part of Bootstrap, knowing its inner workings can help in both extending the existing plugins and making Bootstrap 3 plugins work with Bootstrap 4. Also, understanding the basics of how jQuery plugins work opens a new way of working with interactions in your Bootstrap-powered websites.

Chapter 8, *Bootstrap 4 Flexbox and Layouts*, outlines the amazing changes brought to Bootstrap 4 by the inclusion of the CSS flexbox specification into the framework itself. It is an alternative way of building websites and stepping away from float-based layouts.

Chapter 9, *Workflow Boosters*, focuses on the use of Sass partials, cleaning up unused CSS in your custom Bootstrap 4 builds, and stripping comments. We'll see how the Grunt task runner is used to achieve these goals, which will help in understanding the general way Grunt tasks are structured and run.

Chapter 10, *Creating a Blog with Jekyll and Bootstrap 4*, lists the process of including Bootstrap 4 Sass with Jekyll, splitting it into partials, making Jekyll blog-aware, and finally, serving your Bootstrap 4 Jekyll blog online with the help of GitHub Pages.

Chapter 11, *Bootstrap 4 with ASP.net Core*, takes a look at the process of setting up Bootstrap 4 Sass and Grunt in Visual Studio 2017 and ASP.net Core 1.0/1.1.

Chapter 12, *Integrating Bootstrap 4 with React and Angular*, discusses the integration of Bootstrap 4 with React and Angular. Component-based frontend development is not the future--it is already here. Understanding at least the basics of how it works is crucial. This chapter aims to remove the complexity of these two frameworks and the complexity of their setup, and strives to show how to make these frameworks work with Bootstrap 4 in a simple and understandable manner.

What you need for this book

In almost all the chapters of this book, the following technologies are used:

- Node and NPM
- Bower
- Ruby and Jekyll
- Git and Git Bash
- Harp

Chapter 11, *Bootstrap 4 with ASP.net Core*, is specific because it requires that you have an installation of Visual Studio 2017 Community Edition and a .NET Core 1.x installation.

Chapter 12, *Integrating Bootstrap 4 with React and Angular*, requires installations of React and Angular via npm.

Who this book is for

This book is for both new and seasoned frontend developers. With so many technologies being affected by Bootstrap and affecting Bootstrap itself, there are plenty of ways of putting them together and working with them, as can be seen throughout this book's recipes.

These are just some of the technologies this book covers: CSS and HTML, jQuery, Sass, Harp, Jekyll, Node and NPM, Bower, Grunt, Angular, React, and .NET Core. All of these technologies are looked at through the lens of Bootstrap 4 framework.

Conventions

In this book, you will find a number of text styles that distinguish between different kinds of information. Here are some examples of these styles and an explanation of their meaning. Code words in text, database table names, folder names, filenames, file extensions, pathnames, dummy URLs, user input, and Twitter handles are shown as follows: "After running the npm install command, a number of dependencies will be installed, just as listed in the package.json file."

A block of code is set as follows:

```
{
  "name": "customGrunt",
  "version": "",
  "devDependencies": {
    "grunt": "~1.0.1",
    "grunt-contrib-copy": "^1.0.0"
  }
}
```

Any command-line input or output is written as follows:

```
cd && cd workspace
touch Gruntfile.js package.json
```

New terms and **important words** are shown in bold. Words that you see on the screen, for example, in menus or dialog boxes, appear in the text like this: "Click on **Create a new workspace**, and a new page will appear with only a few things to fill in."

Warnings or important notes appear in a box like this.

 Tips and tricks appear like this.

Reader feedback

Feedback from our readers is always welcome. Let us know what you think about this book-what you liked or disliked. Reader feedback is important for us as it helps us develop titles that you will really get the most out of. To send us general feedback, simply e-mail feedback@packtpub.com, and mention the book's title in the subject of your message. If there is a topic that you have expertise in and you are interested in either writing or contributing to a book, see our author guide at www.packtpub.com/authors.

Customer support

Now that you are the proud owner of a Packt book, we have a number of things to help you to get the most from your purchase.

Downloading the example code

You can download the example code files for this book from your account at http://www.packtpub.com. If you purchased this book elsewhere, you can visit http://www.packtpub.com/support and register to have the files e-mailed directly to you. You can download the code files by following these steps:

1. Log in or register to our website using your e-mail address and password.
2. Hover the mouse pointer on the **SUPPORT** tab at the top.
3. Click on **Code Downloads & Errata**.
4. Enter the name of the book in the **Search** box.
5. Select the book for which you're looking to download the code files.
6. Choose from the drop-down menu where you purchased this book from.
7. Click on **Code Download**.

Once the file is downloaded, please make sure that you unzip or extract the folder using the latest version of:

- WinRAR / 7-Zip for Windows
- Zipeg / iZip / UnRarX for Mac
- 7-Zip / PeaZip for Linux

The code bundle for the book is also hosted on GitHub at `https://github.com/PacktPubl ishing/Bootstrap-4-Cookbook`. We also have other code bundles from our rich catalog of books and videos available at `https://github.com/PacktPublishing/`. Check them out!

Errata

Although we have taken every care to ensure the accuracy of our content, mistakes do happen. If you find a mistake in one of our books-maybe a mistake in the text or the code-we would be grateful if you could report this to us. By doing so, you can save other readers from frustration and help us improve subsequent versions of this book. If you find any errata, please report them by visiting `http://www.packtpub.com/submit-errata`, selecting your book, clicking on the **Errata Submission Form** link, and entering the details of your errata. Once your errata are verified, your submission will be accepted and the errata will be uploaded to our website or added to any list of existing errata under the Errata section of that title. To view the previously submitted errata, go to `https://www.packtpub.com/book s/content/support` and enter the name of the book in the search field. The required information will appear under the **Errata** section.

Piracy

Piracy of copyrighted material on the Internet is an ongoing problem across all media. At Packt, we take the protection of our copyright and licenses very seriously. If you come across any illegal copies of our works in any form on the Internet, please provide us with the location address or website name immediately so that we can pursue a remedy. Please contact us at `copyright@packtpub.com` with a link to the suspected pirated material. We appreciate your help in protecting our authors and our ability to bring you valuable content.

Questions

If you have a problem with any aspect of this book, you can contact us at `questions@packtpub.com`, and we will do our best to address the problem.

1
Installing Bootstrap 4 and Comparing Its Versions

In this chapter, we will cover:

- Installing Bootstrap 4 to c9 IDE using npm
- Installing Bootstrap 4 to c9 IDE via git
- Installing Bootstrap 4 Jekyll-powered docs
- Customizing the styles of Bootstrap 4 docs
- Making custom Grunt tasks in Bootstrap 4
- Comparing Bootstrap 4 versions with Bower
- Installing Bootstrap 4 to c9 IDE with Bower

Introduction

In this chapter, you will learn how to install Bootstrap 4 via the command line on c9.io. The reason for using Cloud9 IDE in this recipe book is that since it is a web-based IDE, it requires you to have only an internet connection and a web browser to run the IDE, which is available at `https://c9.io`.

Once you access c9.io via your web browser, you have at your fingertips a fully functional Ubuntu virtual machine. The nice thing about this setup is, if you are, for example, running Windows on your computer, you can avoid many of the setup headaches this would usually entail, such as downloading and installing Ruby and Node. Using a web-based IDE is also great if there is a need to work with multiple computers, or if collaboration is important.

Finally, because of its ease of use and a plethora of features, using Cloud9 IDE will make it easier for the less advanced readers to follow along in some of the more complex recipes.

 If you decide to use Windows after all, the recipes in this chapter will include notes that are Windows-specific to make it possible to still follow along. In case there are no notes that relate to how things work in Windows, it is implied that the commands work in Windows as well.

In this chapter, besides learning about how to install Bootstrap 4 via the command line, we will also examine the way it utilizes Grunt for commonly performed tasks, Sass to modularize our CSS, and Jekyll to implement a serverless copy of the official Bootstrap docs.

However, all this comes at a cost. In order to use all that Bootstrap 4 has to offer, we need to be familiar with all of these technologies. For more advanced users, this should not be a problem. Still, an ambitious goal of this book is to be useful for as wide an audience as possible, including less advanced users, while at the same time to still prove valuable to those with more experience, as a quick reference to the brand new version of Bootstrap.

Therefore, in this chapter, we will cover the recipes that deal with this advanced setup and explain in simple terms the workings of Grunt, Sass, and Jekyll.

 Note that the official Bootstrap website (`getbootstrap.com`) runs on GitHub's Jekyll platform.

Installing Bootstrap 4 to Cloud9 IDE using npm

This recipe will cover the required steps for installation of Bootstrap 4 via npm on Cloud9 IDE. In order to begin working on this recipe, it is assumed that you have already registered a `c9.io` account.

Getting ready

To begin, log in to your `c9.io` account, which will open your Cloud9 IDE dashboard:

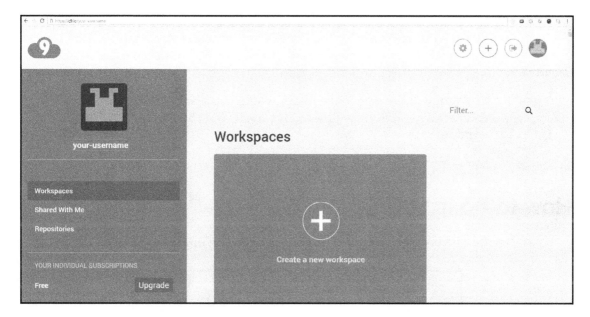

Click on **Create a new workspace**, and a new page will appear with only a few things to fill in. You only need to add the **Workspace name** and **Description**, as you like. You can leave the **Clone from Git or Mercurial URL** empty, as well as leave the default HTML template selected. Finally, click on **Create workspace** to spin up a new container.

Once ready, you will be greeted with the following tree structure of your folders (displayed in the left sidebar):

The largest window (to the right from the sidebar) will have the README.md file open, but you can open any other file in that area as well. Under this largest window, you will see an open Terminal window (titled "bash - <your-project-name>"), and another tab with the JavaScript REPL.

We will make use of Node and npm to install the latest version of Bootstrap via the command line (the readily open Bash Terminal). Both Node and npm come preinstalled in Cloud9 IDE.

 In Windows, navigate to the folder where you want to install Bootstrap 4, and then simply *Shift* + right-click inside it, and choose **Open command window here**.

How to do it...

1. Inspect the versions of Node and npm installed on our virtual machine:

```
bash - "sizif-boot ×        Immediate      ×    ⊕
sizif:~/workspace $ node -v
v4.6.1
sizif:~/workspace $ npm -v
2.15.9
sizif:~/workspace $ █
```

 In Windows, you can check the Node version with node -v, and npm version with npm -v.

2. Inspect the available versions of Bootstrap to be installed:

```
sizif:~/workspace $ npm view bootstrap dist-tags
{ latest: '3.3.7', next: '4.0.0-alpha.5' }
sizif:~/workspace $ █
```

The preceding command shows us that we can either install Bootstrap 3 (latest stable version) or Bootstrap 4 (latest alpha version); we will install Bootstrap 4.

3. To install the latest alpha version of Bootstrap 4, run the following command:

```
sizif:~/workspace $ npm install bootstrap@next
bootstrap@4.0.0-alpha.5 node_modules/bootstrap
├── tether@1.4.0
└── jquery@3.1.1
sizif:~/workspace $ █
```

Running the preceding command will almost instantly install the newest version of Bootstrap 4 in our node_modules directory. Inspect the directory's contents with ll (c9), or dir (Windows).

4. Navigate to the node_modules/bootstrap folder:

cd node_modules/bootstrap

5. Install all the dependencies via npm install:

npm install

After running the npm install command, a number of dependencies will be installed, just as listed in the package.json file. The installation will take some time. The reason why it takes so long is mostly due to the installation of the PhantomJS headless browser, which is used for testing in Bootstrap 4.

Once the installation process is completed, you will be greeted with a large number of folders and files. There are about 40 folders inside the node_modules folder. These folders house specific dependencies, such as grunt-sass or eslint. All of these dependencies are located inside the node_modules/bootstrap/node_modules path.

Here is the structure of the files installed using the npm approach:

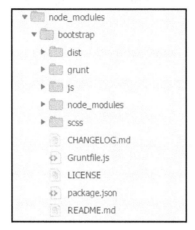

After the installation is completed, the `dist` folder contains all the CSS and JavaScript needed to run a website.

 The `dist` folder is located at `node_modules/bootstrap/dist`.

All that is left now is to add HTML pages, and correctly reference the styles and scripts from the `dist` folder.

Installing Bootstrap 4 to Cloud9 IDE via Git

There is an alternative approach to install Bootstrap via npm and then by running the `npm install` command. This alternative involves downloading the latest Bootstrap release from the official GitHub repository. Contrary to the npm installation approach, this installation contains many additional files and folders, for example, the `nuget` folder. This means that you have downloaded all the available tools for all the platforms supported by Bootstrap. Depending on what you are trying to accomplish, installing via Git might be your preferred approach, as it gives you more options out of the box.

Getting ready

The process starts similarly to the previous recipe. You begin by clicking on **Create a new workspace** at the Cloud9 IDE dashboard.

Alternatively, for Windows, you can follow along using the exact same commands below starting from the tip in step 3, and then from step 6 , provided that you use **Cygwin** or **Git Bash** for Windows to execute those commands.

How to do it...

1. Fill out the **Workspace name** and **Description**.

If you are following this recipe in Windows, start from step 3.

2. In the **Clone from Git or Mercurial URL** input field, enter the address of the official Bootstrap repo on GitHub at `https://github.com/twbs/bootstrap`:

3. Click on **Create workspace**. After clicking on **Create workspace**, a new container will be spun up. Once the environment is ready, you'll be greeted with the tree structure of Bootstrap 3.3.7, cloned from GitHub.

> Windows users should open Cygwin or Git Bash in the folder where you plan to install Bootstrap 4 via git. Execute the `git clone https://github.com/twbs/bootstrap` command. Type `dir` to see the current directory structure. You should see only one directory, titled `bootstrap`. Go into that directory by running the `cd bootstrap` command. Then skip step 4 and go to step 5.

4. Run `git fetch`:

   ```
   git fetch
   ```

5. Checkout the v4-dev branch:

   ```
   git checkout v4-dev
   ```

   Running the preceding command will result in the following notifications in Bash:

   ```
   Branch v4-dev set up to track remote branch v4-dev from
   origin. Switched to a new branch 'v4-dev'
   ```

   In other words, you have now switched to a branch that has the latest installation of Bootstrap 4.

6. Install `grunt-cli`:

   ```
   npm install -g grunt-cli
   ```

7. Run the `package.json` file:

   ```
   npm install
   ```

   Running the preceding command will install PhantomJS, as well as a number of dependencies. At this point, we have the `dist` folder available with all the compiled `.css` and `.js` files. However, to be able to work with Bootstrap docs, we still need to install **Bundler** and **Jekyll**, which is explained in the next recipe.

Installing Bootstrap 4 Jekyll-powered docs

In this recipe, you will see how easy it is to install a copy of the official Bootstrap 4 docs. Running a local copy of the official Bootstrap documentation is a great way to experiment with the available Sass variables, as we will see later in this chapter.

> Windows users, you need to have Ruby, Jekyll, and Bundler installed. If you already have them on your system, and providing that you have completed the previous recipe, there are just a few more things to do to run the Jekyll docs.

> With your console pointing to `chapter3/start/recipe3/bootstrap`, run this command: `gem install nokogiri -v 1.7.2`. Next, run `bundle exec jekyll build`. This command will build your Jekyll site into `./_gh_pages`.
>
> Run `cd _gh_pages`, then run `jekyll serve --watch`. Open your own local copy of Bootstrap docs at `http://127.0.0.1:4000`.

Getting ready

In order to follow this recipe successfully, you should first install Bootstrap 4 via Git. Thus, this recipe assumes that you have a running environment in Cloud9 IDE, and that you have a complete Bootstrap 4 installation as explained in the previous recipe.

How to do it...

1. Verify that Ruby is preinstalled, and Jekyll is not:

   which ruby; which jekyll

   This command will return only the location of Ruby on your VM. Thus, Jekyll needs to be installed.

2. To install Jekyll, you need to install Bundler first:

   gem install bundler

3. Now run `bundle install`, which will install Jekyll:

```
bundle install
```

4. Verify that Jekyll is installed:

```
bundle show jekyll
```

5. Serve Bootstrap 4 Jekyll-powered docs on Cloud9 IDE:

```
bundle exec jekyll serve --host $IP --port $PORT --baseurl ''
```

Upon running this command, a notification will pop up with a link to preview the running webpage. Click on the link and choose one of the display options:

6. Click on the link, and your very own copy of the Bootstrap docs will appear:

Customizing the styles of Bootstrap 4 docs

In the previous recipe, we built our own copy of Bootstrap 4 docs, running on Jekyll. In this recipe, we will see how to change the styling of our Bootstrap 4 docs by making simple changes to Sass variables.

Getting ready

For this recipe to work, you need to complete the previous two recipes, *Installing Bootstrap 4 to c9 IDE using npm* and *Installing Bootstrap 4 to c9 IDE via git*. The following steps will show you how to tweak the look of the docs by changing some of the Sass variables in the `scss` folder.

How to do it...

1. Stop the running Jekyll server by clicking inside the Bash console tab and using *Ctrl + C*.

2. Navigate to the `scss` folder and open the `_variables.scss` file:

   ```
   cd && cd workspace/scss && c9 _variables.scss
   ```

   In Windows, the path is `../bootstrap/scss/`.

3. Find the Sass variable `$enable-rounded`, and uncomment the line it is on, so that it looks like this:

   ```
   // $enable-rounded: true !default;
   ```

4. On the very next line, paste in the following code:

   ```
   $enable-rounded: false !default;
   ```

In Sass, using `!default` is like adding an *unless this is already assigned* qualifier to a variable. Thus, if you are overriding variables in some other file, make sure that there is no `!default` after the changed value of `false` and save the file.

5. Still in console, change directory into the scss folder by running `cd scss` command. Then, run the following command:

```
sass bootstrap.scss ../dist/css/bootstrap.css
```

This command will recompile SCSS into CSS for Bootstrap docs.

In Windows, make sure that you run the preceding command from the `../bootstrap/` folder, that is the root, as cloned earlier using git. On c9.io, you can utilize multiple Bash console tabs, so there is no need to renavigate to root.

6. Go back out from the `scss` folder, by running `cd ..`. Back in the console tab, run the following command:

```
bundle exec jekyll serve --watch --host $IP --port $PORT --
baseurl ''
```

When you refresh the webpage, it will now show the homepage with the **Download Bootstrap** button with sharp edges, instead of rounded ones, as seen in the following screenshot:

7. Back in the _variables.scss file, override the default values by adding more changes:

```
$white: #ddd;
$enable-rounded: false;
$spacer: 8rem;
$font-size-base: 2rem;
```

> You should probably make use of your code editor's search and replace function to complete this step. Once you have completed the step, make sure that you save the file.

8. Recompile SCSS again by pointing your console to the scss folder with cd scss, then running the command from step 6 once again:

```
sass bootstrap.scss ../dist/css/bootstrap.css
```

9. Rebuild Jekyll by running:

```
bundle exec jekyll build;
```

10. Go into _gh_pages and run Jekyll server:

```
jekyll serve --watch --host $IP --port $PORT --baseurl ''
```

This should result in the following changes on the docs website:

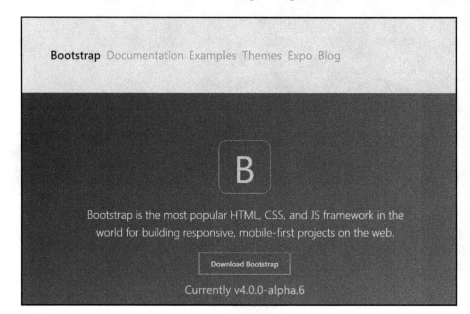

Making custom Grunt tasks in Bootstrap 4

To understand how to better work with a build tool such as Grunt, in this recipe we will customize the available `Gruntfile.js` and `package.json`. We will perform these changes without physically deleting these important files from the default installation. That way, we will be able to play around with customization and not lose the original files.

Getting ready

To start working on this recipe, we first need to navigate to the `workspace` folder, and rename the original `Gruntfile.js` and `package.json`:

```
cd && cd workspace
mv Gruntfile.js Gruntfile.jsORIGINAL
mv package.json package.jsonORIGINAL
```

Now, we are ready to create new versions of these two files and add a custom Grunt task.

How to do it...

1. Let's create new files:

   ```
   cd && cd workspace
   touch Gruntfile.js package.json
   ```

2. Open the `package.json` file:

   ```
   c9 package.json
   ```

    An important thing to note is that if you had the old `package.json` file open before, during, and after the file renaming using the `mv` command, using the `c9 <filename>` command might point to the tab that was not closed, and show the old version of the file. Feel free to close this file's tab by middle-clicking on it (this works just like browser tabs, at least on c9.io running in Chrome).

3. The package file is completely empty, so let's add some code to it:

   ```
   {
     "name": "customGrunt",
     "version": "",
     "devDependencies": {
       "grunt": "~1.0.1"
     }
   }
   ```

   What are we doing in the `package.json` file? We are giving our package just some key:value pairs. Specifically, we are giving it a name, a version, and `devDependencies`. Right now, only the `devDependency` grunt is listed.

4. Now we will add another plugin, `grunt-contrib-copy`, by typing the following command in our Bash console:

   ```
   npm install grunt-contrib-copy --save-dev
   ```

Now, we can see that the `grunt-contrib-copy` plugin has been added to the list of devDependencies in our custom `package.json`:

```
{
  "name": "customGrunt",
  "version": "",
  "devDependencies": {
    "grunt": "~1.0.1",
    "grunt-contrib-copy": "^1.0.0"
  }
}
```

More information about this plugin can be found at `https://www.npmjs.com/package/grunt-contrib-copy`. In a nutshell, this plugin copies files as we specify.

5. Now that we have prepared our `package.json` file, we can tell Grunt how to use it, by coding `Gruntfile.js`. We will begin by opening the currently empty `Gruntfile.js`:

```
c9 Gruntfile.js
```

6. We will add the following code to our `Gruntfile.js`:

```
'use strict';
module.exports = function (grunt) {
  grunt.initConfig({
    pkg: grunt.file.readJSON('package.json'),

    // Define the copy task
    copy: {
      main: {
        expand: true,
        src: 'dist/css/bootstrap.css',
        dest: 'copy',
      },
    },
  });

  grunt.loadNpmTasks("grunt-contrib-copy");
  grunt.registerTask("default", ['copy']);
};
```

If you need a detailed explanation of how the above `Gruntfile.js` code works, take a look at the *How it works...* section.

7. Finally, it is time to run our default Grunt task, with verbose logging:

   grunt -v

   Running the preceding command will create a new folder and will copy the `bootstrap.css` file in the `workspace/copy/dist/css/bootstrap.css` path.

8. Now that we have a basic understanding of just how Grunt runs its tasks, as well as how to modify its tasks to our liking, let's undo the changes we did. However, we will still keep our experimental files, just to have them handy if needed. What follows are the commands used to achieve this. The following commands will get to the root, navigate to `/workspace`, and make a new folder called `GruntExperiment`:

   cd; cd workspace; mkdir GruntExperiment

9. Now, let's move our custom `Gruntfile.js` and `package.json` files, with the following two commands:

```
sizif:~/workspace $ mv node_modules/bootstrap/Gruntfile.jsORIGINAL node_modules/bootstrap/Gruntfile.js
sizif:~/workspace $ mv node_modules/bootstrap/package.jsonORIGINAL node_modules/bootstrap/package.json
```

10. Finally, we need to rename our original files to their original names, running the following commands (note that there are two commands here, for two files; each command was split on two rows so they can fit this page width):

    mv node_modules/bootstrap/Gruntfile.jsORIGINAL
    node_modules/bootstrap/Gruntfile.js;

    mv node_modules/bootstrap/package.jsonORIGINAL
    node_modules/bootstrap/package.json

How it works...

In this recipe, we have provided some custom code needed for a very simple `Gruntfile.js` file to work in step 6 . What follows is the breakdown of what the code does.

On line 1, we use the `strict` mode. On line 3, we call the `grunt` module. Line 4 instructs `grunt` to read our `package.json` file. Lines 7-13 specify the `copy` task. Line 17 is the entry point that registers the `'copy'` task as the `default` task.

Comparing Bootstrap 4 versions with Bower

In this recipe, we will see how to have a fine-grained view of the changes between Bootstrap 4 versions, using **Bower**. We will first install Bower, and then utilize Git to make comparisons.

Getting ready

To begin with, all we need to do is make a new project on Cloud9 IDE, without cloning a repository.

How to do it...

1. Install `bower` using `npm`:

   ```
   npm install -g bower
   ```

2. Verify the `bower` installation:

   ```
   which bower && bower -v
   ```

 Note that both commands should return some values.

3. Install Bootstrap 4 alpha 5 (this is not a typo!):

    bower install bootstrap#v4.0.0-alpha.5

> We are installing an older version on purpose. This will be explained in the next steps.

4. See the list of the installed dependencies:

    bower list

    The preceding command will print out the status of your project's dependencies, including the available update to the currently installed Bootstrap 4 alpha 5.

5. Initialize git in root:

    cd && cd workspace;
git init

6. Stage the files into git's staging area:

    git add --all

7. Commit the changes with a message:

    git commit -m "Add B4, alpha 5"

8. Upgrade Bootstrap 4 to alpha 6 with bower:

    bower install bootstrap#v4.0.0-alpha.6

> To install this update, Windows users will have to use the command prompt (rather than Git Bash for Windows).
>
> When prompted for answer, type "2" and then press ENTER.

9. Now, using `git diff`, we have at our fingertips the full view of changes that happened between alpha 5 and alpha 6 versions of Bootstrap 4. However, it is not feasible to simply use a blanket `git diff` command because too many changes are made to too many files between each version. A much better strategy is to use the `git diff --stat`, with the `--stat` flag giving us a nice overall idea of the changes, as well as which files had the most changes and which had the least. The following screenshot lists only the beginning of the output of the `git diff --stat` command, and does not include all the files affected, but it gives us a nice visual overview of changes made between alpha versions 5 and 6:

```
sizif:~/workspace (master) $ git diff --stat
bower_components/bootstrap/.bower.json                          |   14 +-
bower_components/bootstrap/Gemfile                              |    8 +-
bower_components/bootstrap/Gemfile.lock                         |   38 +-
bower_components/bootstrap/Gruntfile.js                         |  182 +-
bower_components/bootstrap/LICENSE                              |    4 +-
bower_components/bootstrap/README.md                            |   12 +-
bower_components/bootstrap/bower.json                           |    4 +-
bower_components/bootstrap/dist/css/bootstrap-flex.css          | 7381 --------------------------------
bower_components/bootstrap/dist/css/bootstrap-flex.css.map      |    1 -
bower_components/bootstrap/dist/css/bootstrap-flex.min.css      |    7 -
bower_components/bootstrap/dist/css/bootstrap-flex.min.css.map  |    1 -
bower_components/bootstrap/dist/css/bootstrap-grid.css          |  723 ++++++--
bower_components/bootstrap/dist/css/bootstrap-grid.css.map      |    2 +-
bower_components/bootstrap/dist/css/bootstrap-grid.min.css      |    3 +-
bower_components/bootstrap/dist/css/bootstrap-grid.min.css.map  |    2 +-
bower_components/bootstrap/dist/css/bootstrap-reboot.css        |  138 +-
bower_components/bootstrap/dist/css/bootstrap-reboot.css.map    |    2 +-
bower_components/bootstrap/dist/css/bootstrap-reboot.min.css    |    3 +-
```

For Windows users, before listing the result of the `git diff --stat` command, Windows command prompt will throw a bunch of errors--just use the *Page Down* button to move past them.

10. Now we can inspect only the files that we are interested in, for example, the following command:

```
git diff bower_components/bootstrap/scss/_alert.scss
```

The preceding command will show us the changes made only in the `_alert.scss` partial, between Bootstrap 4 Alpha 5 and Alpha 6 versions. In the following screenshot, we can see one of the changes made to this file:

```
@@ -26,13 +26,12 @@
 // Expand the right padding and account for the close button's positioning.

 .alert-dismissible {
-  padding-right: ($alert-padding-x * 2);
-
   // Adjust close link position
   .close {
     position: relative;
-    top: -.125rem;
+    top: -$alert-padding-y;
     right: -$alert-padding-x;
+    padding: $alert-padding-y $alert-padding-x;
     color: inherit;
   }
 }
```

11. With this approach, it is also really simple to track the changes to the `_alert.scss` file in the previous versions of Bootstrap 4 alpha. For example, we can downgrade our Bootstrap 4 installation with the help of Bower, and then repeat our `git diff` for the `_alert.scss` file only, by running the following commands:

```
bower install bootstrap#4.0.0-alpha.4
git diff bower_components/bootstrap/scss/_alert.scss
```

With this recipe, we are able to have complete, fine-grained control of observing the changes made to the framework through its versions. This is an amazing approach to understand the changes that occurred to specific components between different versions of the framework. It can help us understand why bugs occurred in our code, avoid pitfalls when working with legacy code, and learn the approaches taken by the Bootstrap contributors and how to better work with Sass in Bootstrap.

Installing Bootstrap 4 to our Cloud9 IDE with Bower

In this recipe, we will see how to install the newest version of Bootstrap 4 using Bower.

Getting ready

Just like the previous recipe, we will make a new project on Cloud9 IDE without cloning a repo.

How to do it...

1. Install bower using npm:

   ```
   npm install -g bower
   ```

2. Verify the bower installation:

   ```
   which bower && bower -v
   ```

    Note that both commands should return some values.

3. Install Bootstrap 4 alpha 6:

   ```
   bower install bootstrap#v4.0.0-alpha.6
   ```

4. Navigate to the bootstrap folder:

   ```
   cd && cd workspace/bower_components/bootstrap
   ```

5. Run npm install to install all the dependencies:

   ```
   npm install
   ```

    Note that this will take a while.

6. Run grunt verbose:

   ```
   grunt -v
   ```

Now, you can easily reference the dist folder with the necessary styles and scripts for your Bootstrap website to work.

2
Layout Like a Boss with the Grid System

This chapter will cover the following topics:

- Preparing a static server with Bootstrap 4, Harp, and Grunt
- Deploying your web project with Surge
- Splitting up our Harp project into partials
- Using containers with margin and padding utility classes
- Adding columns in a row
- Making col-* classes work
- Building a simple page with the default grid
- Building a real-life web page example with the default grid

Introduction

In this chapter, we will start off by installing a static server with Harp, locally on Windows. Where there are differences between Windows and Ubuntu-based c9, they will be pointed out.

The way we set up Harp will allow for a truly modular approach to develop recipes throughout the rest of this book, helping us keep our code DRY.

Preparing a static server with Bootstrap 4, Harp, and Grunt

In this recipe, we will set up a static server with the help of Harp (available at `https://harp js.com/`). We will use Grunt to set up the foundation for tasks to be run, and we will start with the `grunt-contrib-copy`, `grunt-contrib-sass`, and `grunt-watch` tasks. We will use Bootstrap 4 source code mainly because of its partial Sass files to begin with. This first recipe in this chapter will be the foundation for all the other recipes in this chapter. Hopefully, you will be able to appreciate the power that the combination of these technologies brings when joined with the Cloud9 web-based IDE.

 This recipe is relatively long. If you just want to get up and run as fast as possible, you can skip the setup listed in this recipe and just clone the GitHub repository with all the files set up for you, at `https://github.com /ImsirovicAjdin/bootstrap4-with-sass-harp-grunt`.

To get started quickly, look at the `README.md` available in the repository.

Getting ready

To get ready for this recipe, all we need to do is spin up another Cloud9 IDE HTML5 workspace.

How to do it...

1. Install `bower` using `npm`:

   ```
   npm install -g bower
   ```

2. Verify the `bower` installation:

   ```
   which bower && bower -v
   ```

    Note that both commands should return some values. On Windows, you need Cygwin or Git Bash to run the preceding commands.

3. Install Bootstrap 4 alpha 6:

```
bower install bootstrap#v4.0.0-alpha.6
```

4. Install Harp globally:

```
npm install -g harp
```

5. Make two new folders in the root, and add these files to them as per the following commands:

```
mkdir app grunt &&
touch app/index.html grunt/package.json grunt/Gruntfile.js main.scss
```

6. Add the following code to main.scss:

```
$white: #ffffff;

@import "./bower_components/bootstrap/scss/bootstrap.scss";
```

7. CD into the grunt folder:

```
cd grunt
```

8. Open the package.json file and add the following code to it:

```
{
  "name": "customgrunt",
  "version": "",
  "devDependencies": {
    "grunt": "^1.0.1"
  }
}
```

Then, save the file.

9. In workspace/grunt, install grunt-contrib-sass:

```
npm install grunt-contrib-sass --save-dev
```

10. Also, install grunt **CLI (Command Line Interface)**:

```
npm install grunt-cli -g
```

11. Add the following code to your Gruntfile.js:

```
'use strict';
// Load Grunt
module.exports = function (grunt) {
grunt.initConfig({
pkg: grunt.file.readJSON('package.json'),

// Tasks
sass: { // Begin Sass Plugin
dist: {
options: {
sourcemap: 'inline'
},
files: [{
expand: true,
cwd: '../',
src: ['main.scss'],
dest: '../app/css',
ext: '.css'
}]
}
},
});
// Load Grunt plugins
grunt.loadNpmTasks('grunt-contrib-sass');

// Register Grunt tasks
grunt.registerTask('default', ['sass']);

};
```

Then, save all files.

12. The installation of grunt-cli does not install the grunt task runner. The CLI will only run Grunt if it is installed as a project dependency. We do it by running this command:

```
npm install grunt --save-dev
```

The --save-dev flag lists grunt devDependency to your package.json.

13. In `workspace/grunt`, run the grunt command with verbose logging:

    grunt -v

 Note that this is a very important step, as it will compile Bootstrap's SCSS into a new `.css` file in `app/css/main.css`, as instructed in the sass grunt task in `Gruntfile.js`.

14. Install the `grunt-contrib-copy` plugin:

    npm install grunt-contrib-copy --save-dev

15. Verify that the `package.json` file was updated with the new grunt plugin `devDependencies`; save all files.

16. Update your `Gruntfile.js`, to include the copy task:

```
'use strict';
// Load Grunt
module.exports = function(grunt) {
  grunt.initConfig({
  pkg: grunt.file.readJSON('package.json'),

  // Tasks
  sass: { // Begin Sass Plugin
  dist: {
  options: {
  sourcemap: 'inline'
  },
  files: [{
  expand: true,
  cwd: '../',
  src: ['main.scss'],
  dest: '../app/css',
  ext: '.css'
  }]
  }
  },
  copy: {
  main: {
  files: [{
  cwd: '../bower_components/bootstrap/dist/js/',
  expand: true,
  src: ['**'],
  dest: '../app/js/'
  }]
```

```
        }
    },
});
// Load Grunt plugins
grunt.loadNpmTasks('grunt-contrib-sass');
grunt.loadNpmTasks('grunt-contrib-copy');


// Register Grunt tasks
grunt.registerTask('default', ['sass', 'copy']);

};
```

Save the file.

17. Run grunt without verbose logging:

    grunt

    This time, Bootstrap's JS files, `bootstrap.js` and `bootstrap.min.js`, will be copied into the `app/js/` folder, as described in the new `'copy'` task in our `Gruntfile.js`.

18. Now, make sure that Harp is installed by running the version check:

    harp version

19. Go into the `app` folder and add the following code to the `index.html` file:

```html
<!DOCTYPE html>
<html lang="en">
 <head>
 <meta charset="utf-8">
 <meta name="viewport" content="width=device-width, initial-
 scale=1, shrink-to-fit=no">
 <meta name="description" content="">
 <meta name="author" content="">
 <link rel="icon" href="../../favicon.ico">

 <title>Bootstrap 4 Grid Recipe</title>

 <!-- Bootstrap core CSS -->
 <link href="./css/main.css" rel="stylesheet" type="text/css" >

 <!-- Custom styles for this template -->
 <link href="starter-template.css" rel="stylesheet">
 </head>
```

```
<body>

<nav class="navbar navbar-toggleable-md navbar-light bg-faded">
<button class="navbar-toggler navbar-toggler-right"
type="button" data-toggle="collapse" data-
target="#navbarsExampleDefault" aria-
controls="navbarsExampleDefault" aria-expanded="false" aria-
label="Toggle navigation">
<span class="navbar-toggler-icon"></span>
</button>
<a class="navbar-brand" href="#">Bootstrap 4 Grid Recipe</a>

<div class="collapse navbar-collapse"
id="navbarsExampleDefault">
<ul class="navbar-nav mr-auto">
<li class="nav-item active">
<a class="nav-link" href="#">Home <span class="sr-only">
(current)</span></a>
</li>
<li class="nav-item">
<a class="nav-link" href="#">Link</a>
</li>
<li class="nav-item">
<a class="nav-link disabled" href="#">Disabled</a>
</li>
<li class="nav-item dropdown">
<a class="nav-link dropdown-toggle" href="http://example.com"
id="dropdown01" data-toggle="dropdown" aria-haspopup="true"
aria-expanded="false">Dropdown</a>
<div class="dropdown-menu" aria-labelledby="dropdown01">
<a class="dropdown-item" href="#">Action</a>
<a class="dropdown-item" href="#">Another action</a>
<a class="dropdown-item" href="#">Something else here</a>
</div>
</li>
</ul>
<form class="form-inline my-2 my-lg-0">
<input class="form-control mr-sm-2" type="text"
placeholder="Search">
<button class="btn btn-outline-success my-2 my-sm-0"
type="submit">Search</button>
</form>
</div>
</nav>

<div class="container">

<div class="starter-template">
```

```
<h1>Bootstrap 4 Grid Recipe</h1>
<p class="lead">Use this document as a way to quickly start any
new project.<br> All you get is this text and a mostly barebones
HTML document.</p>
</div>

</div><!-- /.container -->


<!-- Bootstrap core JavaScript
================================================== -->
<!-- Placed at the end of the document so the pages load faster
-->
<script src="https://code.jquery.com/jquery-3.1.1.slim.min.js"
integrity="sha384-A7FZj7v+d/sdmMqp/nOQwliLvUsJfDHW+k9Omg/a/
EheAdgtzNs3hpfag6Ed950n"
crossorigin="anonymous"></script>
<script>window.jQuery || document.write('<script
src="../../assets/js/vendor/jquery.min.js"><\/script>')</script>
<script
src="https://cdnjs.cloudflare.com/ajax/libs/tether/1.4.0/js/
tether.min.js"integrity="sha384-DztdAPBWPRXSA/3eYEEUWrWCy7G5
KFbe8fFjk5JAIxUYHKkDx6Qin1DkWx51bBrb"
crossorigin="anonymous"></script>
<script src="js/bootstrap.min.js"></script>
</body>
</html>
```

Then, save the file.

20. Navigate to the `workspace/app` folder, and run the following code:

```
harp compile
```

 Running this command for the first time will generate a www folder inside the app folder. The www folder will have all the necessary files to run and preview the results in the browser of your choice.

21. Open the compiled `www` folder, and the `index.html` file inside. Click on the round, green **Run** button at the top of the Cloud9 workspace. A new tab will open next to the existing bash tab(s); there will be the **Starting Apache httpd, serving** text inside it. The text is followed by a clickable link, in the following format:
    `https://<project-name>-<c9username>.c9users.io/app/www/index.html`.

Note that this way of running our Harp server is not the suggested one. This is just an intermediary step to enable us to make sure that our setup at this point is running as smoothly as possible. In the next steps, we will look into the preferred approach of serving harp-generated files.

22. Click on the provided link and a new tab will open in your browser, with the following web page:

23. Go to `main.scss`, and change the value of the `$white` variable:

    $white: #bada55;

    Save all files.

To make sure that your `main.scss` file compiles properly, you could use the `grep` and less tools available in the Bash console. Once you have the `main.scss` file saved as per the previous step, all you have to do is run `sass main.scss | grep bada55 | less`. This command compiles the `main.scss` code, and then, instead of outputting it right into the console, it pipes it to `grep`. It is told to look for the `bada55` string and, the result of this `grep` command is output to the less viewer. The less viewer lists all the instances of the `bada55` string in the compiled CSS code, which proves that our `main.scss` file indeed copies the `bootstrap/scss` files and alters them with the new value of the `$white` variable.

24. Now, navigate to the `workspace/grunt` folder, and run the `grunt` command:

```
grunt
```

This will recompile the `.scss` file and copy the `.js` file, from the `bower_components/js/dist` folder, into the `app` folder.

25. Go to the `app` folder, and run `harp compile` again. Open the generated `www/index.html` and run it with the green **Run** button; click on the link and verify that the colors have changed to green, based on the changes made to the `main.scss` file.

26. Now is the time to override more Bootstrap variables in the `main.scss` file. Above the `@include`, replace the override of the `$white` variable with the following code:

```
$enable-rounded: false;
$white: #ccc;
$border-width: 5px;
$font-size-base: 3rem;
```

Save the file. Go back to the `grunt` folder, and run the `grunt` command. Go back to the `app` folder, and run the `harp compile` command.

Obviously, it is not sustainable to keep manually switching between the `grunt` folder and the `app` folder, and to keep saving, recompiling, and rerunning the files. In the next steps, we will automate this process.

27. Now that our setup is working, it is time to organize the Cloud9 workspace in such a way that it makes it easier for us to run the code. This will involve several simple actions. The following screenshot will give us an overview of the actions to do:

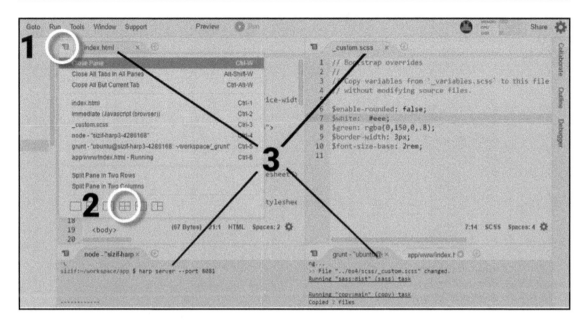

Organizing Cloud9 Workspace

The first thing to do (marked by number **1**) is click on the little icon at the top-left corner, which is the *pane submenu*. Next, click on the *split four ways* button at the bottom of the menu (marked by number **2**). The third action involves dragging and dropping several open tabs, namely, index.html to the top-left corner, _custom.scss to the top-right corner, the Bash console tab that will be used to run the harp server to the lower-left corner, and finally, the bash tab that will run the grunt watch command to the lower-right corner.

28. CD into the grunt folder, and install the grunt-contrib-watch grunt plugin:

    npm install grunt-contrib-watch --save-dev

29. Update the Gruntfile.js file with the following code:

```
'use strict';
// Load Grunt
module.exports = function(grunt) {
  grunt.initConfig({
  pkg: grunt.file.readJSON('package.json'),

  // Tasks
  sass: { // Begin Sass Plugin
  dist: {
```

```
    options: {
    sourcemap: 'inline'
    },
    files: [{
    expand: true,
    cwd: '../',
    src: ['main.scss'],
    dest: '../app/css',
    ext: '.css'
    }]
    }
    },
    copy: {
    main: {
    files: [
    {
    cwd: '../bower_components/bootstrap/dist/js/',
    expand: true,
    src: ['**'],
    dest: '../app/js/'
    }]
    }
    },
    watch: {
    files:
    ['../main.scss','../bower_components/bootstrap/dist/js/*.js'],
    tasks: ['sass', 'copy']
    },
    });
    // Load Grunt plugins
    grunt.loadNpmTasks('grunt-contrib-sass');
    grunt.loadNpmTasks('grunt-contrib-copy');
    grunt.loadNpmTasks('grunt-contrib-watch');

    // Register Grunt tasks
    grunt.registerTask('default', ['watch']);

};
```

30. Everything is now set up to track all the changes. In the bash tab dedicated for running grunt, type the `grunt -v` command. Due to the way it is set up, it will watch for changes, and report its operations with verbose logging. In the lower-left bash tab, we will start running the `harp server`, with the following command:

harp server ./ --port 8080

31. Finally, to view your site, open a new browser tab and type the
    `https://<project-name>-<username>.c9users.io` address. This should
    serve the updated website. To change the look of the website, change the variable
    values in `_custom.scss` and refresh the page. With grunt watching in the lower-
    right console tab, and harp serving in the lower-left console tab, you only need to
    save changes you make to `_custom.scss`, and refresh the browser tab that
    points to your app to view the updates as they are saved.

> It is possible that your page will not serve as expected. That has to do with
> what folder you are in when you run the `harp server ./ --port 8080`
> command. If you are in the `workspace` folder, then you can see your
> running site at the
> `https://<project-name>-<username>.c9users.io` address.
> However, if you are in the `workspace/app` folder, you can see your
> running site at the
> `https://<project-name>-<username>.c9users.io/app/` address.
> To even further improve this workflow, we can make our browser live-
> reload the harp site we just created. A quick solution is to use the **Auto
> Refresh** Chrome extension, from `http://bit.ly/1CvA52G`.

Deploying your web project with Surge

In this recipe, we will serve the web project we created with Surge. For a quick introduction
to the way it works, visit its website, `surge.sh`.

> If you would like to know more about Surge, visit this Medium page--`htt`
> `p://bit.ly/2jDJ7L1` (URL shortened as the original link was too long).

This short recipe will marry the workflow from the previous recipe, the relatively long
setup of Harp on Cloud9 IDE, with a simple way to serve the completed page on a custom
URL. This should be quite a time saver and a powerful way to combine Cloud9 IDE, Harp,
and Surge.

Getting ready

To get ready, we should build on the setup we created in the first recipe, *Preparing a static server with Bootstrap 4, Harp and Grunt*, in this chapter. However, before we start, there are a few clarifications to be made.

The first thing to note is the one major distinction that the web page that was created in the app folder was still serving the index.html page from the root of that folder. In other words, the app/index.html file and the app/css and the app/js folders can all be thought of as our *development environment*, whereas the www folder can be thought of as our *production environment*. Why is that?

To clarify this distinction, we need to remember the end of the previous recipe. At the end of the previous recipe, we have set up the grunt-contrib-watch task as the default task in our custom Gruntfile.js. The watch task was observing our bs4/scss files, including _custom.scss. Any change saved to the bs4/scss/_custom.scss file would lead Grunt to recompile all the SCSS files from the bs4 folder into the app/css/bootstrap.css file. That is why we auto-refreshed our page every X seconds, with the help of that Chrome plugin, because we wanted to be able to live-reload the changes to our app/index.html. However, all of this setup was actually a part of our *development environment*. If you think about it, this makes perfect sense. It is a way to prototype our website and immediately see the changes.

Now, for our *production environment*, all we have to do is stop the harp server ./ --port 8080 command and run the harp compile command. The harp compile command will update our www folder, and we will have a newly compiled www folder. This folder is the one that will be pushed to surge.sh. Without stopping the harp server and rerunning e harp compile, the site that we would have pushed to surge.sh would have been the previously compiled www folder.

Now that we have confirmed how everything works, we can push our static website to Surge.

How to do it...

1. With bash pointed to ~/workspace:, install Surge globally:

```
npm install --global surge
```

2. Run the `surge` command.

3. A message will appear in your console, asking you to either log in or create an account. You can do either of them straight from the console. When prompted for the project path, just append `/app/www` to the path provided. The `surge` command will continue logging a few more things, and in the last logged row, it will write the following message: **Success! Project is published and running at vancouver.surge.sh**.

4. Navigate to the website mentioned in the preceding line (obviously, yours will be different from the one mentioned previously).

5. Change your *development environment* code, then `harp compile` it (make sure that you are in the `worspace/app` folder for the compilation to work).

> Note that at the time of writing, there is a bug in c9 bash that prevents you from running `harp server ./ --port 8080` once you have stopped it to `harp compile`. However, you can still verify that your Grunt command's compilation of `_custom.scss` into `app/css/bootstrap.css` works. To test this, as before, just change the value of the `$white` variable (from say, `gray` to `yellow`). Now, visit the `https://<projectname>-<username>.c9users.io/app/` page and live-refresh your browser to see the changes.

6. Run the `surge` command again. It will prompt you for the project path. Just add `/app/www` to the end of the path and press *Enter*.

7. It will also prompt you for the domain. To avoid having to type the domain name every time you run the `surge` command, run `surge` with the following flag:

```
surge --domain vancouver.surge.sh
```

8. To use a custom domain instead, add a CNAME file (no extensions!) to the root of the `www` folder:

```
echo vancouver.surge.sh > CNAME
```

> When running the preceding command, use your own domain or subdomain instead of `vancouver.surge.sh`.

Splitting up our Harp project into partials

In this recipe, we will split our existing project into partials, to keep our code DRY. Harp uses **Embedded JS (EJS)** format for includes. For more information on .ejs, visit http://www.embeddedjs.com/.

To begin, we can either continue from the previous recipe or clone the available repository for the recipe from the link https://github.com/ImsirovicAjdin/bootstrap4-with-sass-harp-grunt.

It is assumed in this recipe that you are using Cloud9 IDE. However, if that is not the case, then do not include the reference to workspace in commands to be run, as that folder is Cloud9-specific.

How to do it...

1. In workspace/app, add a new folder and call it partial:

   ```
   cd && cd worspace/app && mkdir partial
   ```

2. Add _nav.ejs to the partial folder--touch partial/_nav.ejs.
3. Open the app/index.html and cut all the code starting with <nav> and ending with </nav> (the whole navbar). Paste the code into the _nav.ejs file.
4. In index.html, right where you cut out the <nav> element, paste this include:

   ```
   <%- partial("partial/_nav") %>
   ```

5. Make a new file, _data.json, in workspace/app:

   ```
   touch _data.json
   ```

6. Paste the following code into it:

   ```
   {
       "index": {
           "title": "Welcome to Our Homepage"
       },
       "about": {
           "title": "About Us"
       }
   }
   ```

Note that "index" is the name of the file (index.html), and "title" is the text for the <title> tag of the index page. We can add more pages as needed.

7. Now, let's copy and rename index.html to _layout.ejs:

cp index.html _layout.ejs

8. C9 into index.html and delete everything except the div with the class of container, that is, keep only the following code in index.html:

```
<div class="container">

  <div class="starter-template">
    <h1>Bootstrap 4 Grid Recipe</h1>
    <p class="lead">Use this document to quickly start any new
    project.
    <br> All you get is this text and a barebones HTML document.
    </p>
  </div>

</div><!-- /.container -->
```

9. Change the file extension of index.html to index.ejs:

mv index.html index.ejs

10. In _layout.ejs, add the title of the current page:

```
<title><%- title %></title>
```

11. Also, delete everything under the _nav partial include, all the way up to the comment <!-- Bootstrap core JavaScript ... and place just this one line there:

```
<%- yield %>
```

12. Run the harp compile and harp server commands to verify that everything still works.

In this recipe, we have split our code into includes, making it a lot easier to work with. In the following recipes, we will deal with layouts.

Do not forget to change the variable overrides in the `main.scss` file if you want your recipe code to have a nice background color and your `navbar` to have regular-sized text.

Using containers with margin and padding utility classes

In this recipe, we will build a simple layout, the old-fashioned way, using the default Bootstrap grid (without flexbox).

Getting ready

To get ready for this recipe, we will build from what we made in the first two recipes, *Preparing a static server with Bootstrap 4, Harp* and *Grunt* and *Deploying your web project with Surge*, of this chapter.

For basic information on how the layout works in Bootstrap 4, check out `http://v4-alpha.getbootstrap.com/layout/overview/`.

How to do it...

1. In `workspace/app/index.ejs`, at the end of the file, add a call to another partial:

   ```
   <%- partial("partial/_defaultGrid") %>
   ```

2. Create and open `_defaultGrid.ejs`:

   ```
   cd && cd workspace/app/partial && touch _defaultGrid.ejs && c9
   _defaultGrid.ejs
   ```

3. Add the following code to `_defaultGrid.ejs`:

   ```
   <!--
   Recipe 201 - Classes used: container-fluid, container, bg-*, p-*,
   m-*, mt-*, mb-*, lead, text-center, text-white
   -->
   ```

```
<div class="container-fluid bg-info p-5" id="one"
 data-toggle="tooltip"
 data-placement="bottom"
 data-html="true"

></div>

<div class="container-fluid bg-info p-5 m-5" id="two"
 data-toggle="tooltip"
 data-placement="bottom"
 data-html="true"

></div>

<div class="container-fluid bg-info">
 <div class="container bg-warning p-5" id="three"
 data-toggle="tooltip"
 data-placement="top"
 data-html="true"

 ></div>
</div>

<div class="container bg-warning p-5 mt-5 mb-2" id="four"
 data-toggle="tooltip"
 data-placement="top"
 data-html="true"

></div>

<div class="container-fluid bg-inverse p-5" id="five">
 <p class="lead text-center text-white"> This bottom div is here
 just to help visualise the difference between .mt-5 and .mb-2
 used on the above div.container</p>
</div>
```

4. In `app/_layout.ejs`, add this code at the very bottom:

```
<script>

$('#one').tooltip('toggle');
$('#two').tooltip();
$('#three').tooltip();
$('#four').tooltip();

</script>
</body>
</html>
```

5. Add this code to the bottom of `main.scss`:

```scss
.tooltip-inner {
  text-align: left;
}
```

6. Save everything, run `grunt` and `harp server`. View your layout in the browser. Resize it to see the behavior of the layout at different resolutions.

How it works...

In step 1, we add the `partial _defaultGrid.ejs` to our `index.ejs` layout. This helps us keep our code modular, as discussed before.

In step 2, we add our `_defaultGrid.ejs` partial.

In step 3, we add the HTML structure, and this is the recipe-specific code. The code consists of five `div` tags, with the first four `div` tags having the class of `container-fluid`. Each `div` also has the helper `padding` classes, `p-*`, and the helper `margin` classes, `m-*`. Each `div` also has its own unique ID, assigned based on the position in the HTML structure: one, two, three, four, or five.

In step 4, we add the calls to the four `tooltip` components in the custom `script` tag just above the closing `</body>` tag.

In step 5, we start with the simple `.tooltip-inner` class override, to left-align the text inside the `tooltip` components.

Explanation of the data-* HTML5 attributes

To make things more interesting, each `div` has a `tooltip` component so as to provide clues to what is happening with containers, when viewing the page in a browser.

The `tooltip` components are activated through the self-explanatory jQuery calls in step 4 of the recipe.

To make the `tooltip` components work, their specific options are set in HTML5 `data-*` attributes. The `data-toggle` attribute specifies that the component we are using is indeed a `tooltip`. The `data-placement` attribute can be set to the following four directions: top, right, bottom, or left. Setting the `data-html` attribute to `"true"` allows us to insert HTML inside our `tooltip`. As can be seen in the browser, this creates a pretty good effect.

The `tooltip` function in the custom `script` can be passed several parameters, as explained in the Bootstrap docs.

There's more...

To keep this chapter's code as modular as possible while still making it work as an example website to showcase the recipes, we will have to make a few tweaks, such as renaming some files and changing the `Gruntfile.js` options accordingly.

Renaming main.scss

This step might not look that important, but it is actually crucial. To keep things as modular as possible, we need to make a different `main.scss` file for each recipe. To start with, let's rename the `main.scss` file to `main-02-04.scss`:

```
mv main.scss main-02-04.scss
```

Now, just copy `main-02-04.scss` and rename it `main-02-05.scss`. This second file will be used to test if everything is correctly automated from our `Gruntfile`. In our `Gruntfile`, we need to account for this multiplicity of files. We will do that by simply changing just one line in the `sass:files` code, as follows:

```
src: ['main.scss'],
```

We will change the line of code to this:

```
src: ['main-*.scss'],
```

Similarly, we will start our `watch` task with this line of code:

```
watch: {
files: ['../main-*.scss','../bower_components/bootstrap/dist/js/*.js'],
```

We are now watching for changes, and compiling all the `scss` files that start with `main-`. To test whether it works, let's change the `$white` variable in `main-02-04.scss` to `whitesmoke`, and in `main-02-05.scss` to `#faced1`.

Finally, in _layout.ejs, let's change the stylesheet href to mirror the changes we made:

```
<!-- Bootstrap core CSS -->
<link href="./css/main-02-04.css" rel="stylesheet" type="text/css" >
<!--
<link href="./css/main-02-05.css" rel="stylesheet" type="text/css" >
-->
```

Note that the first href is valid, whereas the other one is commented out. It is easy to switch between the two, as grunt has compiled both .css files in app/css/, as previously described.

Now, run grunt and harp server and verify that the changes are taking place. To test whether both files are served properly, you do not need to recompile everything. You can do it in the browser, while the page is served, by simply changing the recipe number.

We can improve our setup even further. This time, we will create another include that will call all the individual recipe style sheets as .ejs partials.

In _layout.ejs, add the following code in place of the regular style sheet hrefs:

```
<!-- Bootstrap core CSS -->
<%- partial("partial/_recipe02-04-css") %>
<%# partial("partial/_recipe02-05-css") %>
<%# partial("partial/_recipe02-06-css") %>
<%# partial("partial/_recipe02-07-css") %>
<%# partial("partial/_recipe02-08-css") %>
```

In the preceding calls, only the code for recipe 02-04 will be included, as the rest of them are commented out with a proper .ejs syntax. Let's now add the content to the _recipe02-04-css.ejs file, as follows:

```
<link href="./css/main-02-04.css" rel="stylesheet" type="text/css" >
```

The other preceding listed numbered .ejs files should be created accordingly.

In conclusion, we can now just change the # sign into a – sign in our _layouts.ejs partial calls, and thus serve the proper .css file. Even though it takes some upfront setup, the long-term benefits are great.

This approach will allow us to easily reuse the CSS code from multiple recipes.

Adding columns in a row

In this recipe, we will add five columns in a row. At the end of the recipe, you should have a fully customized modular page.

Getting ready

To get ready for this recipe, we will build from what we made in the first three recipes, the *Preparing a static server with Bootstrap 4, Harp and Grunt* recipe, the *Deploying your web project with Surge* recipe, and the *Splitting up our Harp project into partials* recipe in this chapter. To get started quickly, refer to the code provided with the book (folder: chapter2-5).

For basic information on how the layout works in Bootstrap 4, check out `http://v4-alpha.getbootstrap.com/layout/overview/`.

How to do it...

1. In `workspace/app/index.ejs`, at the bottom of the file, let's comment out the EJS code. The current code looks like this:

   ```
   <%- partial("partial/_defaultGrid") %>
   ```

   We will comment it out by replacing the third character from – to #:

   ```
   <%# partial("partial/_defaultGrid") %>
   ```

   If you save your `index.ejs` file now (and if the `harp server` command is running), when you refresh your Cloud9 users page, the grid that is called by the `_defaultGrid` partial will be gone.

2. Add another line to `index.ejs`, and reference another include:

   ```
   <%- partial("partial/_chapter2-5-html") %>
   ```

3. In `main-02-05.scss`, add the following code:

   ```
   // Recipe 2-5
   $enable-rounded: false;
   $white: whitesmoke;
   $border-width: 1px;
   $font-size-base: 1rem;
   ```

```
@import "./bower_components/bootstrap/scss/bootstrap.scss";

$grid-columns: 5;
$grid-gutter-width-base: 0;
.img-fluid {margin: 0; }
```

4. In `app/partial`, create the `_chapter2-5-html.ejs` partial, and c9 into it:

    **cd && cd workspace/app/partial && touch _chapter2-5.ejs && c9
    _chapter2-5.ejs**

5. Add the following code to the file:

```
<div class="container-fluid">
 <div class="row">
 <div class="col-md-1">
 <img class="img-fluid"
 src="http://placehold.it/767x767/613d7c/ffffff?text=COL-MD-1">
 </div>
 <div class="col-md-1">
 <img class="img-fluid"
 src="http://placehold.it/767x767/5bc0de/ffffff?text=COL-MD-1">
 </div>
 <div class="col-md-1">
 <img class="img-fluid"
 src="http://placehold.it/767x767/0275d8/ffffff?text=COL-MD-1">
 </div>
 <div class="col-md-1">
 <img class="img-fluid"
 src="http://placehold.it/767x767/f0ad4e/ffffff?text=COL-MD-1">
 </div>
 <div class="col-md-1">
 <img class="img-fluid"
 src="http://placehold.it/767x767/d9534f/ffffff?text=COL-MD-1">
 </div>
 </div>
</div>
```

6. Save the changes and preview them in your web page.

In the two previous recipes, *Splitting up our Harp project into partials* and *Using containers with margin and padding utility classes*, we have set up our Bootstrap 4 workflow so that we can easily turn on and off multiple style sheets and HTML includes, which will significantly cut down our development time and help us stay organized.

Making col-* classes work

In this recipe, we will only use the default Bootstrap 4 classes to demonstrate some basic gotchas related to the *default*, non-flexbox-enabled grid. Practically, this means that we will not even have to touch any CSS, as all the styling will be set through the class attributes in the appropriate HTML elements.

Getting ready

To follow the recipe easier, refer to the code provided with the book (folder: chapter02-06 of the codebase).

How to do it...

1. Let's add all the files we'll use in this recipe:

```
touch app/partial/_chapter-02-06-html.ejs app/partial/_recipe02-
06-css.ejs main-02-06.scss
```

2. Add the following code to `app/partial/_chapter-02-06-html.ejs`:

```
<div class="container-fluid">
 <div class="row bg-inverse m-4 p-4 lead">
 <div class="col-md-6 bg-success p-3 text-white">This div takes
 up 6 of 12 columns above the <code>md</code> breakpoint. Below
 the <code>md</code> breakpoint, it stacks horizontally (since it
 takes up the full width of the screen at those resolutions).
 </div>
 <div class="col-md-6 bg-danger text-white p-3">This column acts
 exactly like the previous one, but a different effect is
 achieved using different classes to color the text and the
 background.</div>
 </div>
<div>

 <div class="container-fluid bg-success pt-4 pb-4 mb-5 lead">
 <div class="row p-2 m-2 bg-faded">
 <div class="col-12 col-sm-10 col-md-8 col-lg-6 col-xl-4 bg-info
 text-white p-3">This column starts off as 100% wide on extra-
 small screens. This is set with the class <code>.col-12</code>.
 On every additional breakpoint above <code>xs</code>, it is made
 narrower by additional 2 of 12 columns for the specific
 resolution. At the widest resolution, it takes up 4 of 12
```

```
columns, as set with the <code>.col-xl-4</code> class.</div>
<div class="col-12 col-sm-2 col-md-4 col-lg-6 col-xl-8 bg-
warning p-2">This div too starts off as 100% wide on extra small
screens, so it is stacking under the first column. On every
additional breakpoint, it starts off only one-third of the
screen, and grows by one-sixth for every higher breakpoint. Note
that the first div has all-arround padding set to <code>.p-
3</code>, and the second div has all-around padding set to
<code>.p-2</code>. <mark>The sum of all the paddings of divs in
a row cannot be greater than p-5 (simply, .p-2 + .p-3).</mark>
Otherwise, the layout would break.</div>
</div>

<div class="row p-5 m-3 bg-faded lead">
<div class="col-6 bg-danger text-white display-4 pt-5 ">The
width of this div is set with <code>.col-6</code>. Only at this
smallest resolution is the pattern of col-* different from all
the other ones.</div>
<div class="col-6 col-sm-4 col-md-4 col-lg-4 col-xl-4 h4 bg-info
text-white pt-5">At this smallest resolution, there is no
breakpoint specified between the "col" and the number. Thus,
<code>.col-6</code>. On all the other resolutions above
<code>xs</code>, the breakpoint abbreviation is also used in the
class name. For example:
<ul>
<li class="">.col-sm-4</li>
<li class="">.col-md-4</li>
<li class="">.col-lg-4</li>
<li class="">.col-xl-4</li>
</ul>
Note: In practice, it is obvious that adding all these columns
is redundant. If we set the width for this div to 4 of 12
columns at the <code>sm</code> resolution, it will keep the same
width for all the above resolutions too, since Bootstrap is
mobile-first.
This code was obviously used to simply show the naming pattern
for all the .col-* classes. In the next recipes, we will show
the right way to actually use these classes.
</div>
</div>
</div>
```

3. Add the following code to `partial/_recipe-02-06-css.ejs`:

```
<link href="./css/main-02-06.css" rel="stylesheet"
type="text/css" >
```

Note that this `.ejs` file is calling the recipe-specific `.css` file. As mentioned in the introduction of the recipe, we are not adding any custom styles, but we still need to import and process Bootstrap sass. We also need to keep everything organized and modular, and that is why we are making the files in steps 3 and 4 of this recipe.

4. Add the following code to `main-02-06.scss`:

```
// Recipe 02-06

@import "./bower_components/bootstrap/scss/bootstrap.scss";
```

5. Change the last three lines of `app/index.ejs` so that they look like this:

```
<%# partial("partial/_defaultGrid") %>
<%# partial("partial/_chapter02-05-html") %>
<%- partial("partial/_chapter02-06-html") %>
```

6. In `app/_layout.ejs`, call the correct `.css` file, and comment out the rest:

```
<%# partial("partial/_recipe02-04-css") %>
<%# partial("partial/_recipe02-05-css") %>
<%- partial("partial/_recipe02-06-css") %>
<%# partial("partial/_recipe02-07-css") %>
<%# partial("partial/_recipe02-08-css") %>
```

7. Save, run `grunt` and `harp server`, and inspect the result in your browser. Using the developer tools, examine the way that the layout behaves at different resolutions.

Building a simple page with the default grid

In this recipe, we will build a simple, well-rounded page to demonstrate how easy it is to work with Bootstrap 4 to create layouts. It is assumed that you are using Cloud9 IDE, but you can follow this recipe in any environment. At the end of the recipe, you should have a fully customized modular page.

Getting ready

To get started quickly, refer to the code provided with the book (folder: chapter02-07).

For basic information on how layouts work in Bootstrap 4, check out `http://v4-alpha.get bootstrap.com/layout/overview/`.

How to do it...

1. In `workspace/app/index.ejs`, change the code to look like this:

```
<!--
<div class="container">

<div class="starter-template">
<h1>Bootstrap 4 Grid Recipe</h1>
<p class="lead">Use this document as a way to quickly start any
new project.<br> All you get is this text and a mostly barebones
HTML document.</p>
</div>

</div>
-->

<%# partial("partial/_defaultGrid") %>
<%# partial("partial/_chapter02-05-html") %>
<%# partial("partial/_chapter02-06-html") %>
<%# partial("partial/_chapter02-06-html") %>
<%- partial("partial/_chapter02-07-html") %>
```

2. In `app/_layout.ejs`, the updated code from the opening `!DOCTYPE` to the `<%-yield %>` should look like this:

```
<!DOCTYPE html>
<html lang="en">
 <head>
 <meta charset="utf-8">
 <meta name="viewport" content="width=device-width, initial-
 scale=1, shrink-to-fit=no">
 <meta name="description" content="">
 <meta name="author" content="">
 <link rel="icon" href="../../favicon.ico">

 <title><%- title %></title>
```

```
<!-- Bootstrap core CSS -->
<%# partial("partial/_recipe02-04-css") %>
<%# partial("partial/_recipe02-05-css") %>
<%# partial("partial/_recipe02-06-css") %>
<%- partial("partial/_recipe02-07-css") %>
<%# partial("partial/_recipe02-08-css") %>

</head>

<body>

<%# partial("partial/_nav") %>
<%- partial("partial/_nav02-07") %>

<%- yield %>
```

3. Make a new file, app/partial/_nav02-07.ejs, and add the following code to it:

```
<div class="container mt-5 bg-inverse">
 <nav class="navbar navbar-toggleable-md navbar-light">
 <button class="navbar-toggler navbar-toggler-right text-white
 mt-1" type="button" data-toggle="collapse" data-
 target="#navbarSupportedContent" aria-
 controls="navbarSupportedContent" aria-expanded="false" aria-
 label="Toggle navigation">
 ≡
 </button>
 <a class="navbar-brand text-white" href="#">Navbar</a>


 <div class="collapse navbar-collapse"
 id="navbarSupportedContent">
 <ul class="navbar-nav mr-auto">
 <li class="nav-item active">
 <a class="nav-link text-white" href="#">Home <span class="sr-
 only">(current)</span></a>
 </li>
 <li class="nav-item">
 <a class="nav-link text-white" href="#">Link</a>
 </li>
 <li class="nav-item">
 <a class="nav-link disabled text-white" href="#">Disabled</a>
 </li>
 </ul>
 </div>
 </nav>
</div>
```

4. Make a new file, `app/partial/_chapter02-07-html.ejs`, and add the following code to the file:

```
<div class="container mt-lg-5 mt-sm-0 p-5 bg-faded">
<div class="row">
<div class="col-md-8">
<h1>This is the main section</h1>
<p class="lead">Just a paragraph with a .lead class</p>
<p>Lorem ipsum dolor sit amet, consectetur adipisicing elit.
Repudiandae, alias mollitia impedit. Consequatur blanditiis,
reprehenderit laboriosam, esse aliquid possimus aut culpa
adipisci, quia officiis placeat at dolorem numquam. Adipisci
eligendi eos tempora facere dicta, quidem libero numquam rerum,
obcaecati expedita, deserunt commodi vero nesciunt. Repudiandae
cumque molestiae magni doloribus nesciunt, aliquam. Dolor
accusamus vel voluptatibus, soluta, eligendi quaerat maxime
facilis itaque tempore placeat pariatur, a sint! Reiciendis
dicta sit, enim est consequatur, iusto quod. Adipisci eligendi
culpa error dicta explicabo placeat beatae nemo harum suscipit
voluptas deleniti, esse vero necessitatibus voluptatem nesciunt
itaque cumque facere blanditiis quidem, distinctio neque ut?
Doloremque minus eum veritatis, adipisci, dignissimos, expedita
recusandae sequi dolor optio error placeat incidunt id maiores
autem ad quam earum asperiores magnam quis voluptatem
consequuntur numquam vero at? Velit illo, porro! Maiores cum
sunt exercitationem tenetur illum, vel non illo fuga laudantium
aperiam nihil dolores facere quos error minus sequi porro minima
dolorum corporis. Quibusdam quo aperiam commodi consequuntur
amet incidunt iusto totam odio nisi, repellendus, odit facere.
Modi, asperiores. Molestias necessitatibus aperiam
exercitationem praesentium voluptate modi reprehenderit odio
nisi eaque nostrum, ut illum consectetur perferendis unde culpa
similique eveniet consequatur accusantium error officiis quasi
dolorem! Eius consequatur, esse amet!</p>
<p>Lorem ipsum dolor sit amet, consectetur adipisicing elit.
 ...
</p>
</div>
<div class="col-md-4">
<h2>Sidebar</h2>
<p>Lorem ipsum dolor sit amet, consectetur adipisicing elit.
Quos aspernatur repellendus autem molestias maxime quaerat quo
praesentium dolorum laborum odit! Fuga cum ea consequuntur
harum, sunt debitis a nesciunt perspiciatis.</p>
<p>Lorem ipsum dolor sit amet, consectetur adipisicing elit.
Pariatur nam nostrum quibusdam sit in reprehenderit. Nesciunt,
dolor suscipit aspernatur qui officia quam illo, placeat impedit
ipsa non debitis aperiam doloribus.</p>
```

```
    </div>
    </div>
  </div>

  <div class="container mt-5 p-3">
  <div class="row">
  <div class="col-md-7 bg-faded mr-auto p-5">
  <h1>This is the main section</h1>
  <p class="lead">Just a paragraph with a .lead class</p>
  <p>Lorem ipsum dolor sit amet, consectetur adipisicing elit....
  </p>
  </div>
  <div class="col-md-4 bg-faded p-5">
  <h2>Sidebar</h2>
  <p>Lorem ipsum dolor sit amet, consectetur adipisicing elit.
  Quos aspernatur repellendus autem molestias maxime quaerat quo
  praesentium dolorum laborum odit! Fuga cum ea consequuntur
  harum, sunt debitis a nesciunt perspiciatis.</p>
  <p>Lorem ipsum dolor sit amet, consectetur adipisicing elit.
  Pariatur nam nostrum quibusdam sit in reprehenderit. Nesciunt,
  dolor suscipit aspernatur qui officia quam illo, placeat impedit
  ipsa non debitis aperiam doloribus.</p>
  </div>
  </div>
  </div>

  <footer class="text-white text-center mt-5 p-5">
  Copyright &copy; Navbar 2017
  </footer>
```

5. Make a new file, in `app/partial/_recipe02-07-css.ejs`, and add this code to it:

```
<link href="./css/main-02-07.css" rel="stylesheet"
type="text/css" >
```

6. Add a new file, `main-02-07.scss`, and add the subsequent code to it:

```
// Recipe 02-07

@import url('https://fonts.googleapis.com/css?family=Rock+Salt');


@import "./bower_components/bootstrap/scss/bootstrap.scss";


body {
  background: #E55D87; /* fallback for old browsers */
```

```
   background: -webkit-linear-gradient(45deg, #E55D87 , #5FC3E4);
   /* Chrome 10-25, Safari 5.1-6 */
   background: linear-gradient(45deg, #E55D87 , #5FC3E4); /* W3C,
   IE 10+/ Edge, Firefox 16+, Chrome 26+, Opera 12+, Safari 7+ */
   }

   nav {
    text-color: white;

   }
   .bg-faded {
    opacity: .95;
   }
   h1, h2, h3 {
    font-family: 'Rock Salt', cursive;
   }
```

7. Run `grunt` and `harp compile`/`harp server`, and view the final result in the browser.

How it works...

Step 1 is part of our regular preparation to build the code in the recipe. Step 2 involves adding the needed partial, including the addition of an alternate `navbar`. Steps 3 and 4 add the specific `navbar` and main content code.

Step 6 is our custom SCSS. We demonstrate here how to import a Google font, and how to add some background gradient to our body element, in plain CSS.

Building a real-life web page example with the default grid

In this recipe, we will build a real-life example web page.

Getting ready

To get ready for this recipe, check out the following links to the official Bootstrap docs:

- https://v4-alpha.getbootstrap.com/layout/grid/
- https://v4-alpha.getbootstrap.com/examples/grid/

We will also use an example image from pexels.com, and the Font Awesome icon font, at h ttp://fontawesome.io/.

How to do it...

1. Create new files and folders, as follows:

   ```
   touch app/partial/_recipe02-08-css.ejs app/partial/_chapter02-08-
   html.ejs app/partial/_nav02-08.ejs  main-02-08.scss;
   mkdir app/css/img
   ```

2. Let's now update our bower_components. In the root of your project, run the following command to install the font-awesome library:

   bower install font-awesome

3. Download the image to use in this recipe from https://www.pexels.com/photo /box-business-celebrate-celebration-296878/. Pick the large size (with the width of 1920 pixels) in the download options. Paste the image in the app/css/img folder.

4. Paste the following code into main-02-08.scss:

   ```
   // Recipe 02-08

   @import "./bower_components/bootstrap/scss/bootstrap.scss";
   @import "./bower_components/font-awesome/scss/font-awesome.scss";


   .jumbotron-background {
   color: white;
   background: linear-gradient(to bottom, rgba(0,0,0,0.55)
    0%,rgba(0,0,0,0.35) 100%),
   url('img/pexels-photo-296878.jpeg') no-repeat center center
    fixed;
    -webkit-background-size: cover;
    -moz-background-size: cover;
   ```

```
-o-background-size: cover;
background-size: cover;
}
```

5. Add the following code into `app/partial/_nav02-08.ejs`:

```
<nav class="navbar navbar-toggleable-md navbar-light fixed-top
bg-info">
<div class="container">
<button class="navbar-toggler navbar-toggler-right text-white
mt-1" type="button" data-toggle="collapse" data-
target="#navbarSupportedContent" aria-
controls="navbarSupportedContent" aria-expanded="false" aria-
label="Toggle navigation">
≡
</button>
<a class="navbar-brand text-white" href="#">Navbar</a>


<div class="collapse navbar-collapse"
id="navbarSupportedContent">
<ul class="navbar-nav mr-auto"></ul>
<ul class="navbar-nav mr-sm-2">
<li class="nav-item active">
<a class="nav-link text-white" href="#">Banking Services <span
class="sr-only">(current)</span></a>
</li>
<li class="nav-item">
<a class="nav-link text-white" href="#">Consulting Services</a>
</li>
<li class="nav-item">
<a class="nav-link text-white" href="#">Archived Data Access</a>
</li>
</ul>
</div>
</div>
</nav>
```

6. Open `app/partial/_chapter-02-08-html.ejs`, and paste this code:

```
<div class="jumbotron jumbotron-fluid mt-5 jumbotron-background">
<div class="container text-center p-5">
<h1 class="h2">This is the <code>h1</code> heading used in our
jumbotron component</h1>
<p class="lead">Fluid jumbotron has been added in Bootstrap 4.
</p>
<p class="">This addition makes creating promotional content on
websites that much easier.</p>
```

```
<p><a class="btn btn-info btn-lg mt-5" href="#"
role="button">Call to Action Button</a></p>
</div>
</div>

<section id="details" class="details text-center">
<div class="container">
<h2 class="m-5 h3">Discover Possibilities With Us</h2>
<div class="row m-5">
<div class=" col-xs-12 col-md-4">
<h3 class="text-info">Banking Services</h3>
<i class="fa fa-bar-chart fa-5x text-info mt-3 mb-4" aria-
hidden="true"></i>
<p>Lorem ipsum dolor sit amet, consectetur adipisicing elit.
Odio ipsam, impedit est fugiat ratione incidunt delectus illo
aperiam sunt temporibus!</p>
</div>
<div class=" col-xs-12 col-md-4">
<h3 class="text-info">Consulting Services</h3>
<i class="fa fa-comments fa-5x text-info mt-3 mb-4" aria-
hidden="true"></i>
<p>Lorem ipsum dolor sit amet, consectetur adipisicing elit.
Harum blanditiis omnis distinctio doloribus dolore eum
repellendus minus excepturi, quo magni?</p>
</div>
<div class=" col-xs-12 col-md-4">
<h3 class="text-info">Archived Data Access</h3>
<i class="fa fa-archive fa-5x text-info mt-3 mb-4" aria-
hidden="true"></i>
<p>Lorem ipsum dolor sit amet, consectetur adipisicing elit.
Quibusdam quidem ab quo porro quod recusandae perferendis sit
doloremque consequatur minus.</p>
</div>
</div>
</div>
</section>

<div class="jumbotron jumbotron-fluid mt-5">
<div class="container pt-3 pt-1">
<h1 class="h2 mb-5">This is the h1 heading used in the regular
jumbotron component.</h1>
<div class="row">
<div class="col-md-6 pr-5">
<p class="lead">Lorem ipsum dolor sit amet.</p>
<p>Lorem ipsum dolor sit amet, consectetur adipisicing elit. Hic
quos eos voluptatum nihil architecto, maxime quo quod alias non
fugiat, pariatur voluptas repellat aspernatur eligendi quae
libero recusandae consequuntur dignissimos, facilis nam minus
```

```
nemo totam incidunt distinctio optio! Ut harum nihil quisquam
porro reprehenderit ipsam labore reiciendis perspiciatis.</p>
</div>
<div class="col-md-6 pl-5">
<p class="lead">Lorem ipsum dolor.</p>
<p>Lorem ipsum dolor sit amet, consectetur adipisicing elit. Hic
quos eos voluptatum nihil architecto, maxime quo quod alias non
fugiat, pariatur voluptas repellat aspernatur eligendi quae
libero recusandae consequuntur dignissimos, facilis nam minus
nemo totam incidunt distinctio optio! Ut harum nihil quisquam
porro reprehenderit ipsam labore reiciendis perspiciatis.</p>
</div>
</div>
<p class="text-center"><a class="btn btn-info btn-lg mt-5"
href="#" role="button">Call to Action Button</a></p>
</div>
</div>

<div class="container">
<div id="tables">
<h2>Just Another Responsive Table</h2>
<p>IN Bootstrap 4, you can use the class of <code>.table-
responsive</code> on the table element. In Bootstrap 3, you had
to use it on the parent element.</p>

<table class="table table-responsive">
<thead>
<tr>
<th>Header 1</th>
<th>Header 2</th>
<th>Header 3</th>
<th>Header 4</th>
<th>Header 5</th>
</tr>
</thead>
<tbody>
<tr>
<td>Cell</td>
<td>Cell</td>
<td>Cell</td>
<td>Cell</td>
<td>Cell</td>
</tr>
<tr>
<td>Cell</td>
<td>Cell</td>
<td>Cell</td>
<td>Cell</td>
```

```
    <td>Cell</td>
    </tr>
    </tbody>
    </table>
</div>
</div>


<footer class="container-fluid bg-inverse p-5 text-white">
  <p>&copy; Navbar 2017</p>
</footer>
```

7. In `index.ejs`, change the code so that it looks like this:

```
<%# partial("partial/_defaultGrid") %>
<%# partial("partial/_chapter02-05-html") %>
<%# partial("partial/_chapter02-06-html") %>
<%# partial("partial/_chapter02-06-html") %>
<%# partial("partial/_chapter02-07-html") %>
<%- partial("partial/_chapter02-08-html") %>
```

8. In `_layout.ejs`, the last two links that call `css` should look like this:

```
<%# partial("partial/_recipe02-07-css") %>
<%- partial("partial/_recipe02-08-css") %>
```

9. We are commenting our `css` for the previous recipe, and adding the link to the new `css` include, served from `partial/_recipe02-08-css.ejs`. Still, in `_layout.ejs`, we need to add the link to the `nav` for this recipe. Just under the body tag, comment out the call to the previous recipe's `nav`, and call the current recipe-specific `nav`, as follows:

```
<body>

<%# partial("partial/_nav") %>
<%# partial("partial/_nav02-07") %>
<%- partial("partial/_nav02-08") %>
```

10. In `app/partial/_recipe02-08-css.ejs`, add the call to the `.css` file, titled `main-02-08.css`, which will be compiled by our Grunt tasks:

```
<link href="./css/main-02-08.css" rel="stylesheet"
type="text/css" >
```

11. Run `grunt` and `harp compile` / `harp server`, and view the completed web page.

How it works...

In step 1 of this recipe, we start off with the addition of all the new files and folders needed for it to work.

In step 2, we add the `font-awesome` bower component. This will allow us to call `font-awesome` classes locally (without linking to a CDN).

In step 3, we download the image that we will use as our `jumbotron` background, just under the `navbar`.

In step 4, we add the recipe-specific SCSS code. This code calls our Bootstrap 4 default SCSS and `font-awesome` from `bower_components`.

In step 5, we add the code to the recipe-specific navbar.

Step 6 is very important, as it introduces a new concept in Bootstrap 4 related to the `jumbotron` component. In Bootstrap 4, `jumbotron` makes it easier to create a great call-to-action space, with headings, paragraphs, buttons, and so on. The most important thing to remember is that all this content needs to be surrounded with a `div` tag, with the `jumbotron` and `jumbotron-fluid` classes. We also include the call to a custom class of `jumbotron-background`:

```
<div class="jumbotron jumbotron-fluid mt-5 jumbotron-background">
...
</div>
```

The rest of the code in step 6 is pretty easy to understand. We are using font-awesome icons for better visual effects and a table as an example of a responsive table that can be added easily to a web page such as this.

The remaining steps in this recipe will make all the includes work.

 If you are interested in learning more about Harp in general, refer to `http ://chloi.io/open/`.

3
Power Up with the Media Object, Text, Images, and Tables

In this chapter, we will cover the following topics:

- Extending the text classes of `.display-*` and adding hover effects with `Hover.css`
- Creating comment sections using Bootstrap media objects
- Enriching text content with Bootstrap typography classes
- Customizing the blockquote element with CSS
- Extending the blockquote styles with Sass
- Aligning text around images
- Wrapping text around rounded images
- Styling a pricing section using Bootstrap's default table classes

Introduction

In this chapter, we will set up a website that will hold all the aforementioned recipes. Each recipe will be a link in that website's navbar's dropdown. The structure for the complete website, with all the recipes included, is available in the code for this chapter. To preview this structure, navigate to the `chapter3/app` folder, and run the `harp server` command from the console. Then, click on the about link in the navbar. The **about** page lists all the files and folders in this chapter's code.

Looking at the code structure for this chapter, it is important to note the most important parts.

The `app` folder comprises all the recipes' files. The `app` folder has the following subfolders and files:

- `css` (created by the `grunt sass` command)
- `js` (copied by the `grunt copy` command)
- `partial` (this folder holds the following partial files:`_js.ejs` and `_nav.ejs`, called by `_layout.ejs`)
- `www` (compiled by the `harp compile` and/or `harp server` commands)
- `about.ejs` (holds the file tree overview)
- `index.ejs`
- `recipe1.ejs` and `recipe2.ejs` (these files are accessible for preview via the navigation bar in the local website that can be run via `harp server`)

The `bower_components` folder comprises the following subfolders:

- `bootstrap` (to install it, the `bower install bootstrap#4.0.0-alpha.6` command was run)
- `font-awesome` (to install it, the `bower install font-awesome` command was run)
- `hover` (to install it, `bower install hover` was run)
- `jquery` (installed with Bower's Bootstrap installation)
- `tether` (installed with Bower's Bootstrap installation)

The `grunt` folder has the `node_modules` subfolder, as well as the following two files: `Gruntfile.js` and `package.json`.

Take a look at `package.json`; we can see the necessary `devDependencies`, which were installed via console, from the `chapter3/grunt` folder, running the following command:

```
npm install grunt-contrib-concat grunt-contrib-copy grunt-contrib-sass
grunt-contrib-watch --save-dev
```

The root of the document holds the SCSS file `main.scss`, which includes `main-03-01.scss`, `main-03-02.scss`, `main-03-03.scss`, `main-03-04.scss`, and `main-03-07.scss`.

Having this detailed overview of the files and folders included in this chapter's code is important, as it will help us complete the recipes faster.

For that reason, all the files and folders in the `chapter3-start` folder have already been created. However, most of the files are empty, and in the recipes that follow, we will add code to them.

Extending the text classes of .display-* and adding hover effects with Hover.css

In this recipe, we will extend the text classes of `.display-*` and add hover effects to our links, using the `Hover.css` library.

Getting ready

To get ready, download the starter code for this chapter, and refer to this chapter's starter code in the folder titled `chapter03-start`. Open the `app/partial/_nav.ejs` file, which is already saved with its final code. The reason for this is to have a working `navbar` with links to all the recipes used in this chapter.

> Note that when including the `.ejs` files in HTML, you can just call the filename. There is no need to use the `.ejs` extension. You can see plenty of examples of this in the `app/partial/_nav.ejs` anchor tags.

It is also important to note that our `Gruntfile.js` is somewhat different than the one in the preceding chapter. This time, you will need to manually run `grunt copy` to copy all the necessary JS dependencies. However, this needs to be done only once. Then, later on, you need to run `grunt copy` only when you change your `bower_components`, which will probably not happen very often.

Also, to compile SCSS into CSS, you can run `grunt sass`. To both watch and compile changes, you can still use `grunt` or `grunt watch`.

How to do it...

1. Navigate to the `bower_components` folder and make sure that you can see all the folders as described in this chapter's introduction. For more information on the `Hover.css` library, visit its GitHub page at `https://github.com/IanLunn/Hover`. For examples of effects in use, check out the examples page at `http://ianlunn.github.io/Hover/`.

2. In `app/_layout.ejs`, add the following code:

```
<!DOCTYPE html>
<html lang="en">

<head>
 <meta charset="utf-8">
 <meta name="viewport" content="width=device-width, initial-
 scale=1, shrink-to-fit=no">
 <meta name="description" content="">
 <meta name="author" content="">
 <link rel="icon" href="../../favicon.ico">
 <title>
 <%- title %>
 </title>

 <!-- Bootstrap core CSS -->
 <link href="css/main.css" rel="stylesheet">

</head>

<body class="bg-faded-green">

 <%- partial("partial/_nav") %>

 <%- yield %>

 <%- partial("partial/_js") %>

</body>
</html>
```

3. In `app/index.ejs`, add this code:

```
<div class="container">

 <div class="mt-5">
 <h1>Welcome to Chapter 3</h1>
 <div class="mt-2 text-justify">This webpage contains the recipes
```

```
from the 3rd chapter of <a href="#" class="bg-faded">Bootstrap 4
Cookbook</a>:
<ul class="mt-2">
<li>Author: <a href="#" class="bg-faded">Ajdin Imsirovic</a>
</li>
<li>Technical Reviewer: <a href="#" class="bg-faded">Zlatko
Alomerovic</a></li>
<li>Publisher: <a href="#" class="bg-faded">Packt Publishing</a>
</li>
</ul>
</div>
</div>

</div><!-- /.container -->
```

4. In app/recipe1.ejs, add the following code that is very similar to the code in
   step 3:

```
<div class="container">

<div class="mt-5">
<h1>Chapter 3, Recipe 1:</h1>
<p class="lead">Extend the Text Classes of .display-* and Add
Hover Effects with Hover.css</p>
<div class="display-7 mt-2 text-justify">This webpage contains
the recipes from the 3rd chapter of <a href="#" class="bg-faded
hvr-buzz">Bootstrap 4 Cookbook</a>:
<ul class="display-8 mt-2">
<li>Author: <a href="#" class="bg-faded hvr-underline-from-
left">Ajdin Imsirovic</a></li>
<li>Technical Reviewer: <a href="#" class="bg-faded hvr-
underline-from-left">Zlatko Alomerovic</a></li>
<li>Publisher: <a href="#" class="bg-faded hvr-underline-from-
left">Packt Publishing</a></li>
</ul>
</div>
</div>

</div><!-- /.container -->
```

If you take a look at the preceding code, you will see that the only difference between step 3 and step 4 is that we have inserted additional CSS classes to the HTML elements. As can be seen in step 4, we added custom `.display-*` text classes. We have also included hover effects from `Hover.css`.

5. In the root of our folder, in `main-03-01.scss`, add the following code:

```
a:focus, a:hover {
  text-decoration: none;
}

.display-5 {
  font-size: 3rem;
}
.display-6 {
  font-size: 2.5rem;
}
.display-7 {
  font-size: 2rem;
}
.display-8{
  font-size: 1.5rem;
}
```

6. In `main.scss`, we will include all the SCSS files we need, using the `@import` statement:

```
// @import "main-03-04.scss";

@import "./bower_components/bootstrap/scss/bootstrap.scss";
@import "./bower_components/font-awesome/scss/font-awesome.scss";
@import "./bower_components/hover/scss/hover.scss";
@import "main-03-01.scss";
// @import "main-03-02.scss";
// @import "main-03-03.scss";

// @import "main-03-07.scss";
```

7. Finally, add the following code to `app/partial/_js.ejs`:

```
<!-- Bootstrap core JavaScript
================================================== -->
<!-- Placed at the end of the document so the pages load faster
-->
<script src="js/jquery.js"></script>
<script src="js/tether.js"></script>
<script src="js/bootstrap.js"></script>
```

```
<script src="https://raw.githubusercontent.com/adobe-
webplatform/css-shapes-polyfill/master/shapes-polyfill.min.js">
</script>
```

How it works...

In this recipe, we start out with a lot of prebuilt code and structure, which is a good starting point for DRY development, and it is the foundation that we will build upon in the coming recipes in this chapter. We have preinstalled font-awesome and Hover.css as bower_components, and these are included in the starter code for this example.

In step 2 of this recipe, we are calling the main.css file that will be compiled into the app/www/css folder (via grunt).

In step 3, we are adding the HTML structure for the index page. The CSS classes in this HTML structure are only those that exist in the default Bootstrap code. There are no additions and no overrides for css.

Once we serve our website via Harp, this index page is the one that will greet us in the browser.

In step 4, we are adding recipe1.ejs with the same structure as the index.ejs from step 3. The only difference here is that we are adding additional custom CSS classes in our HTML elements.

In step 5, we are declaring these custom CSS classes, namely the classes of display-5, display-6, display-7, and display-8. In step 6, the @include declarations call the SCSS files for Bootstrap 4, Font Awesome, and Hover.css from the bower_components folder. They also call the code from step 5, thereby extending the .display-* classes. The @include calls for other recipes are present, but are currently commented out so that we can focus on the recipe at hand.

When we compare between the index.html and recipe1.html pages, we can note that our text is much larger on the recipe1.html page, thanks to us making new, custom .display-* classes. We can also see that all our anchor tags have hover effects, since we are calling specific CSS classes from the Hover.css library in our HTML code.

Finally, to make everything work, we add the JavaScript dependencies in app/partial/_js.ejs, as called from _layout.ejs.

In conclusion, although the `recipe1.html` site is not outstanding from the design perspective, it is a proof of concept for inclusion of a third-party SCSS library (`hover.scss`), as well as for meaningful addition of new classes to the default Bootstrap 4 css.

Creating comment sections using media objects

In this recipe, we will create a responsive comments section using media objects. We will enhance the design with the help of the HTML's `<time>` element and Bootstrap's badge component. We will also use Font Awesome's icons for comment liking and sharing. We will add interactivity using Bootstrap's `alert` component, which will be triggered after clicking on a Font Awesome icon.

Getting ready

Everything is already set up in our `chapter3-start` folder to start working on this recipe. Now that all the files are there, we just need to add code to them.

How to do it...

1. Navigate to `app/recipe2.ejs` and add the following code to it:

```
<!-- Create Comment Areas Using Media Objects -->
<div class="container mt-5">
 <h1>Chapter 3, Recipe 2:</h1>
 <p class="lead">Create Comment Sections Using Media Objects</p>
 <ul class="custom-media">
 <li class="media list-group-item media p-4">
 <img class="media-object mr-3 align-self-start rounded img-
 thumbnail" src="http://placehold.it/80x80/bada55">

 <div class="media-body">
 <div class="media-heading">
 <p class="lead mb-1"><em>John Doe</em>
 <span class="float-right"><i class="fa fa-heart text-faded-
 green"></i> <i class="fa fa-twitter text-faded-green"></i> <i
 class="fa fa-facebook text-faded-green"></i></span>
 </p>
```

```
<time class="badge badge-faded-green mb-1" datetime="2017-02-17
T10:10">7 am last week</time>
</div>
<p>
Lorem ipsum dolor sit amet, consectetur adipisicing elit. Omnis
tempore culpa voluptate quos laborum laudantium, quas dolore
fuga temporibus inventore rerum aliquid voluptatum! Omnis minus
consequuntur mollitia impedit cumque aliquam porro expedita, nam
assumenda repellat!
</p>
<img class="media-body-inline-img img-fluid img-thumbnail mt-3
mb-4" src="http://placehold.it/800x400/eeeeee/aaaaaa/&text=►">
<ul class="custom-media">
<li class="media">
<img class="media-object mr-3 align-self-start rounded"
src="http://placehold.it/60x60/bada55">
<div class="media-body">
<p class="lead-small"><em>Jane Doe</em>
<span class="float-right">
<a href="#" id="comment-3-like"><i class="fa fa-heart text-
faded-green"></i></a>
<a href="#" id="comment-3-tweet"><i class="fa fa-twitter text-
faded-green"></i></a>
<a href="#" id="comment-3-add-to-fb"><i class="fa fa-facebook
text-faded-green"></i></a>
</span>
</p>
<time class="badge badge-faded-green mb-1" datetime="2017-02-17
T10:10">3 pm, two days ago</time>
<div id="custom-alert-3-like"></div>
<div id="custom-alert-3-tweet"></div>
<div id="custom-alert-3-facebook"></div>
<p>Lorem ipsum dolor sit amet, consectetur adipisicing elit. Ut
placeat quas facilis labore, repellendus!</p>
</div>
</li>
</ul>
</div>
</li>
</ul>
</div>
```

2. Paste the following code to `main-03-02.scss`:

```
.bg-faded-green {
background: rgba(80, 134, 67, 0.04);
}
.badge-faded-green {
```

```css
background: rgba(80, 134, 67, 0.14);
color: #5cb85c!important;
border: 1px solid rgba(80, 134, 67, 0.24);
}
.text-faded-green {
color: rgba(80, 134, 67, 0.34);;
}
.text-faded-green:hover, .text-faded-green:focus {
color: rgba(80, 134, 67, 0.64);
cursor: pointer;
}
.lead-small {
font-size: 1.14rem;
margin-bottom: .25rem;
font-weight: 300;
}

@media (min-width: 48em) {
 .container {
max-width: 46rem;
 }
}
ul.custom-media {
 -webkit-padding-start: 4px;
 padding-left: 0 !important;
}
.alert-twitter {
 background-color: rgba(29, 161, 242, .25);
 border-color: rgba(29, 161, 242, .50);
 color: rgba(29, 161, 242, .90);
}
.alert-facebook {
 background-color: rgba(66, 103, 178, 0.25);
 border-color: rgba(66, 103, 178, 0.50);
 color: rgba(66, 103, 178, 0.90);
}
```

3. In `main.scss`, uncomment the `@import "main-03-02.scss"` line.

4. Add the following `<script>` at the bottom of `app/partial/_js.ejs`:

```html
<script>
$('#comment-like').on("click", function (e) {
e.preventDefault();
$('#custom-alert-like').hide().html('<div class="alert alert-
success alert-dismissible fade show mt-3" role="alert"><button
type="button" class="close" data-dismiss="alert" aria-
label="Close"><span aria-hidden="true">&times;</span></button>
<strong>You have liked this comment!</strong>
```

```
</div>').fadeIn(800);
});
$('#comment-tweet').on("click", function (e) {
e.preventDefault();
$('#custom-alert-tweet').hide().html('<div class="alert alert-
twitter alert-dismissible fade show mt-3" role="alert"><button
type="button" class="close" data-dismiss="alert" aria-
label="Close"><span aria-hidden="true">&times;</span></button>
<strong>You have tweeted this comment!</strong>
</div>').fadeIn(800);
});
$('#comment-add-to-fb').on("click", function (e) {
e.preventDefault();
$('#custom-alert-facebook').hide().html('<div class="alert
alert-facebook alert-dismissible fade show mt-3" role="alert">
<button type="button" class="close" data-dismiss="alert" aria-
label="Close"><span aria-hidden="true">&times;</span></button>
<strong>You have shared this comment on Facebook!</strong>
</div>').fadeIn(800);
});
</script>
```

5. Run `grunt sass` and `grunt copy`. In your browser, navigate to
`localhost:9000/recipe2` and inspect the page. Click on the three icons on the
right from Jane Doe's comment. You should see alerts popping up, powered by
`jquery` code from step 4.

How it works...

There are a lot of things happening in this recipe. In step 1, we add the recipe-specific
HTML structure. To achieve the desired effect, we are using Bootstrap 4's media object. The
structure is pretty easy to grasp, so we will not delve into details here. For some basic
examples, refer to `https://v4-alpha.getbootstrap.com/layout/media-object/`.

Part of the HTML structure worth mentioning is the `<img>` tag, which calls the
`placehold.it` as its source, with the custom size, background color, and text (the *play*
symbol) passed to the `src` attribute as parameters.

We also use a paragraph with the class of `lead` to make the names more prominent, followed with the span with the `float-right` Bootstrap class. The three icons on the right use of Font Awesome styles, and we are adding our own custom color class of `text-faded-green`. A similar custom color background class is used on Bootstrap's `badge` class, which is added to the HTML's `<time>` element.

The lower half of the HTML structure is a made-up comment by Jane Doe, as a *response* to the notification posted by John Doe. Contrary to John Doe's icons, Jane Doe's icons are clickable, and clicking on any of the three icons (like Twitter or Facebook) will make custom alerts pop up underneath.

All of these `css` customizations are done in step 2. We can note that the `*-faded-green` class declarations dominate the top half of the style sheet. The `custom-media` class significantly changes the behavior of the media object by removing the left padding, thereby allowing it to take up more space, which is really important on smaller screens.

Finally, `alert-twitter` and `alert-facebook` are the added custom `alert` classes. The **like** button uses the regular `alert-success` class.

In step 3, we include the custom `css`, and in step 4, we make a smooth appearance of the alert boxes possible, triggered by clicking on the icons. The code is a bit clunky, and it is possible to improve it. However, just as it is, it is a great example of what is happening on each click and how all the parts come together. Since this example is already pretty advanced, we will not deal with refactoring of the `jQuery` code.

Enriching text content with Bootstrap typography classes

In this recipe, we demonstrate the use of Bootstrap's typography classes. Bootstrap 4 offers a number of different classes, which allow for easy manipulation of text styles out of the box.

Getting ready

Navigate to the third recipe of Chapter 3 website (you can access it by navigating to `chapter3/complete/app` in the code files then running the `harp server` command, which will allow you to visit the completed website for the this chapter, at `localhost:9000` in your browser). Here, you can click on the **Recipe** dropdown in the navbar, click on the recipe 3 link, and preview the final result that we are trying to achieve.

To get this look, we will combine text color classes, background color classes, display classes, and vertical text alignment classes. We will create this look from the empty files readily available in our `chapter3/start/recipe3` folder.

How to do it...

1. Open `chapter3/start/app/recipe3.ejs` and add the following code to it:

```
<div class="container bg-white mt-5 rounded">
<h1>Chapter 3, Recipe 3:</h1>
 <p class="lead">Style Text Content with Bootstrap Typography
 Classes</p>

<!-- Let's apply the exisiting default Bootstrap styles to a
paragraph of text, as follows: -->

 <p class="display-4">This is just a regular paragraph.</p>
 <p class="display-3"><span class="text-muted">This is an example
of muted text</span>.</p>
 <p class="display-2">
 <span class="text-primary">All the </span>
 <span class="text-success"> contextual Bootstrap</span>
 <span class="text-info bg-primary"> colors have</span>
 <span class="text-warning"> their specific</span>
 <span class="text-danger"> text color</span>
 <span class="text-white bg-inverse"> classes</span>.
 </p>
 <p class="h3">Just another h3 <mark>paragraph</mark>.</p>
 <p class="h3">And <mark>here is <span class="align-text-
bottom">another</span><span class="align-text-top"> one</span>
 </mark>.
</div>

<!-- Let's play around with those now -->
<div class="container mt-5">
 <div>
```

```
<div class="d-inline">Lorem ipsum dolor sit amet, <span
class="d-block">consectetur</span> adipisicing elit. Dolor
ratione, voluptatibus debitis veniam rem suscipit.
</div>
</div>

<div class="container mt-5">
<!-- Use $font-family-base, $font-size-base, $line-height-base
attributes as our typographic base applied to the <body> -->

<!-- Set the global link color via $link-color and apply link
underlines only on :hover -->

<!-- These styles can be found within _reboot.scss, and the
global variables are defined in _variables.scss -->

</div>
```

2. In `main-03-03.scss`, add the following code:

```
.bg-white {
background-color: white;
}
```

3. In `main.scss`, uncomment the `@include` call to the `scss` file updated in step 2.
4. Run `harp compile` / `harp server`, and preview the recipe in your browser.

How it works...

In this simple recipe, we have only made one custom class to color the wrapping container white. All the other classes are readily available in the default Bootstrap 4 code.

In the website with the completed recipe, we can see that the several available color classes that Bootstrap 4 has out of the box offer plenty of possibilities for creating decent-looking layouts on the fly.

Toward the bottom of the page, we can see examples of vertical text alignment, achieved with the use of Bootstrap's own `align-text-top` and `align-text-bottom` classes. The highlighted effect is the result of using the `<mark>` element in our HTML code.

At the very bottom of the page, we can see Bootstrap's helper classes of d-block and d-inline used on the <span> and <div> elements respectively, as examples of the possibility provided in Bootstrap 4 to easily change the regular display property of HTML elements with appropriate CSS classes.

Finally, as a hint to how to start experimenting with text and Sass in Bootstrap 4, there are some guidelines in the HTML comments at the bottom of recipe3.ejs.

Customizing the blockquote element with CSS

In this recipe, we will examine how to use and modify Bootstrap's blockquote element. The technique we'll employ is using the :before and :after CSS pseudo-classes. We will add HTML entities to the CSS content property, and then style their position, size, and color.

Getting ready

Navigate to the **recipe4** page of the **chapter 3** website, and preview the final result that we are trying to achieve (its preview is available in chapter3-complete/app, after running harp server in the said folder). To get this look, we are using all the regular Bootstrap 4 CSS classes, with the addition of .bg-white, added in the preceding recipe. In this recipe, we will add custom styles to .blockquote.

How to do it...

1. In the empty chapter3/start/app/recipe4.ejs file, add the following code:

```
<div class="container mt-5">
 <h1>Chapter 3, Recipe 4:</h1>
 <p class="lead">Customize the Blockquote Element with CSS</p>
</div>

<!-- Customizing the blockquote element -->
<div class="container">
 <div class="row mt-5 pt-5">
 <div class="col-lg-12">
 <blockquote class="blockquote">
```

```html
<p>Blockquotes can go left-to-right. Lorem ipsum dolor sit amet,
consectetur adipisicing elit. Repellat dolor pariatur,
distinctio doloribus aliquid recusandae soluta tempore. Vero a,
eum.</p>
<footer class="blockquote-footer">Some Guy,
<cite>A famous publication</cite>
</footer>
</blockquote>
</div>
<div class="col-lg-12">
<blockquote class="blockquote blockquote-reverse bg-white">
<p>Blockquotes can go right-to-left. Lorem ipsum dolor sit amet,
consectetur adipisicing elit. Quisquam repellendus sequi officia
nulla quaerat quo.</p>
<footer class="blockquote-footer">Another Guy,
<cite>A famous movie quote</cite>
</footer>
</blockquote>
</div>
<div class="col-lg-12">
<blockquote class="blockquote card-blockquote">
<p>You can use the <code>.card-blockquote</code> class. Lorem
ipsum dolor sit amet, consectetur adipisicing elit. Aliquid
accusamus veritatis quasi.</p>
<footer class="blockquote-footer">Some Guy,
<cite>A reliable source</cite>
</footer>
</blockquote>
</div>
<div class="col-12">
<blockquote class="blockquote bg-info">
<p>Blockquotes can go left-to-right. Lorem ipsum dolor sit amet.
</p>
<footer class="blockquote-footer">Some Guy,
<cite>A famous publication</cite>
</footer>
</blockquote>
</div>
</div>
</div>
```

2. In `main-03-04.scss`, add the following code:

```scss
blockquote.blockquote {
padding: 2rem 2rem 2rem 4rem;
margin: 2rem;
quotes: "\201C" "\201D";
position: relative;
```

```
  }

  blockquote:before {
    content: open-quote;
    font-family: Georgia,  serif;
    font-size: 12rem;
    opacity: .04;
    font-weight: bold;
    position:absolute;
    top:-6rem;
    left: 0;
  }
  blockquote:after {
    content: close-quote;
    font-size: 12rem;
    opacity: .04;
    font-family: Georgia,  serif;
    font-weight: bold;
    position:absolute;
    bottom:-11.3rem;
    right: 0;
  }
```

3. In `main.scss`, uncomment `@include` for `main-03-04.scss`.

4. Run `grunt sass` and `harp server`.

How it works...

In this recipe, we are using the regular `blockquote` HTML element and Bootstrap's classes for styling it. To make it look different, we primarily use the following tweaks:

- Setting the `blockquote.blockquote` position to `relative`
- Setting the `:before` and `:after` pseudo-classes, position to `absolute`
- In `blockquote.blockquote`, setting the `padding` and `margin`. Also, assigning the values for opening and closing quotes, using CSS (ISO) encoding for the two HTML entities
- Using `Georgia` font to style the content property in pseudo-classes
- Setting the `font-size` of pseudo-classes to a very high value and giving the font a very high opacity, so as to make it become more background-like
- With absolute positioning in place, it is easy to place the quotes in the exact location, using negative `rem` values

Extending the blockquote styles with Sass

In this recipe, we will show how to extend the `blockquote` styles using Sass. To make this work, we will have to rely both on the `@include` for `main-03-04.scss` and the `@include` for `main-03-05.scss`. Also, since we are overriding Bootstrap variables, our `@include` element for this recipe has to be added before the addition of the Bootstrap SCSS files.

Getting ready

Navigate to the **recipe5** page of the **chapter 3** website, and preview the final result that we are trying to achieve. To get this look, we need to override several SCSS variables from Bootstrap 4, as well as declare a new variable to be used in the `box-shadow` effect applied around the `blockquote` element.

How to do it...

1. Open `main-03-05.scss` and add the following code to it:

```
/*
FROM _type.scss, line 110:

.blockquote {
 padding: ($spacer / 2) $spacer;
 margin-bottom: $spacer;
 font-size: $blockquote-font-size;
 border-left: $blockquote-border-width solid $blockquote-border-
 color;
}
*/
$white: white;
// $white: darksalmon;
$blockquote-border-width: 1rem;
$blockquote-border-color: rgba(80, 134, 67, 0.35);
$faded-green: rgba(80, 134, 67, 1);

.blockquote {
 background: $white;
 -webkit-box-shadow: 0px 10px 5px -8px $faded-green;
 -moz-box-shadow: 0px 10px 5px -8px $faded-green;
 box-shadow: 0px 10px 5px -8px $faded-green;
}
```

2. Navigate to `main.scss` and comment out the `@include` for `main-03-04.scss`, and uncomment the `@include` for `main-03-05.scss`.

3. Run `grunt sass`, followed by `harp compile`, and view the result in your browser.

How it works...

Note the CSS comment at the top of the `main-03-05.scss` file. This comment was placed there so as to make it easier to remember the original `.blockquote` settings as specified in `_type.scss`. Knowing the logic of the original file allows us to better understand how to use the code in the recipe.

Note that the `$white` variable is set to `white`. This is its default value, but it is placed there as another reminder since the next line changes the value of `$white` to HTML color `darksalmon`. Commenting out the first value, and uncommenting the second one, will quickly show us an interesting color scheme in our browser.

Finally, several SCSS variables are overwritten. Background is set to white on all `.blockquote` elements (in contrast to the previous recipe). A custom variable of `$faded-green` is declared on line 16 and used in the `.blockquote` declaration on lines 20-22.

Finally, note that in order to view the previous recipe again (*Customizing the blockquote element with CSS*) the way it was meant, you would have to comment out the `@include` for `main-03-05.scss` in `main.scss`, and run `grunt sass` and `harp server` again.

Aligning text around images

In this recipe, we will align text around images using default Bootstrap classes.

Getting ready

Navigate to the **recipe6** page of the **chapter 3** website, and preview the final result that we are trying to achieve. The key section of this recipe is the `<img>` HTML element, and its CSS classes, as specified in its `class` attribute.

How to do it...

1. Open `chapter3/start/app/recipe6.ejs` and insert the following code:

```
<div class="container mt-5">
 <h1>Chapter 3, Recipe 6:</h1>
 <p class="lead">Align Text Around Images</p>
<section class="bg-success text-white clearfix mb-3">
 <img src="http://placehold.it/150x150" alt="" class="img-fluid
 rounded-circle float-left float-sm-right float-md-left float-lg-
 right float-xl-left p-5">
 <p>Lorem ipsum dolor sit amet, consectetur adipisicing elit. Qui
 temporibus aliquid dignissimos dolor aut at, libero est
 obcaecati atque culpa, sequi reiciendis nostrum cumque magnam
 nulla in molestias nesciunt illo?/p>
</section>
```

2. In the same file, the closing `</section>` tag, add another section as per this code snippet:

```
<section class="bg-warning clearfix mb-3">
 <img src="http://placehold.it/150x150" alt="" class="img-fluid
 rounded-circle p-5">
 <p>Lorem ipsum dolor sit amet, consectetur adipisicing elit.
 Fugit iusto quis inventore. Sint ipsum consectetur molestias
 consequuntur veritatis earum voluptates officia pariatur, saepe
 quae illum ipsam omnis ab deleniti, eum.</p>
</section>
```

3. Follow it up by adding the third `<section>` element:

```
<section class="bg-danger clearfix mb-3">
 <img src="http://placehold.it/150x150" alt="" class="img-fluid
 rounded-circle p-5">
 <p class="d-inline">Lorem ipsum dolor sit amet, consectetur
 adipisicing elit. Fugit iusto quis inventore. Sint ipsum
 consectetur molestias consequuntur veritatis earum voluptates
 officia pariatur, saepe quae illum ipsam omnis ab deleniti, eum.
 </p>
</section>
```

4. Finally, let's wrap up this recipe by adding the fourth `<section>` and then closing `</div>` for the wrapping container:

```
<section class="bg-info text-white clearfix mb-3">
<img src="http://placehold.it/150x150" alt="" class="img-fluid
rounded float-left float-sm-none float-md-left float-lg-none
float-xl-left p-5">
<p>Lorem ipsum dolor sit amet, consectetur adipisicing elit.
Voluptate illum praesentium quam aliquam adipisci in ullam,
accusantium itaque rem quasi consequatur esse suscipit
consequuntur est ad vel enim omnis quibusdam!</p>
</section>

</div>
```

5. Save the file and run `harp server`. Navigate to `localhost:9000/recipe6` in your browser and view the result.

How it works...

In this simple recipe, we have four areas that repeat the same HTML structure, with the exception of different `.float-*-*` classes used on the `<img>` tags in each of the four sections.

 To clear floats, we use the `.clearfix` class on each of the `<section>` elements. These elements are parents of the floated `<img>` tags. As explained in the documentation, you need to use the `.clearfix` class on the parent of a floated element. For more information, please refer to the following address: `https://v4-alpha.getbootstrap.com/utilities/clearfix/`.

The first image has the following `.float-*-*` classes present: `.float-left`, `.float-sm-right`, `.float-md-left`, `.float-lg-right`, and `.float-xl-left`. If we resize the browser window, we can observe the effect these classes have on our floated `<img>` element. This results in our image being floated left on the smallest screens, which is determined by the `.float-left` class. Next, on the sm breakpoint and up, it is floated right. For md breakpoint and up, it is again floated left. This goes on, with the image switching to the opposite side on each wider breakpoint.

To understand this behavior better, we need to look at the official docs which list the breakpoint sizes, found at `https://v4-alpha.getbootstrap.com/layout/overview/#res ponsive-breakpoints`.

Looking at the docs, we can see that the image is floated left until it reaches the `sm` breakpoint, at about 575 pixels. Then, it floats right and it stays right till about 767 pixels. At `md` sizes (767-991 pixels), it is floated left. Between 991 and 1199 pixels, it is floated right, and finally, over 1199 pixels, at `xl` sizes, it is floated left again.

In section two of the recipe (in step 2), there are no `.float-*-*` classes in use, and thus the image stacks on top of the paragraph. Even though `<img>` is an inline element, it still stacks on top of the `<p>` tag since `<p>` is a block element.

In section three of the recipe (in step 3), we change this behavior of the `<p>` tag, by adding the `.d-inline` class to it. It is interesting to observe the result of this change.

Finally, in section four, we are alternating the float classes, just like in section one. However, this time we are also adding the `.float-*-none` classes, which add the `float: none !important;` to the image at `sm` screen widths (between about 551 pixels and 767 pixels), and at `lg` screen widths (between about 991 pixels and 1199 pixels).

Besides the various `.float-*` classes used in this recipe, we also use the `.img-fluid` class, which in Bootstrap 4 does what `.img-responsive` did in Bootstrap 3, which is to make sure that the image responds to `viewport` changes.

We also use the class of `.rounded-circle`, which turns our image into a circle (by giving the image it is applied to a `border-radius` property with the value of `50%`).

In section four, instead of `.rounded-circle`, we use just the class of `.rounded`, which results in our image having its original squared shape, with rounded corners.

Wrapping text around rounded images

In this recipe, we will align text around images using default Bootstrap classes with the addition of the `shape-outside` CSS property. With `shape-outside`, we can change the shape of a float area for a floated element, from a square into a circle or even a polygon.

For advanced uses of the shape-outside property, check out the Adobe Brackets editor extension at `http://brackets.dnbard.com/extension/br ackets-css-shapes-editor`.

Getting ready

Navigate to the **recipe6** page of the **chapter 3** website, and preview the final result that we are trying to achieve. To get this look, we are combining Bootstrap's default `.float-*`, `.img-fluid` and `.rounded-circle` classes, with our custom `.wrap-text-around`, `.circle-placed-right`, and `.circle-placed-left` classes. We will create this look from the empty files readily available in our `chapter3-start` folder.

How to do it...

1. Navigate to `chapter3/start/app/recipe7.ejs` and add the following code to the currently empty file:

```
<div class="container mt-5">
 <h1>Chapter 3, Recipe 7:</h1>
 <p class="lead mb-5">Wrap Text Around Rounded Images</p>

<h1 class="h2 mb-4">Some Heading</h1>
```

2. Follow this up by adding a `<div>` tag that wraps the `<img>` and `<p>` tags inside:

```
<div class="wrap-text-around clearfix">
 <img src="http://placehold.it/250x250" alt="" class="img-fluid
 rounded-circle float-right circle-placed-right">
 <p class="float-left">Lorem ipsum dolor sit amet, consectetur
 adipisicing elit. Tempora facilis vero iusto quis ut pariatur
 dicta voluptas cupiditate, fuga ullam adipisci assumenda
 architecto voluptatem, at magni repellat dolorem reiciendis
 ratione numquam optio quam iste. Sed temporibus, eaque nostrum
 alias deserunt?</p>
 <p class="mb-5">Lorem ipsum dolor sit amet, consectetur
 adipisicing elit. Unde minus eius sunt eveniet voluptatem
 corrupti corporis quia sit! Quae neque dolores repellendus unde
 ea voluptates asperiores accusantium fugit nisi ratione saepe
 doloremque dolor incidunt, facere aliquid magni. Sit, soluta,
 deleniti!</p>
 </div>
```

3. Complete the `recipe7.ejs` file by adding the following code at the bottom:

```
<div class="wrap-text-around clearfix">
<img src="http://placehold.it/250x250" alt="" class="img-fluid
rounded-circle float-left circle-placed-left">
<p class="float-right">Lorem ipsum dolor sit amet, consectetur
adipisicing elit. Tempora facilis vero iusto quis ut pariatur
dicta voluptas cupiditate, fuga ullam adipisci assumenda
architecto voluptatem, at magni repellat dolorem reiciendis
ratione numquam optio quam iste. Sed temporibus, eaque nostrum
alias deserunt?</p>
<p class="mb-5">Lorem ipsum dolor sit amet, consectetur
adipisicing elit. Unde minus eius sunt eveniet voluptatem
corrupti corporis quia sit! Quae neque dolores repellendus unde
ea voluptates asperiores accusantium fugit nisi ratione saepe
doloremque dolor incidunt, facere aliquid magni. Sit, soluta,
deleniti!</p>
</div>
```

4. Open the `main-03-07.scss` file and add the following code to it:

```
.wrap-text-around .circle-placed-right {
margin-left: 3rem;
-webkit-shape-outside:circle();
shape-outside:circle();
}
.wrap-text-around .circle-placed-left {
margin-right: 3rem;
-webkit-shape-outside:circle();
shape-outside:circle();
}
```

5. In `main.scss`, uncomment the `@include` for `main-03-07.scss`.

6. Save everything, and run `grunt sass` and `harp server`. Open the page with recipe7 in your browser.

How it works...

Similarly to the previous recipe, we are adding an `<img>` tag, followed by a `<p>` tag, in a wrapping element. This time, the wrapping HTML element is a `<div>` in both cases.

The first image is floated right. The second image is floated left. To make the text follow the circular outline of the image, we use custom CSS classes, with their styles set in `main-03-07.scss`. To prevent paragraph text from touching the rounded image, we use the `margin-right` or the `margin-left` CSS property, based on where the image is floated.

The CSS shapes W3C specification can be found at `https://www.w3.org/TR/css-shapes/`. This CSS property allows for creation of such layouts that were previously only possible in print. More information on the topic can be found on the Mozilla Developer Network, at `https://developer.mozilla.org/en/docs/Web/CSS/shape-outside`.

To see the list of browsers that support this feature, check out the *Can I use...* web page, at `http://caniuse.com/#feat=css-shapes`.

If you want to support older browsers, it might be useful to look into the CSS shapes polyfill by Adobe, available at `https://github.com/adobe-webplatform/css-shapes-polyfill`.

Styling a pricing section using Bootstrap's default table classes

In this recipe, we will utilize default table-specific Bootstrap classes to achieve several variations on the same HTML structure.

Getting ready

Navigate to the **recipe8** page of the **chapter 3** website, and preview the final result that we are trying to achieve. To get this look, we will use several Bootstrap 4 classes, as follows:

- `.table-responsive` and `.table`
- `.table-striped`, `.table-bordered`, and `.table-hover`
- `.table-inverse`, `.table-warning`, `.table-info`, `.table-danger`, `.table-success`, and `.table-sm`
- `.thead-default` and `.thead-inverse`

The basic HTML structure will be repeated several times, with changes involving the use of various combinations of the aforementioned Bootstrap 4 classes.

How to do it...

1. Open the empty `chapter3/start/app/recipe8.ejs` file and add the following code to it:

```
<div class="container mt-5">
 <h1>Chapter 3, Recipe 8:</h1>
 <p class="lead mb-5">Style a Price Section Using Bootstrap's
 Default Table Classes</p>
```

    In the preceding code, just like in the previous recipes, we are setting up the heading and lead paragraph for this recipe.

2. Add the table inside a `div` tag with the classes of `.table-responsive`, `.text-center`, and `.mb-5`:

```
<div class="table-responsive text-center mb-5">
 <table class="table table-striped table-sm ">
 <thead>
 <tr>
 <!-- https://github.com/twbs/bootstrap/issues/16146 -->
 <th class="text-center">Free Plan</th>
 <th class="text-center">Basic Plan</th>
 <th class="text-center">Pro Plan</th>
 </tr>
 </thead>
 <tbody>
 <tr>
 <td>1 website</td>
 <td>10 websites</td>
 <td>Unlimited websites</td>
 </tr>
 <tr>
 <td>Code Checker</td>
 <td>Code Checker</td>
 <td>Code Checker</td>
 </tr>
 <tr>
 <td><i class="fa fa-minus"></i></td>
 <td>Website Analytics</td>
 <td>Website Analytics</td>
 </tr>
 <tr>
 <td><i class="fa fa-minus text-muted"></i></td>
 <td><i class="fa fa-minus text-muted"></i></td>
 <td>Encryption</td>
```

```
</tr>
<tr>
<td>
<i class="fa fa-star text-success"></i>
</td>
<td>
<i class="fa fa-star text-success"></i>
<i class="fa fa-star text-success"></i>
</td>
<td>
<i class="fa fa-star text-success"></i>
<i class="fa fa-star text-success"></i>
<i class="fa fa-star text-success"></i>
</td>
</tr>
<tr>
<td>free</td>
<td>$9 / month</td>
<td>$29 / month</td>
</tr>
</tbody>
</table>
</div>
```

The preceding code is the basis of this recipe. We will reuse this code several times.

3. Copy the table code from step 2 of this recipe and paste it to the bottom of the file. Right now, you should have two identical tables in `recipe8.ejs`.

4. In the second table, locate the `<table class="table table-striped table-sm ">` code and replace it with `<table class="table table-hover table-bordered ">`. This will remove the alternating stripes from the table and add the hover effect when hovering over rows in table 2.

5. While you are still in the second table, locate the last `<tr>` tag and add `class="h5"`. This will make the prices listed in the last row stand out in comparison to the rest of the table.

6. Copy the contents of the second table and paste them to the third table at the bottom of the recipe code.

7. In the third table, find the `<table class="table table-hover table-bordered ">` code and replace it with `<table class="table table-inverse table-hover table-sm ">`. After this change, table 3 will have smaller rows, black background color, and no borders.

8. In table 3, in the very next row, extend the existing `<thead>` with the `<thead class="bg-info">` code. Doing this will color the `<thead>` element with Bootstrap's information color (`#5bc0de`).

9. Again in table 3, for the table cells that have no features (`fa-minus` icon), add the class of `.text-muted`. This will make the minus icons in those cells less intrusive, but still visible.

10. Copy table 3 and paste it in as table 4.

11. In table 4, find the line `<table class="table table-inverse table-hover table-sm ">`, and replace it with the following:

    ```
    <table class="table table-striped table-bordered table-warning">
    ```

    This will give our table a pale yellow background, with alternating light and dark stripes, and a light gray border on all the cells. There will be no hover effects.

12. When we copy table 4 and paste it in as table 5, the only difference we will make is still on the `<table>` element. Replace the `<table class="table table-striped table-bordered table-warning">` code in table 5 with the following:

    ```
    <table class="table table-striped table-hover table-bordered
    table-danger">
    ```

13. Copy table 5 and paste it below as table 6.

14. Locate this code in table 6:

    ```
    <table class="table table-striped table-hover table-bordered
    table-danger">
    <thead>
    ```

15. Replace the preceding code with this code:

    ```
    <table class="table table-striped table-hover table-bordered
    table-info">
     <thead class="thead-inverse">
    ```

    This change will give our `<thead>` element a black background and white text. The rest of the table will have a light blue background, with alternating light and dark rows, and a hover effect for the currently hovered row.

16. Copy table 6 and paste it in as table 7.

17. In table 7, locate this code:

```
<table class="table table-striped table-hover table-bordered
  table-info">
  <thead class="thead-inverse">
```

18. Replace the preceding code with this one:

```
<table class="table table-striped table-hover table-bordered
  table-success">
  <thead class="thead-default">
```

How it works...

In this recipe, we have used default Bootstrap 4 table-specific classes to create a number of color combinations. To center the text in the tables, we used the `.text-center` class. However, this still does not center the text in `<thead>`, so we had to follow the advice on how to solve it as explained on the Bootstrap issue page, at `https://github.com/twbs/boo tstrap/issues/16146`.

With the use of Font Awesome icons, we further improved our tables.

It is important to note that if we used just the `.table-responsive` class on its own, our table would shrink to wrap its content. This means that the table in our example would never span 100% of its parent container. To rectify this, and make the tables span 100% of the available space while still remaining responsive, we had to place the `.table-responsive` class in the wrapping `div`, with all the remaining table-specific classes in the `<table>` element and the subsequent HTML elements (such as `<thead>`, `<tbody>`, `<tr>`, and so on), which are all encapsulated by the top-most `div.table-responsive` for each of our example tables.

Another great feature of `.table-responsive` is the fact that on smaller screens, we get horizontal scrollbars, which makes it a lot easier to view the contents of our tables on mobile devices.

Since the class of `.table-responsive` is dealing with an aspect of accessibility, this is a good opportunity to mention `aria` roles, which were not the focus of this chapter and will be discussed in a later chapter.

Finally, it is worth noting that the SCSS styles that define table-specific styling can be found in two Sass partials: `_reboot.scss` and `_tables.scss`.

Reboot is an opinionated extension of Normalize. The detailed explanation is available at `http://v4-alpha.getbootstrap.com/content/reboot/`. As one comment at the top of `_reboot.scss` reads, Reboot contains global resets to common HTML elements. This, of course, includes the `<table>` element.

The `_tables.scss` is a relatively short Sass partial that further defines the final styling for Bootstrap 4 tables out of the box. It has only about 150 lines of code and it's worth checking out to garner a better understanding of how it works.

4
Diving Deep into Bootstrap 4 Components

In this chapter, we will cover:

- Creating custom alerts and positioning them in the viewport
- Making full-page modals
- Altering the behavior of popups using tether options
- Controlling the color and opacity of ToolTips using Sass variables
- Using Bootstrap's Sass mixins to create custom buttons
- Adjusting the rounding of corners on buttons and button groups
- Controlling the number of card columns on different breakpoints with SCSS
- Making cards responsive
- Easily positioning inline forms

Creating custom alerts and positioning them in the viewport

In this recipe, we will create four alerts that will appear in the top-right corner of a web page. To see the final result, open the `chapter4/complete` code's `app` folder, and run the `git bash` command on it. Follow it up with the `harp server` command, and navigate to `localhost:9000` in your browser to see the result we will achieve in this recipe.

Upon opening the web page as explained in the preceding paragraph, you should see the four alerts appearing one after the other. Click on the close button to close any of them, and note how they are being closed with various jQuery effects.

Getting ready

To get acquainted with the alert component of the Bootstrap 4 framework, refer to the official documentation at https://v4-alpha.getbootstrap.com/components/alerts/.

A quick tip regarding code formatting on Cloud9 IDE: There is a simple solution for users to format code in Cloud9 IDE. The user should align all the copy/pasted code to the left margin with a couple of strokes of *Shift* + *Tab*. Then, to format the code, simply use the keyboard shortcut *Ctrl* + *Shift* + *B*.

How to do it...

1. Open the currently empty file located at chapter4/start/app/recipe04-01.ejs, and add the following code:

```
<div class="container">

  <div class="mt-5">
  <h1><%- title %></h1>
  <p><a href="https://v4-
  alpha.getbootstrap.com/components/alerts/" target="_blank">Link
  to bootstrap alerts docs</a></p>
  </div>
</div><!-- /.container -->
```

2. Still in the same file, add any additional content. If you choose to do so, you can add the content from the chapter4/complete/app/recipe04-01.ejs folder.

3. Open the chapter4/start folder and navigate to app/partial/_js.ejs. Add the following code to the bottom of the file:

```
<%- partial("_recipe-04-01-js") %>
```

4. Open the empty _recipe-04-01-js.ejs file, located in the app/partial folder.

5. Add the following code to the file opened in the preceding step:

```
<script>

$(document).ready(function() {
  $(".alert-warning").delay(1000).fadeIn(500);
  $(".alert-info").delay(3000).fadeIn(500);
  $(".alert-success").delay(4000).fadeIn(500);
  $(".alert-danger").delay(5500).fadeIn(500);
});

$(".alert-warning").on("click", "button.close", function() {
  $(this).parent().hide('fast', function() {
  $(this).remove();
  });
});

$(".alert-info").on("click", "button.close", function() {
  $(this).parent().hide('slow', function() {
  $(this).remove();
  });
});

$(".alert-success").on("click", "button.close", function() {
  $(this).parent().animate({opacity: 0}, 1500).hide('fast',
  function() {
  $(this).remove();
  });
});

$(".alert-danger").on("click", "button.close", function() {
  $(this).parent().slideUp('slow', function() {
  $(this).remove();
  });
});
</script>
```

6. Open the SCSS file `recipe04-01.scss` and add the following code to it:

```
// hide the .alert class so that it can be displayed with jQuery
.alert {
 display: none;
}

// position the div that holds all the alerts in the top-right
corner of the window
.top-right {
 position: fixed;
```

```
    z-index: 9999;
    top: 20px;
    right: 20px;
    padding-left: 50px;
    transition: all 0.5s ease;
}
```

How it works...

This is an example of alerts popping up in the top-right corner, with a high z-index so that they appear above all the other elements on the page.

There are four alerts that will show up in the top-right corner of this recipe's web page.

The first is a warning alert, the second is an info alert, the third is a success alert, and the fourth is a danger alert.

On all the alerts, the HTML attribute of `data-dismiss="alert"` is removed from the HTML.

We added a custom class of `.top-right` on the alert container. We also used the classes of `.col-12` and `.col-md-5` so that on the screen under the md breakpoint, the alert spans the full width of the viewport, minus the `50px` padding (set in the `.top-right` class). Above the md breakpoint, the alert will take up 5 of 12 columns of the available screen space.

To make the alerts behave the way we want, we will use custom jQuery.

Looking at the jQuery code used for this recipe, we can see that we are setting delays on the appearance of each of the alerts, followed by the `.fadeIn()` jQuery function. This is how the alerts get onto our screen. Note that in our SCSS file for the recipe, we added `display: none;` to the `alert` class in order to prevent the alerts from showing via CSS.

Once the alerts are on the screen, we need to somehow allow the user to remove them. Since we are overriding the default Bootstrap behavior, in order to remove the alert, we will target `button.close` of each individual alerts, and apply various jQuery effects on each of them. Try closing each of the alerts to see the effects in practice.

The default Bootstrap behavior when using `data-dismiss="alert"` is that it removes the alert from the **Document Object Model** (**DOM**). Since we are overriding this behavior, we must make sure that the element is not only hidden from the screen but also removed. We achieve that in our jQuery using the following line of code: `$(this).remove();`. This way, we get the same end result as with the default Bootstrap alerts behavior so that the alert element in question is removed from the DOM.

Making full-page modals

In this recipe, we will alter the behavior of the modal component, so as to have it completely cover the available screen space.

To see the final result, open the `chapter4/complete` code's `app` folder, and run the `git bash` on it. Follow it up with the `harp server` command, and navigate to `localhost:9000` in your browser to see the result we will achieve in this recipe.

Upon opening the web page as explained in the preceding paragraph, you should see a large **Click Me** button that will trigger the modal, which will then appear and cover the entire viewport.

Getting ready

To get acquainted with the modal component in Bootstrap 4, visit `https://v4-alpha.getbootstrap.com/components/modal/`.

How to do it...

1. Open the empty `recipe-04-02.ejs` file, located in the `chapter4/start/app` folder.
2. Add the following code to it:

```
<div class="container">

<div class="mt-5">
<h1><%- title %></h1>
<p><a href="https://v4-alpha.getbootstrap.com/components/modal/"
target="_blank">Link to bootstrap modal docs</a></p>

</div><!-- /.container -->
```

```html
<button type="button" class="btn btn-primary btn-lg" data-
toggle="modal" data-target="#myModal">
Click Me
</button>

<!-- Modal -->
<div class="modal fade modal-fullscreen" id="myModal" tabindex="-1"
role="dialog" aria-labelledby="exampleModalLabel" aria-
hidden="true">
 <div class="modal-dialog modal-lg" role="document">
 <div class="modal-content">
 <div class="modal-header">
 <h5 class="modal-title" id="exampleModalLabel">Modal title</h5>
 <button type="button" class="close" data-dismiss="modal" aria-
label="Close">
 <span aria-hidden="true">&times;</span>
 </button>
 </div>
 <div class="modal-body">
 <h1>Modal content goes here</h1>
 </div>
 <div class="modal-footer">
 <button type="button" class="btn btn-secondary" data-
dismiss="modal">Close</button>
 <button type="button" class="btn btn-primary">Save
changes</button>
 </div>
 </div>
 </div>
</div>
```

3. Open the empty SCSS file, `recipe04-02.scss`, and paste the following code in it:

```scss
// Scale up the modal
@include media-breakpoint-up(sm) {
 // Automatically set modal's width for larger viewports
 .modal-dialog {
 max-width: 100%;
 height: 100%;
 margin: 0;
 }

 .modal-content {
 @include box-shadow($modal-content-sm-up-box-shadow);
 }

 .modal-sm { max-width: 100%; }
```

```
}

@include media-breakpoint-up(lg) {
  .modal-lg { max-width: 100%; }
}


.modal.modal-fullscreen {
  /* Maximize the main wrappers on the screen */
  /* Make the parent wrapper of the modal box a full-width block */
  /* Remove borders and effects on the content */
  /**
   * /! By using this feature, you force the header and footer to be
placed
   * in an absolute position. You must handle by yourself the margin
of the
   * content.
   */
  opacity: .98;
  filter: alpha(opacity=98);
}
.modal.modal-fullscreen .modal-dialog,
.modal.modal-fullscreen .modal-content {
  bottom: 0;
  left: 0;
  position: absolute;
  right: 0;
  top: 0;
}
.modal.modal-fullscreen .modal-dialog {
  margin: 0;
  width: 100%;
}
.modal.modal-fullscreen .modal-content {
  border: none;
  -moz-border-radius: 0;
  border-radius: 0;
  -webkit-box-shadow: inherit;
  -moz-box-shadow: inherit;
  -o-box-shadow: inherit;
  box-shadow: inherit;
}
.modal.modal-fullscreen.force-fullscreen {
  /* Remove the padding inside the body */
}
.modal.modal-fullscreen.force-fullscreen .modal-body {
  padding: 0;
}
```

```
.modal.modal-fullscreen.force-fullscreen .modal-header,
.modal.modal-fullscreen.force-fullscreen .modal-footer {
  left: 0;
  position: absolute;
  right: 0;
}
.modal.modal-fullscreen.force-fullscreen .modal-header {
  top: 0;
}
.modal.modal-fullscreen.force-fullscreen .modal-footer {
  bottom: 0;
}

.modal-backdrop.modal-backdrop-fullscreen.in {
  opacity: .97;
  filter: alpha(opacity=97);
}
```

4. Recompile the Sass code, restart the `harp server` command, and preview the result in your browser.

How it works...

In this recipe, we are using code from the example modal provided by the official Bootstrap website, at `https://v4-alpha.getbootstrap.com/components/modal/#live-demo`.

We alter the appearance of the sample modal by changing its SCSS and CSS properties. There is no JavaScript involved in this recipe.

We start off the `recipe04-02.scss` file by setting the `.modal-dialog` class to be 100% of the larger viewports.

We follow this up by setting the opacity to a high value of `.98`, which gives us a nice overlay effect with the content under the modal almost invisible. Changing the background color and/or this opacity setting might produce interesting results, which could be a further exercise as an extension of this recipe.

Finally, we override the css properties of `.modal-fullscreen` class and position the `.modal-header` and `.modal-footer` absolutely.

The beauty of this recipe is that we have a fully working full-page overlay that works both on mobile and desktop, and that can have versatile uses. For example, we could use it to display blog posts, or as an alternative to the usual ways of displaying menus in Bootstrap.

Altering the behavior of popups using tether options

In this recipe, we will alter the pop-up component so that it can be dismissed by clicking anywhere on the page.

To see the final result, open the `chapter4/complete` code's `app` folder, and run the `git bash` on it. Follow it up with the `harp server` command, and navigate to `localhost:9000` in your browser to see the result we will achieve in this recipe.

Upon opening the web page as explained in the previous paragraph, you should see a large **Dismissible popover** button. Clicking on the button will make the popover appear. Clicking again (anywhere on the page) will close the popover.

Getting ready

To get acquainted with the popover component in Bootstrap 4, visit `https://v4-alpha.getbootstrap.com/components/popovers/`. Also, visit `http://tether.io/` for additional information, as popovers rely on this third-party library to work.

Test the default behavior of the popover component by checking out the live demo section at `https://v4-alpha.getbootstrap.com/components/popovers/#live-demo`.

How to do it...

1. Open the currently empty file located at `chapter4/start/app/recipe04-03.ejs`, and add the following code:

    ```
    <div class="container">

    <div class="mt-5">
    <h1><%- title %></h1>
    <p><a
    href="https://v4-alpha.getbootstrap.com/components/popovers/"
    ```

```
target="_blank">Link to bootstrap popovers docs</a></p>

</div><!-- /.container -->

<a tabindex="0"
 class="btn btn-lg btn-danger"
 role="button" data-toggle="popover"
 data-trigger="focus"
 data-container="body"

 data-content="Lorem ipsum dolor sit amet, consectetur adipisicing
 elit. Vel, temporibus fugiat modi quia provident aut? Labore, minus
 hic sapiente animi vero tempora odio fugit consectetur porro. Dolor
 fuga, consectetur facere aliquid veniam, distinctio nam
 perspiciatis explicabo quam ipsum obcaecati sequi nostrum tempora.
 Minima modi, dignissimos nam facilis eum cupiditate nisi?">
 Dismissible popover
</a>
```

2. Still in the same file, add any additional content. If you choose to do so, you can add the content from the `chapter4/complete/app/recipe04-03.ejs` folder. This step is optional; the recipe will still work if you skip it.

3. Open the `chapter4start` folder and navigate to `app/partial/_js.ejs`. Add the following code to the bottom of the file:

```
<%- partial("_recipe-04-03-js") %>
```

4. Open the empty `_recipe-04-03-js.ejs` file, located in the `app/partial` folder.

5. Add the following code to the file opened in the preceding step:

```
<script>
$(function () {
$('[data-toggle="popover"]').popover({
trigger: 'hover', // trigger: 'focus',
delay: { "show": 500, "hide": 100 },
attachment: 'top left',
targetAttachment: 'top right',
constraints: [
{
to: 'window',
pin: true
}
] // constraints
}); // popover
}); // function
```

```
</script>
```

6. Start the `harp server`, and preview the result in your browser.

How it works...

In this simple recipe, we utilized the options provided by the tether library to alter the behavior of our popup.

The options we adjusted involve both using the HTML `data-*` attributes and the JavaScript options as described in the tether documentation, namely **constraint options** and **offset options**.

Looking at the HTML attributes, we can see that the options we can use include the `title` attribute, which gives a card-like styling to the popover's heading (`title`).

Looking at the JS options, we can inspect the code called on document ready:

```
$(function () {
  $('[data-toggle="popover"]').popover({
  trigger: 'hover', // trigger: 'focus',
  delay: { "show": 500, "hide": 100 },
  attachment: 'top left',
  targetAttachment: 'top right',
  constraints: [
  {
  to: 'window',
  pin: true
  }
  ] // constraints
  }); // popover
}); // function
```

The above code is pretty easy to understand. Among other things, we can set the trigger for the popover. The trigger is set to `hover`.

This changes the usual behavior of having to click on the button to toggle the popover on and off, as seen in the **Live preview** section of the official Bootstrap documentation.

Another change added in the JavaScript options is the delay to show and hide the popover based on the triggerable events.

Controlling the color and opacity of ToolTips using Sass variables

In this recipe, we will change the ToolTip component so that it has a different color, as well as a different opacity, from what we have in the default options.

To see the final result, open the `chapter4/complete` code's `app` folder, and run the `git bash` on it. Follow it up with the `harp server` command, and navigate to `localhost:9000` in your browser to see the result we will achieve in this recipe.

Upon opening the web page as explained in the previous paragraph, you should see four buttons. Hovering over each of the buttons will trigger ToolTips in four different directions.

Getting ready

To get started with the ToolTip component in Bootstrap 4, visit `https://v4-alpha.getboot strap.com/components/ToolTips/`. Also, visit `http://tether.io/` for additional information, as ToolTips relies on this third-party library to work.

Test the default behavior of the ToolTip component by checking out the interactive demo section at `https://v4-alpha.getbootstrap.com/components/ToolTips/#interactive-d emo`.

How to do it...

1. Open the currently empty file located at `chapter4/start/app/recipe04-04.ejs`, and add the following code:

   ```
   <div class="container">

    <div class="mt-5">
    <h1><%- title %></h1>
    <p><a
   href="https://v4-alpha.getbootstrap.com/components/ToolTips/"
   target="_blank">Link to bootstrap ToolTips docs</a></p>

    </div><!-- /.container -->

    <button type="button" class="btn btn-secondary" data-
   toggle="ToolTip" data-placement="top" >
   ```

```
 Tooltip on top
</button>
<button type="button" class="btn btn-secondary" data-
toggle="ToolTip" data-placement="right" >
 Tooltip on right
</button>
<button type="button" class="btn btn-secondary" data-
toggle="ToolTip" data-placement="bottom" >
 Tooltip on bottom
</button>
<button type="button" class="btn btn-secondary" data-
toggle="ToolTip" data-placement="left" >
 Tooltip on left
</button>
```

2. While you are still in the same file, add any additional content. If you choose to do so, you can add the content from the chapter4/complete/app/recipe04-04.ejs folder. This step is optional; the recipe will work if you skip it.

3. Open the chapter4/start folder and navigate to app/partial/_js.ejs. Add the following code to the bottom of the file:

```
<%- partial("_recipe-04-04-js") %>
```

4. Open the empty _recipe-04-01-js.ejs file, located in the app/partial folder.

5. Add the following code to the file opened in the previous step:

```
<script>
// Enable ToolTips everywhere
$(function () {
$('[data-toggle="ToolTip"]').ToolTip()
})
</script>
```

6. Open the recipe04-04.scss file and add the following code to it:

```
$ToolTip-arrow-color: tomato;
$ToolTip-bg: tomato;
$ToolTip-opacity: 1;
```

7. Compile Sass and run the harp server command. You should see the changed ToolTips, with the colors and opacity as you set them in step 6 of this recipe.

How it works…

In this recipe, we used the tether library to call our ToolTips. However, we did not set options or specify behavior via JavaScript. Instead, we used the HTML `data-*` attributes to position the ToolTips in all the buttons at different locations.

First, we used the `data-toggle` attribute and passed it the value of `ToolTip`. Second, we used the `data-placement` attribute to position our respective ToolTips with one of four values (depending on the button): `top`, `right`, `bottom`, and `left`. The HTML `title` attribute is used to display the ToolTip text.

So far, we have set all our ToolTips just as per the official Bootstrap documentation. Then, we added our own twist by changing the value of the Sass variables, as shown in step 6 of this recipe.

Using Bootstrap's Sass mixins to create custom buttons

To create custom buttons, we will use Bootstrap's Sass mixins in this recipe.

To see the final result, open the `chapter4completed` code's `app` folder, and run the `git bash` on it. Follow it up with the `harp server` command, and navigate to `localhost:9000` in your browser to see the result we will achieve in this recipe.

Upon opening the web page as explained in the preceding paragraph, you should see six fully functional custom buttons at the bottom of the page.

Getting ready

To get started with the custom buttons in Bootstrap 4, first visit the official documentation on the buttons component in Bootstrap 4, available at `https://v4-alpha.getbootstrap.com/components/buttons/`.

Default buttons are showcased at `https://v4-alpha.getbootstrap.com/components/buttons/#examples`. Bootstrap 4 also introduces outline buttons. To see them in practice, navigate to `https://v4-alpha.getbootstrap.com/components/buttons/#outline-buttons`.

How to do it...

1. Open the currently empty file located at
   `chapter4/start/app/recipe04-05.ejs`, and add the following code:

   ```html
   <div class="container">

    <div class="mt-5">
    <h1 class="mb-2"><%- title %></h1>
    <h3 class="text-info mb-3">List of recipe-related official
   Bootstrap documentation</h3>
    <p><a href="https://v4-alpha.getbootstrap.com/components/buttons/"
   target="_blank">Link to bootstrap buttons docs</a></p>

   </div><!-- /.container -->

   <h3 class="mt-5 mb-3">Here is an example of using the Bootstrap
   sass mixin to create a custom button</h3>

   <p>First, we will import the mixins into our <code>main.scss</code>
   file, using the following <code>@import</code> statement:
   <code>@import
   "./bower_components/bootstrap/scss/_mixins.scss";</code></p>

   <p>Next, we will add the <code>@import</code> for the custom scss
   file for this recipe (recipe 5 of chapter 4).</p>

   <p>Finally, we'll add the custom code for the button, by specifying
   the values as described in the code comment.</p>

   <a class="btn btn-tomato" href="#" role="button">Custom Button
   (Tomato)</a>
   <button class="btn btn-green" type="button">Custom Button
   (Green)</button>
   <input class="btn btn-purple" type="button" value="Custom Button
   (Purple)">
   <br>
   <br>
   <a class="btn btn-outline-tomato" href="#" role="button">Custom
   Button (Tomato)</a>
   <button class="btn btn-outline-green" type="button">Custom Button
   (Green)</button>
   <input class="btn btn-outline-purple" type="button" value="Custom
   Button (Purple)">
   ```

2. Open the `main.scss` file and import the mixins into it, using the `@import` statement:

```
@import "./bower_components/bootstrap/scss/_mixins.scss";
```

3. Next, we will add `@import` for the custom SCSS file for this recipe:

```
@import "recipe04-05.scss";
```

Note that the above `@import` statement should go at the very end of the file.

4. Finally, we add the custom code for the button using the `button-variant` mixin:

```
// The button-variant mixin takes 3 parameters (as follows):
// @include button-variant($btn-primary-color, $btn-primary-bg,
$btn-primary-border);

.btn-tomato {
 @include button-variant(white, salmon, tomato);
}
.btn-green {
 @include button-variant(white, #1CB51C, #0DA60D);
}
.btn-purple {
 @include button-variant(white, #BA21ED, #AB12DE);
}

// The button-outline-variant mixin only takes one parameter, as
follows:
// @include button-outline-variant($color);

.btn-outline-tomato {
 @include button-outline-variant(salmon);
}
.btn-outline-green {
 @include button-outline-variant(#1CB51C);
}
.btn-outline-purple {
 @include button-outline-variant(#BA21ED);
}
```

5. Recompile Sass and start the `harp server` command to view the result.

How it works...

In step 1, we set up our HTML structure. To create buttons, we used HTML's a tag, and assigned them `btn` classes in the usual way. However, instead of assigning them the existing button classes, such as `class="btn btn-primary"`, we changed the second class to a custom class name, such as btn-tomato. This way, we are mirroring Bootstrap's button naming convention, which is great for productivity and collaboration.

Similarly, we set up outline buttons using `class="btn btn-outline-*"`, where * represents the custom color (tomato, green, or purple).

In step 2, we imported the mixins into our `main.scss` file, in order to be able to use the mixins to make our custom buttons.

In steps 3 and 4, we imported the SCSS file for this recipe and added code to it.

As mentioned in the code comments, we are using two mixins in this recipe: the `button-variant` mixin for custom buttons, and the `button-outline-variant` mixin for custom outline buttons.

The `button-variant` mixin takes three parameters: `$btn-primary-color`, `$btn-primary-bg`, and `$btn-primary-border`, whereas the `button-outline-variant` mixin takes only one parameter.

To define our custom css button classes, we simply start with the custom class name we used in our HTML structure in step 1 of this recipe, and inside the curly brackets, we pass an `@include` statement using the `@include mixin-name(parameter1, parameter2, parameter3)` pattern.

Adjusting the rounding of corners on buttons and button groups

There are several components that this recipe can be used on. The official documentation for these components is available at `https://v4-alpha.getbootstrap.com/components/buttons/`, `https://v4-alpha.getbootstrap.com/components/button-group/`, `https://v4-alpha.getbootstrap.com/components/dropdowns/`, and `https://v4-alpha.getbootstrap.com/components/pagination/`.

Getting ready

To make this recipe work, you will need to include the SCSS code from the preceding recipe. The reason for this is that the previous recipe already specifies the custom button classes used in this recipe too (classes of `btn-tomato`, `btn-green`, and `btn-purple`).

An alternative approach would be to use Bootstrap's default buttons, but if you choose to do it this way, bear in mind that you will need to change the references to `btn-tomato`, `btn-green`, and `btn-purple` in the following code to any of the default Bootstrap button classes, such as `btn-primary`, `btn-info`, and so on.

How to do it...

1. Open the currently empty file located at `chapter4/start/app/recipe04-06.ejs`, and add the following code:

```
<div class="container">

 <div class="mt-5">
 <h1><%- title %></h1>
 <p><a href="https://v4-alpha.getbootstrap.com/components/buttons/"
target="_blank">Link to bootstrap buttons docs</a></p>
 <p><a
href="https://v4-alpha.getbootstrap.com/components/button-group/"
target="_blank">Link to bootstrap button-groups docs</a></p>
 <p><a
href="https://v4-alpha.getbootstrap.com/components/dropdowns/"
target="_blank">Link to bootstrap dropdowns docs</a></p>
 <p><a
href="https://v4-alpha.getbootstrap.com/components/pagination/"
target="_blank">Link to bootstrap pagination docs</a></p>

</div><!-- /.container -->

<h3 class="mt-5 mb-3">Here is an example of using a Bootstrap sass
mixin to ccustomize the rounding of buttons.</h3>

<p>Add the <code>@import</code> for the custom scss file for this
recipe (recipe 6 of chapter 4).</p>

<p>Finally, we'll add the custom code for the button, by specifying
the values as described in the code comments.</p>

<a class="btn btn-tomato" href="#" role="button">Custom Rounded
```

```
Button (Tomato)</a>

<div class="btn-group" role="group" aria-label="Basic example">
 <button type="button" class="btn btn-green">Custom</button>
 <button type="button" class="btn btn-green">Rounded</button>
 <button type="button" class="btn btn-green">Green</button>
 <button type="button" class="btn btn-green">Button</button>
 <button type="button" class="btn btn-green">Group</button>
</div>


<div class="dropup mt-2">
 <button class="btn btn-purple dropdown-toggle" type="button"
id="dropdownMenuButton" data-toggle="dropdown" aria-haspopup="true"
aria-expanded="false">
 A Square Dropup button
 </button>
 <div class="dropdown-menu" aria-labelledby="dropdownMenuButton">
 <a class="dropdown-item" href="#">Action</a>
 <a class="dropdown-item" href="#">Another action</a>
 <a class="dropdown-item" href="#">Something else here</a>
 </div>
</div>
```

2. Open the `main.scss` file and import the mixins into it, using the `@import` statement:

```
@import "./bower_components/bootstrap/scss/_mixins.scss";
```

3. Next, we will add `@import` for the custom SCSS file for this recipe:

```
@import "recipe04-06.scss";
```

4. Finally, we will add the custom code for the recipe, as follows:

```
// For this mixin, it is enough to pass one parameter to the
border-radius mixin. The parameter is specified (in round brackets)

.btn-tomato {
 @include border-radius(2em)
}

.btn-green {
 @include border-radius(1.2em)
}

.btn-purple {
 @include border-radius(0)
```

```
        }
```

5. Recompile Sass and start the `harp server` command to view the result.

How it works...

Similarly to *Using Bootstrap's Sass mixins to create custom buttons* recipe of this chapter, we will utilize Bootstrap's Sass mixins to alter the look of our buttons. In this recipe, we will change the radius of borders on buttons, button groups, and drop-down components.

To achieve this, we are employing Bootstrap's border-radius mixin using the following pattern:

```
.classname {
    @incude border-radius(#em);
}
```

Controlling the number of card columns on different breakpoints with SCSS

This recipe will involve some SCSS mixins, which will alter the behavior of the card-columns component. To be able to showcase the desired effect, we will have to have a few hundred lines of compiled HTML code.

This poses an issue; how do we show all that code inside a recipe? Here, Harp partials come to the rescue! Since most of the code in this recipe is repetitive, we will make a separate file. The file will contain the code needed to make a single card. Then, we will have a `div` with the class of card-columns, and this div will hold 20 cards, which will, in fact, be 20 calls to the single card file in our source code before compilation. This will make it easy for us to showcase how the number of cards in this card-columns div will change, based on screen width.

To see the final result, open the `chapter4/complete` code's `app` folder, and run the console (that is, `bash`) on it. Follow it up with the `harp server` command, and navigate to `localhost:9000` in your browser to see the result we will achieve in this recipe.

Upon opening the web page as explained in the preceding paragraph, you should see 20 cards in a varying number of columns, depending on your screen size.

Getting ready

To get acquainted with how card-columns work, navigate to the card-columns section of the Bootstrap documentation at `https://v4-alpha.getbootstrap.com/components/card/#card-columns`.

How to do it…

1. Open the currently empty file located at `chapter4start/app/recipe04-07.ejs`, and add the following code:

```
<div class="container-fluid">

 <div class="mt-5">
 <h1><%- title %></h1>
 <p><a
href="https://v4-alpha.getbootstrap.com/components/card/#card-colum
ns" target="_blank">Link to bootstrap card-columns docs</a></p>

</div><!-- /.container-fluid -->


<div class="container-fluid mt-5 mb-5">
 <div class="card-columns">
 <!-- cards 1 to 5 -->
 <%- partial("partial/_recipe04-07-samplecard.ejs") %>
 <%- partial("partial/_recipe04-07-samplecard.ejs") %>
 <%- partial("partial/_recipe04-07-samplecard.ejs") %>
 <%- partial("partial/_recipe04-07-samplecard.ejs") %>
 <%- partial("partial/_recipe04-07-samplecard.ejs") %>

 <!-- cards 6 to 10 -->
 <%- partial("partial/_recipe04-07-samplecard.ejs") %>
 <%- partial("partial/_recipe04-07-samplecard.ejs") %>
 <%- partial("partial/_recipe04-07-samplecard.ejs") %>
 <%- partial("partial/_recipe04-07-samplecard.ejs") %>
 <%- partial("partial/_recipe04-07-samplecard.ejs") %>

 <!-- cards 11 to 15 -->
 <%- partial("partial/_recipe04-07-samplecard.ejs") %>
```

```
<%- partial("partial/_recipe04-07-samplecard.ejs") %>
<%- partial("partial/_recipe04-07-samplecard.ejs") %>
<%- partial("partial/_recipe04-07-samplecard.ejs") %>
<%- partial("partial/_recipe04-07-samplecard.ejs") %>

<!-- cards 16 to 20 -->
<%- partial("partial/_recipe04-07-samplecard.ejs") %>
<%- partial("partial/_recipe04-07-samplecard.ejs") %>
<%- partial("partial/_recipe04-07-samplecard.ejs") %>
<%- partial("partial/_recipe04-07-samplecard.ejs") %>
<%- partial("partial/_recipe04-07-samplecard.ejs") %>
</div>
</div>
```

2. Open the `main.scss` file, and comment out all the other imports since some of them clash with this recipe:

```
@import "recipe04-04.scss";


@import "./bower_components/bootstrap/scss/bootstrap.scss";
@import "./bower_components/bootstrap/scss/_mixins.scss";
@import "./bower_components/font-awesome/scss/font-awesome.scss";
@import "./bower_components/hover/scss/hover.scss";

// @import "recipe04-01.scss";
// @import "recipe04-02.scss";
// @import "recipe04-03.scss";

// @import "recipe04-05.scss";
// @import "recipe04-06.scss";
@import "recipe04-07.scss";
// @import "recipe04-08.scss";
// @import "recipe04-09.scss";
// @import "recipe04-10.scss";
// @import "recipe04-11.scss";
// @import "recipe04-12.scss";
```

3. Next, we will add the partial file with the single card code in `app/partial/_recipe04-07-samplecard.ejs`:

```
<div class="card">
<img class="card-img-top img-fluid"
 src="http://placehold.it/300x250"
 alt="Card image description">
<div class="card-block">
<h4 class="card-title">Lorem ipsum dolor sit amet.</h4>
```

```
<p class="card-text">Lorem ipsum dolor sit amet, consectetur
   adipisicing elit. Officia autem, placeat dolorem sed praesentium
   aliquid suscipit tenetur iure perspiciatis sint?</p>
</div>
</div>
```

> If you are serving the files on Cloud9 IDE, then reference the
> `placehold.it` images from HTTPS so you don't have the warnings
> appearing in the console.

4. Open this recipe's SCSS file, titled `recipe04-07.scss`, and paste the following code:

```
.card-columns {
@include media-breakpoint-only(sm) {
column-count: 2;
}
@include media-breakpoint-only(md) {
column-count: 3;
}
@include media-breakpoint-only(lg) {
column-count: 5;
}
@include media-breakpoint-only(xl) {
column-count: 7;
}
}
```

5. Recompile Sass and start the `harp server` command to view the result.

How it works...

In step 1, we added our recipe's structure in `recipe04-07.ejs`. The focus in this file is the div with the class of `card-columns`, which holds 20 calls to the sample card partial file.

In step 2, we included the SCSS file for this recipe, and to make sure that it works, we comment out the imports for all the other recipes' SCSS files.

In step 3, we made our single card, as per the Bootstrap documentation.

Finally, we customized the `.card-columns` class in our SCSS by changing the value of the `card-columns` property using the `media-breakpoint-only` mixin. The `media-breakpoint-only` mixin takes the `sm`, `md`, `lg`, and `xl` values as its parameter. This allows us to easily change the value of the `column-count` property in our layouts.

Making cards responsive

This recipe is closely connected with the preceding one. To show how to make cards responsive, we will use the preceding recipe's single card include.

To see the final result, open the `chapter4/complete` code's `app` folder, and run the `git bash` on it. Follow it up with the `harp server` command, and navigate to `localhost:9000` in your browser to see the result we will achieve in this recipe.

Upon opening the web page as explained in the previous paragraph, you should see two rows of cards in two card decks. The container that holds them is styled with the `.container-fluid` class. Open the dev tools with *F12* and drag its edge from right to left to see the decks respond to the change of the viewport.

Getting ready

To get acquainted with how card decks work, navigate to the card decks section of the Bootstrap documentation at `https://v4-alpha.getbootstrap.com/components/card/#card-decks`.

How to do it...

1. Open the currently empty file located at `chapter4/start/app/recipe04-08.ejs`, and add the following code:

```
<div class="container">

<div class="mt-5">
<h1><%- title %></h1>
<p><a href="https://v4-
 alpha.getbootstrap.com/components/card/#card-decks"
 target="_blank">Link to bootstrap card deck documentation</a></p>
</div>
```

```
</div><!-- /.container -->


<div class="container-fluid mt-5 mb-5">
 <div class="card-deck mt-5">
 <%- partial("partial/_recipe04-07-samplecard.ejs") %>
 <%- partial("partial/_recipe04-07-samplecard.ejs") %>
 <%- partial("partial/_recipe04-07-samplecard.ejs") %>
 <%- partial("partial/_recipe04-07-samplecard.ejs") %>
 </div>
 <div class="card-deck mt-5">
 <%- partial("partial/_recipe04-07-samplecard.ejs") %>
 <%- partial("partial/_recipe04-07-samplecard.ejs") %>
 <%- partial("partial/_recipe04-07-samplecard.ejs") %>
 <%- partial("partial/_recipe04-07-samplecard.ejs") %>
 </div>
</div>
```

2. Open the `main.scss` file, and comment out all the other imports since some of them clash with this recipe:

```
@import "recipe04-04.scss";


@import "./bower_components/bootstrap/scss/bootstrap.scss";
@import "./bower_components/bootstrap/scss/_mixins.scss";
@import "./bower_components/font-awesome/scss/font-awesome.scss";
@import "./bower_components/hover/scss/hover.scss";

// @import "recipe04-01.scss";
// @import "recipe04-02.scss";
// @import "recipe04-03.scss";

// @import "recipe04-05.scss";
// @import "recipe04-06.scss";
// @import "recipe04-07.scss";
 @import "recipe04-08.scss";
// @import "recipe04-09.scss";
// @import "recipe04-10.scss";
// @import "recipe04-11.scss";
// @import "recipe04-12.scss";
```

3. Open this recipe's SCSS file, titled `recipe04-08.scss`, and paste the following code:

```
.card {
img {
width: 100%;
}
}
```

4. Recompile Sass and start the `harp server` command to view the result.

How it works...

This is one of the simplest recipes in this book. It is important to know that it is so easy to achieve this effect. However, in order for it to work, make sure that you wrap your card decks in an HTML element styled with `.container-fluid`.

Easily positioning inline forms

In this recipe, we will position an inline form in the center of the viewport, on the left, and on the right. To achieve that, we will be using flexbox classes of `justify-content-center`, `justify-content-start`, and `justify-content-end`.

Getting ready

To get acquainted with how forms work, navigate to the forms component section of the Bootstrap documentation at `https://v4-alpha.getbootstrap.com/components/forms/`.

How to do it...

1. Open the currently empty file located at
   `chapter4/start/app/recipe04-09.ejs`, and add the following code:

```
<div class="container-fluid">

  <div class="mt-5">
  <h1><%- title %></h1>
  <p><a href="https://v4-alpha.getbootstrap.com/components/forms/"
    target="_blank">Link to bootstrap forms docs</a></p>
  </div>

</div><!-- /.container -->
```

2. In the same file, add the following code to the bottom to position the first form in the center:

```
<div class="container-fluid mt-5">
  <h2 class="text-center">Centered inline form</h2>
  <form class="form-inline justify-content-center">
  <label class="sr-only" for="inlineFormInput">Name</label>
  <input type="text" class="form-control mb-2 mr-sm-2 mb-sm-0"
    id="inlineFormInput" placeholder="Jane Doe">

  <label class="sr-only" for="inlineFormInputGroup">Username</label>
  <div class="input-group mb-2 mr-sm-2 mb-sm-0">
  <div class="input-group-addon">@</div>
  <input type="text" class="form-control" id="inlineFormInputGroup"
    placeholder="Username">
  </div>

  <div class="form-check mb-2 mr-sm-2 mb-sm-0">
  <label class="form-check-label">
  <input class="form-check-input" type="checkbox"> Remember me
  </label>
  </div>

  <button type="submit" class="btn btn-primary">Submit</button>
  </form>
</div>
```

3. In the same file, position the next form to the left:

```
<div class="container-fluid mt-5">
 <h2 class="text-left">Left-aligned inline form</h2>
 <form class="form-inline justify-content-start">
 <label class="sr-only" for="inlineFormInput">Name</label>
 <input type="text" class="form-control mb-2 mr-sm-2 mb-sm-0"
   id="inlineFormInput" placeholder="Jane Doe">

 <label class="sr-only" for="inlineFormInputGroup">Username</label>
 <div class="input-group mb-2 mr-sm-2 mb-sm-0">
 <div class="input-group-addon">@</div>
 <input type="text" class="form-control" id="inlineFormInputGroup"
   placeholder="Username">
 </div>

 <div class="form-check mb-2 mr-sm-2 mb-sm-0">
 <label class="form-check-label">
 <input class="form-check-input" type="checkbox"> Remember me
 </label>
 </div>

 <button type="submit" class="btn btn-primary">Submit</button>
 </form>
</div>
```

4. Follow it up by adding the form that will touch the right-hand side of the viewport:

```
<div class="container-fluid mt-5">
 <h2 class="text-right">Right-aligned inline form</h2>
 <form class="form-inline justify-content-end">
 <label class="sr-only" for="inlineFormInput">Name</label>
 <input type="text" class="form-control mb-2 mr-sm-2 mb-sm-0"
   id="inlineFormInput" placeholder="Jane Doe">

 <label class="sr-only" for="inlineFormInputGroup">Username</label>
 <div class="input-group mb-2 mr-sm-2 mb-sm-0">
 <div class="input-group-addon">@</div>
 <input type="text" class="form-control" id="inlineFormInputGroup"
  placeholder="Username">
 </div>

 <div class="form-check mb-2 mr-sm-2 mb-sm-0">
 <label class="form-check-label">
 <input class="form-check-input" type="checkbox"> Remember me
 </label>
 </div>
```

```
<button type="submit" class="btn btn-primary">Submit</button>
</form>
</div>
```

5. Recompile Sass and start the `harp server` command to view the result.

How it works...

The code for all the three inline forms is the same. To position the whole form, we simply use flexbox-enabled classes of `justify-content-*`.

5
Menus and Navigations

In this chapter, we will cover:

- Adding Font Awesome to Bootstrap navbar
- Placing a single Bootstrap navbar dropdown to the right
- Centering navbar links
- Making a transparent navbar on a darker background
- Creating A Navbar with Icons and Flexbox
- Adding another row of links to the navbar
- Adding Yamm3 Megamenu list of links to a navbar dropdown
- Adding Yamm3 Megamenu images to a navbar dropdown

Adding Font Awesome to Bootstrap navbar

In this recipe, we will build a navbar with a dropdown that will hold recipes for the chapter, and two additional links to showcase different navigation scenarios. To see the final result, open the `chapter5/complete` code's `app` folder, and run the `git bash` on it. Follow it up with the `harp server` command, and navigate to `localhost:9000` in your browser to see the result we will achieve in this recipe.

Upon opening the web page as explained in the preceding paragraph, there will be four top-level links, and each of them will have an icon next to it. The second link is a dropdown, whereas the others are regular links.

Getting ready

In this recipe, we are using a customized version of the navbar used on the official Bootstrap 4 site at `https://v4-alpha.getbootstrap.com/`. Feel free to inspect the home page in developer tools and get yourself acquainted with the structure of the navbar on the site.

How to do it...

1. Open the currently empty file located at `chapter5/start/main.scss`, and add the following code:

```
@import "./bower_components/bootstrap/scss/bootstrap.scss";
@import "./bower_components/bootstrap/scss/_mixins.scss";
@import "./bower_components/font-awesome/scss/font-awesome.scss";
@import "./bower_components/hover/scss/hover.scss";

    @import "recipe05-01.scss";
//  @import "recipe05-02.scss";
//  @import "recipe05-03.scss";
//  @import "recipe05-04.scss";
//  @import "recipe05-05.scss";
//  @import "recipe05-06.scss";
//  @import "recipe05-07.scss";
//  @import "recipe05-08.scss";
```

2. Open another blank file located at `chapter5/start/app/recipe05-01.ejs`, and add the following code:

```
<div class="container">

 <div class="mt-5">
 <h1><%- title %></h1>
 <p><a href="https://v4-alpha.getbootstrap.com/components/alerts/"
    target="_blank">Link to bootstrap alerts docs</a></p>

 </div><!-- /.container -->


 <p>We are using a customized version of the navbar used on the
    official bootstrap 4 website.</p>

 <p>It is customized by adding the <code>&lt;span&gt;</code> tags
    with the fa classes to display specific icons, on either side of
```

different links.</p>

<p>Finally, we are using a dropdown link on the navbar, and that dropdown is holding all the recipes used in this chapter.</p>

3. Navigate to the `partial` folder inside the `chapter5/start/app` folder, and add the following code to `_nav1.ejs`:

```
<header class="navbar navbar-light navbar-toggleable-md navbar-
light bg-faded">
 <nav class="container">
 <div class="d-flex justify-content-between">
 <a class="navbar-brand" href="/">
 <span class="fa fa-database"></span>
 Chapter 5
 </a>
 <button class="navbar-toggler collapsed" type="button" data-
  toggle="collapse" data-target="#bd-main-nav" aria-controls="bd-
  main-nav" aria-expanded="false" aria-label="Toggle navigation">
 <span class="navbar-toggler-icon"></span>
 </button>
 </div>

 <div class="navbar-collapse collapse" id="bd-main-nav" aria-
  expanded="false">
 <ul class="nav navbar-nav">
<li class="nav-item dropdown">
 <a class="nav-link dropdown-toggle" href="#" id="dropdown01" data-
  toggle="dropdown" aria-haspopup="true" aria-expanded="false">
 <span class="fa fa-book"></span>
 Recipes
 </a>
 <div class="dropdown-menu" aria-labelledby="dropdown01">
 <a class="dropdown-item" href="recipe05-01">1 - Adding Font
  Awesome to Bootstrap navbar</a>
 <a class="dropdown-item" href="recipe05-02">2 - Positioning
  Bootstrap navbar Items to the Right</a>
 <a class="dropdown-item" href="recipe05-03">3 - Centering an
  Element in the Bootstrap 4 navbar</a>
 <a class="dropdown-item" href="recipe05-04">4 - Background Overlap
  on navbar</a>
 <a class="dropdown-item" href="recipe05-05">5 - Changing the
navbar
  Toggle on Different Breakpoints</a>
 <a class="dropdown-item" href="recipe05-06">6 - Bootstrap Side
  Menu Collapse with navbar</a>
 <a class="dropdown-item" href="recipe05-07">7 - Bootstrap 4 navbar
  with 2 Rows at Right</a>
```

```
      <a class="dropdown-item" href="recipe05-08">8 - Decrease the
      Height of Bootstrap navbar</a>
      <a class="dropdown-item" href="recipe05-09">9 - Adding a Custom
      Burger Icon</a>
      </div>
      </li>
      <li class="nav-item">
      <a class="nav-item nav-link" href="#">
      <span class="fa fa-briefcase"></span>
      Example Link
      </a>
      </li>
      <li class="nav-item">
      <a class="nav-item nav-link" href="#">
      Another Link
      <span class="fa fa-bullhorn"></span>
      </a>
      </li>
      </ul>
      </div>
      </nav>
  </header>
```

4. Run `harp server` to preview the result.

How it works...

We used the navbar from the official Bootstrap website as the starting point. We customized this navbar by adding the `span` tags with the Font Awesome classes of `fa fa-*` to specify individual icons next to the navbar links.

Finally, we used a drop-down link on the navbar, and that drop-down link holds the links to all the recipes used in this chapter.

 It has been a practice for some time to put icons inside the `<i>` tags. However, that is not the preferred way of adding icons. The official Bootstrap documentation suggests using the `<span>` tags instead.

Placing a single Bootstrap navbar dropdown to the right

In this recipe, we are also using a customized version of the navbar used on the official Bootstrap 4 website. The navbar is somewhat similar to the one used in the preceding recipe.

Getting ready

In this recipe, we will deal with the drop-down issue for the drop-down bubble (secondary links) in the navbar. Refer to the official documentation regarding dropdowns at `https://v4-alpha.getbootstrap.com/components/dropdowns/#menu-alignment`.

How to do it…

1. Open `chapter5/start/main.scss` and comment out all the `@import` statements except the one that pertains to this recipe:

    ```
    @import "./bower_components/bootstrap/scss/bootstrap.scss";
    @import "./bower_components/bootstrap/scss/_mixins.scss";
    @import "./bower_components/font-awesome/scss/font-awesome.scss";
    @import "./bower_components/hover/scss/hover.scss";

    // @import "recipe05-01.scss";
       @import "recipe05-02.scss";
    // @import "recipe05-03.scss";
    // @import "recipe05-04.scss";
    // @import "recipe05-05.scss";
    // @import "recipe05-06.scss";
    // @import "recipe05-07.scss";
    // @import "recipe05-08.scss";
    ```

2. Open another blank file located at `chapter5/start/app/recipe05-02.ejs`, and add the following code:

    ```
    <div class="container">

    <div class="mt-5">
    <h1><%- title %></h1>
    <p><a href="https://v4-alpha.getbootstrap.com/components/modal/"
      target="_blank">Link to bootstrap modal docs</a></p>
    ```

```
</div><!-- /.container -->


<p>We are using a customized version of the navbar used on the
official bootstrap 4 website.</p>

<p>The navbar is somewhat similar to the one used in the previous
recipe.</p>

<p>To achieve the navbar as it is in this recipe, we are using the
usual div with classes .navbar-collapse.collapse.</p>

<p>Inside of that div, we are using two ul elements. The first ul
element is styled using the classes of .nav.navbar-nav and .mr-
auto.</p>

<p>The third class, .mr-auto, is the key here. This class will
increase the right margin on the ul element to stretch so that it
pushes the next ul all the way to the right edge of the navbar.</p>

<p>This raises another issue, which is, since the second ul element
holds the dropdown items, clicking the "Recipes" dropdown will
display the items in the dropdown with the right-side cut-off.</p>

<p>Therefore, we need to re-align the dropdown bubble, and we
achieve it by using the class of .dropdown-menu-right.</p>
```

3. Navigate to the `partial` folder inside the `chapter5/start/app` folder, and add the following code to `_nav2.ejs`:

```
<header class="navbar navbar-light navbar-toggleable-md navbar-
light bg-faded">
 <nav class="container">
 <div class="d-flex justify-content-between">
 <a class="navbar-brand" href="/">
 Chapter 5
 </a>
 <button class="navbar-toggler collapsed" type="button" data-
  toggle="collapse" data-target="#bd-main-nav" aria-controls="bd-
  main-nav" aria-expanded="false" aria-label="Toggle navigation">
 <span class="navbar-toggler-icon"></span>
 </button>
 </div>

 <div class="navbar-collapse collapse" id="bd-main-nav" aria-
   expanded="false">

 <ul class="nav navbar-nav mr-auto">
```

```
<li class="nav-item">
<a class="nav-item nav-link active" href="#">
Example Link
</a>
</li>
<li class="nav-item">
<a class="nav-item nav-link active" href="#">
Another Link
</a>
</li>
</ul>


<ul class="nav navbar-nav">
<li class="nav-item dropdown">
 <a class="nav-link dropdown-toggle" href="#" id="dropdown01" data-
   toggle="dropdown" aria-haspopup="true" aria-expanded="false">
 Recipes
 </a>
 <div class="dropdown-menu dropdown-menu-right" aria-
   labelledby="dropdown01">
 <a class="dropdown-item" href="recipe05-01">1 - Adding Font
   Awesome to Bootstrap navbar</a>
 <a class="dropdown-item" href="recipe05-02">2 - Positioning
   Bootstrap navbar Items to the Right</a>
 <a class="dropdown-item" href="recipe05-03">3 - Centering an
   Element in the Bootstrap 4 navbar</a>
 <a class="dropdown-item" href="recipe05-04">4 - Background Overlap
   on navbar</a>
 <a class="dropdown-item" href="recipe05-05">5 - Changing the
   navbar Toggle on Different Breakpoints</a>
 <a class="dropdown-item" href="recipe05-06">6 - Bootstrap Side
   Menu Collapse with navbar</a>
 <a class="dropdown-item" href="recipe05-07">7 - Bootstrap 4 navbar
   with 2 Rows at Right</a>
 <a class="dropdown-item" href="recipe05-08">8 - Decrease the
   Height of Bootstrap navbar</a>
 <a class="dropdown-item" href="recipe05-09">9 - Adding a Custom
   Burger Icon</a>
 </div>
 </li>
 </ul>
 </div>

 </nav>
</header>
```

4. Run `harp server` to preview the result.

How it works...

To achieve the navbar as it is in this recipe, we are using the usual div with classes of
`.navbar-collapse.collapse`. Inside of that `div`, we are using two `ul` elements. The first
`ul` element is styled using the classes of `.nav.navbar-nav` and `.mr-auto`.

The third class, `.mr-auto`, is the key here. This class will increase the right margin on the
`ul` element to stretch so that it pushes the second `ul` element all the way to the right edge of
the navbar.

This raises another issue, which is, since the second `ul` element holds the drop-down items,
clicking on the **Recipes** dropdown will display the items in the dropdown with their right
edges cut-off.

Therefore, we need to realign the drop-down bubble, and we achieve this using the class of
`.dropdown-menu-right`.

Centering navbar links

In this recipe, we continue using a customized version of the navbar used on the official
Bootstrap 4 website. However, in each recipe, we also tweak the navbar slightly, thereby
making it easier to note the similarities and differences between each recipe, while still
working with the exact same links throughout this chapter.

Getting ready

In this recipe, we will be using the flex CSS property to position navbar items. A useful
overview of the flex property can be found at `https://css-tricks.com/snippets/css/a-guide-to-flexbox/`.

How to do it...

1. Comment out all the `@import` statements except the one that pertains to this
   recipe, and add the following code to `chapter5/start/recipe05-03.scss`:

   ```
   .flex-links {
     flex: auto;
   }
   ```

2. Open the empty file located at `chapter5/start/app/recipe05-03.ejs`, and add the following code:

```
<div class="container">

 <div class="mt-5">
 <h1><%- title %></h1>
 <p><a
href="https://v4-alpha.getbootstrap.com/components/popovers/"
  target="_blank">Link to bootstrap popovers docs</a></p>

</div><!-- /.container -->


<p>In this recipe, we continue using a customized version of the
navbar used on the official bootstrap 4 website. However, in each
recipe, we are also tweaking the navbar slightly, thereby making it
easier to notice the differences between each recipe while still
working with the exact same links throughout this chapter.</p>

<p>To achieve that, we are setting the flex property to the value
of auto, in the custom class of flex-links. This class is used on
the ul element inside the div with the class of .navbar-
collapse.collapse.</p>
```

3. Navigate to the `partial` folder inside the `chapter5/start/app` folder, and add the following code to `_nav3.ejs`:

```
<header class="navbar navbar-light navbar-toggleable-md navbar-
light bg-faded">
 <nav class="container">
 <div class="d-flex justify-content-between">
 <a class="navbar-brand" href="/">
 <span class="fa fa-database"></span>
 Chapter 5
 </a>
 <button class="navbar-toggler collapsed" type="button" data-
  toggle="collapse" data-target="#bd-main-nav" aria-controls="bd-
  main-nav" aria-expanded="false" aria-label="Toggle navigation">
 <span class="navbar-toggler-icon"></span>
 </button>
 </div>

 <div class="navbar-collapse collapse" id="bd-main-nav" aria-
 expanded="false">
 <ul class="nav navbar-nav flex-links justify-content-center">
 <li class="nav-item dropdown">
```

```
      <a class="nav-link dropdown-toggle" href="#" id="dropdown01" data-
      toggle="dropdown" aria-haspopup="true" aria-expanded="false">
      <span class="fa fa-book"></span>
      Recipes
      </a>
      <div class="dropdown-menu" aria-labelledby="dropdown01">
      <a class="dropdown-item" href="recipe05-01">1 - Adding Font
Awesome
       to Bootstrap navbar</a>
      <a class="dropdown-item" href="recipe05-02">2 - Positioning
       Bootstrap navbar Items to the Right</a>
      <a class="dropdown-item" href="recipe05-03">3 - Centering an
       Element in the Bootstrap 4 navbar</a>
      <a class="dropdown-item" href="recipe05-04">4 - Background Overlap
       on navbar</a>
      <a class="dropdown-item" href="recipe05-05">5 - Changing the
navbar
       Toggle on Different Breakpoints</a>
      <a class="dropdown-item" href="recipe05-06">6 - Bootstrap Side
Menu
       Collapse with navbar</a>
      <a class="dropdown-item" href="recipe05-07">7 - Bootstrap 4 navbar
       with 2 Rows at Right</a>
      <a class="dropdown-item" href="recipe05-08">8 - Decrease the
Height
       of Bootstrap navbar</a>
      <a class="dropdown-item" href="recipe05-09">9 - Adding a Custom
       Burger Icon</a>
      </div>
      </li>
      <li class="nav-item">
      <a class="nav-item nav-link" href="#">
      <span class="fa fa-briefcase"></span>
      Example Link
      </a>
      </li>
      <li class="nav-item">
      <a class="nav-item nav-link" href="#">
      Another Link
      <span class="fa fa-bullhorn"></span>
      </a>
      </li>
      </ul>
      </div>
      </nav>
   </header>
```

4. Run `harp server` to preview the result.

How it works...

To achieve the effect of centering links in Bootstrap 4's navbar, we will set the `flex` property to the value of `auto`, in the custom class of `.flex-links`. This class is used on the `ul` element inside the `div` with the class of `.navbar-collapse.collapse`.

Making a transparent navbar on a darker background

In this recipe, we continue using a customized version of the navbar used on the official Bootstrap 4 website. This recipe will result in a completely different look based on the HTML structure that is almost the same as in the previous recipes in this chapter. To achieve this, we will be relying heavily on SCSS.

Getting ready

To get ready for this recipe, search for the `scss` folder inside the `bower_components/bootstrap` folder. We will take some bits and pieces from the code in this folder and override its behavior to get the desired effect.

How to do it...

1. Open `chapter5/start/main.scss` and comment out all the `@import` statements except the one that pertains to this recipe:

```
@import "./bower_components/bootstrap/scss/bootstrap.scss";
@import "./bower_components/bootstrap/scss/_mixins.scss";
@import "./bower_components/font-awesome/scss/font-awesome.scss";
@import "./bower_components/hover/scss/hover.scss";

// @import "recipe05-01.scss";
// @import "recipe05-02.scss";
// @import "recipe05-03.scss";
   @import "recipe05-04.scss";
// @import "recipe05-05.scss";
// @import "recipe05-06.scss";
// @import "recipe05-07.scss";
// @import "recipe05-08.scss";
```

2. Open `chapter5/start/recipe05-04.scss` and add the following code:

```scss
// White links against a dark background
.navbar-inverse {

  .navbar-nav {
  .nav-link {
  color: $navbar-inverse-active-color;
  }
  }
  .navbar-toggler {
  border-color: $navbar-inverse-toggler-bg;
  }

  .navbar-toggler-icon {
  background-image: $navbar-inverse-active-color;
  }
}


// Generate series of `.navbar-toggleable-*` responsive classes for
configuring
// where your navbar collapses.
.navbar-toggleable {
  @include media-breakpoint-up(sm) {
  .navbar-nav {
  .dropdown-menu {
  position: static;
  float: none;
  }
  }
  }
}

nav.container {
  width: 200px;
}
```

3. Open the empty file located at `chapter5/start/app/recipe05-04.ejs`, and add the following code:

```html
<div class="container">

  <div class="mt-5">
  <h1><%- title %></h1>
  <p><a href="https://v4-alpha.getbootstrap.com/components/alerts/"
  target="_blank">Link to bootstrap alerts docs</a>
```

```
</p>

</div>
<!-- /.container -->


<p>We are using a customized version of the navbar used on the
  official bootstrap 4 website.</p>

<p>It is customized by adding the <code>&lt;span&gt;</code> tags
  with the fa classes to display specific icons, on either side of
  different links.</p>

<p>Finally, we are using a dropdown link on the navbar, and that
  dropdown is holding all the recipes used in this chapter.</p>
</div>
```

4. Navigate to the `partial` folder inside the `chapter5/start/app` folder, and add the following code to `_nav4.ejs`:

```
<header class="navbar navbar-inverse">
<nav class="container">
<div>
<a class="navbar-brand mr-auto" href="/">
<span class="fa fa-database"></span> Chapter 5
</a>
<button class="navbar-toggler" type="button"
 data-toggle="collapse"
 data-target="#bd-main-nav" aria-controls="bd-main-nav" aria-
 expanded="true" aria-label="Toggle navigation">
  ≡
</button>
</div>

<div class="navbar-collapse collapse" id="bd-main-nav" aria-
 expanded="true">
<ul class="nav navbar-nav">
<li class="nav-item dropdown">
<a class="nav-link dropdown-toggle" href="#" id="dropdown01" data-
 toggle="dropdown" aria-haspopup="true" aria-expanded="false">
<span class="fa fa-book"></span> Recipes
</a>
<div class="dropdown-menu" aria-labelledby="dropdown01">
<a class="dropdown-item" href="recipe05-01">1 - Adding Font
 Awesome to Bootstrap navbar</a>
<a class="dropdown-item" href="recipe05-02">2 - Positioning
 Bootstrap navbar Items to the Right</a>
<a class="dropdown-item" href="recipe05-03">3 - Centering an
```

```
Element in the Bootstrap 4 navbar</a>
<a class="dropdown-item" href="recipe05-04">4 - Background Overlap
 on navbar</a>
<a class="dropdown-item" href="recipe05-05">5 - Changing the
 navbar Toggle on Different Breakpoints</a>
<a class="dropdown-item" href="recipe05-06">6 - Bootstrap Side
 Menu Collapse with navbar</a>
<a class="dropdown-item" href="recipe05-07">7 - Bootstrap 4 navbar
 with 2 Rows at Right</a>
<a class="dropdown-item" href="recipe05-08">8 - Decrease the
 Height of Bootstrap navbar</a>
<a class="dropdown-item" href="recipe05-09">9 - Adding a Custom
 Burger Icon</a>
</div>
</li>
<li class="nav-item">
<a class="nav-item nav-link" href="#">
<span class="fa fa-briefcase"></span> Example Link
</a>
</li>
<li class="nav-item">
<a class="nav-item nav-link" href="#">
Another Link
<span class="fa fa-bullhorn"></span>
</a>
</li>
</ul>
</div>
</nav>
</header>
```

5. Add the following code to _layout.ejs:

```
<!DOCTYPE html>
<html lang="en">

<head>
 <meta charset="utf-8">
 <meta name="viewport" content="width=device-width, initial-
  scale=1, shrink-to-fit=no">
 <meta name="description" content="">
 <meta name="author" content="">
 <link rel="icon" href="../../favicon.ico">
 <title>
 <%- title %>
 </title>

 <!-- Bootstrap core CSS -->
```

```
    <link href="css/main.css" rel="stylesheet">

</head>

<body class="bg-warning">

 <%# partial("partial/_nav1") %>
 <%# partial("partial/_nav2") %>
 <%# partial("partial/_nav3") %>
 <%- partial("partial/_nav4") %>
 <%# partial("partial/_nav5") %>
 <%# partial("partial/_nav6") %>
 <%# partial("partial/_nav7") %>
 <%# partial("partial/_nav8") %>

 <%- yield %>

 <%- partial("partial/_js") %>

</body>
</html>
```

6. Run `harp server` to preview the result.

How it works...

In step 1, we add the recipe-specific SCSS include, as usual. In step 2, we add the code to this include, which contains overrides of font colors so that all the links become completely white, without transparency. Again, in step 2, we use the `media-breakpoint-up` mixin and pass it the value of `sm`, to override the default behavior and have the burger menu appear at all resolutions. Finally, to place the `nav.container` in the center, we will give it a width in pixels.

Creating a Navbar with Icons and Flexbox

In this recipe, we will create a wonderful navbar. It will have large icons as links. The text to describe the icons will be placed below each icon. The icons used will be Font Awesome.

Getting ready

To get ready for this recipe, preview the completed navbar in `chapter5/complete/recipe05` folder. Run the hard server and preview the navbar in your browser. Resize the browser window to see the behavior of the navbar. On smaller resolutions, click the toggle menu button to see the positioning of navbar links.

How to do it...

1. Open `chapter5/start/main.scss` and comment out all the `@import` statements except the one that pertains to this recipe:

   ```
   @import "./bower_components/bootstrap/scss/bootstrap.scss";
   @import "./bower_components/bootstrap/scss/_mixins.scss";
   @import "./bower_components/font-awesome/scss/font-awesome.scss";
   @import "./bower_components/hover/scss/hover.scss";

   // @import "recipe05-01.scss";
   // @import "recipe05-02.scss";
   // @import "recipe05-03.scss";
   // @import "recipe05-04.scss";
      @import "recipe05-05.scss";
   // @import "recipe05-06.scss";
   // @import "recipe05-07.scss";
   // @import "recipe05-08.scss";
   ```

2. Open the empty file located at `chapter5/start/app/recipe05-05.ejs`, and add the following code:

   ```
   <div class="container">

     <div class="mt-5">
     <h1 class="mb-2"><%- title %></h1>

     </div><!-- /.container -->
   ```

3. Navigate to the `partial` folder inside the `chapter5/start/app` folder, and add the following code to `_nav5.ejs`:

   ```
   <nav class="navbar navbar-toggleable-sm navbar-light bg-faded fixedsticky
   fixed-top">
     <button class="navbar-toggler navbar-toggler-right" type="button"
     data-toggle="collapse" data-target="#navbarText" aria-
     controls="navbarText" aria-expanded="false" aria-label="Toggle
   ```

```
   navigation">
     <span class="navbar-toggler-icon"></span>
   </button>
   <a href="#" class="hidden-md-upX ml-autoX navbar-brand">
     <img src="https://v4-alpha.getbootstrap.com/assets/brand/bootstrap-
     solid.svg" class="brand-img" width="30" height="30" />
   </a>

<div class="collapse navbar-collapse" id="navbarText">

<ul class="navbar-nav ml-auto mr-auto text-center">

<li class="nav-item">
        <a class="nav-link" href="#"><span class="d-block text-center
          fa fa-address-book fa-2x"></span> Address Book <span
          class="sr-only">(current)</span></a>
      </li>
      <li class="nav-item">
        <a class="nav-link" href="#"><span class="d-block text-center
          fa fa-archive fa-2x"></span> Archive</a>
      </li>
      <li class="nav-item">
        <a class="nav-link" href="#"><span class="d-block text-center
          fa fa-area-chart fa-2x"></span> Charts and Graphs</a>
      </li>
      <li class="nav-item">
        <a class="nav-link" href="#"><span class="d-block text-center
          fa fa-balance-scale fa-2x"></span> Legal Docs</a>
      </li>
      <li class="nav-item">
        <a class="nav-link" href="#"><span class="d-block text-center
          fa fa-bell-o fa-2x"></span> Alerts</a>
      </li>
      <li class="nav-item">
        <a class="nav-link" href="#"><span class="d-block text-center
          fa fa-bullhorn fa-2x"></span> Announcements</a>
      </li>
      <li class="nav-item">
        <a class="nav-link" href="#"><span class="d-block text-center
          fa fa-archive fa-2x"></span> Online Docs</a>
      </li>
    </ul>
</div>
</nav>
```

4. Add the following code to _layout.ejs:

```
<!DOCTYPE html>
```

```
<html lang="en">

<head>
 <meta charset="utf-8">
 <meta name="viewport" content="width=device-width, initial-
  scale=1, shrink-to-fit=no">
 <meta name="description" content="">
 <meta name="author" content="">
 <link rel="icon" href="../../favicon.ico">
 <title>
 <%- title %>
 </title>

 <!-- Bootstrap core CSS -->
 <link href="css/main.css" rel="stylesheet">

</head>

<body>

 <%# partial("partial/_nav1") %>
 <%# partial("partial/_nav2") %>
 <%# partial("partial/_nav3") %>
 <%# partial("partial/_nav4") %>
 <%- partial("partial/_nav5") %>
 <%# partial("partial/_nav6") %>
 <%# partial("partial/_nav7") %>
 <%# partial("partial/_nav8") %>

 <%- yield %>

 <%- partial("partial/_js") %>

</body>
</html>
```

5. Add the following code to `main-05-05.scss`:

```
.navbar-nav {
  flex-flow: column wrap;

  li.nav-item {
    flex: 1 6%;
    text-align: center;
    padding: 1em;
    flex-wrap: wrap;
    display: flex;
    .nav-link {
```

```
      display: flex;
      span:first-child {
        margin-left: 20px;
        margin-right: 30px;
      }
    }
  }

@media (min-width: 568px) {
  li.nav-item {
    flex: 1 14%;
  }
  .nav-link {
    display: block;
  }
}

@media (min-width: 768px) {
  li.nav-item {
    flex: 1 34%;
  }
}

@media (min-width: 992px) {
  li.nav-item {
    flex: 1 33%;
  }
}

@media (min-width: 1200px) {
  li.nav-item {
    flex: 1 25%;
  }
}

@media (min-width: 1400px) {
  li.nav-item {
    flex: 1 auto;
  }
}
}

.navbar-nav {
  flex-direction: column-reverse;
}
```

Run `harp server` to preview the result.

How it works...

In step 1, we include the recipe-specific SCSS. In step 2 we add the code to `recipe05-05.ejs` file. In step 3 we add the navbar, in step 4 we add the `_layout.ejs`, and in step five we add the recipe specific SCSS, with a lot of nesting involving media queries and the flex property to position the icons correctly on different resolutions.

Adding another row of links to the navbar

In this recipe, we will add an additional list of links above the main links in the navbar and make those additional links smaller. We will add different hover effects to links in the navbar. Finally, we will add underline effects to main links only, using media queries.

Getting ready

To get ready for this recipe, take a look at the drop-down component documentation available at `https://v4-alpha.getbootstrap.com/components/dropdowns/`. Also, refer to the navbar component documentation at `https://v4-alpha.getbootstrap.com/componen ts/navbar/`.

How to do it...

1. Open `chapter5/start/main.scss` and comment out all the `@import` statements except the one that pertains to this recipe:

```
@import "./bower_components/bootstrap/scss/bootstrap.scss";
@import "./bower_components/bootstrap/scss/_mixins.scss";
@import "./bower_components/font-awesome/scss/font-awesome.scss";
@import "./bower_components/hover/scss/hover.scss";

// @import "recipe05-01.scss";
// @import "recipe05-02.scss";
// @import "recipe05-03.scss";
// @import "recipe05-04.scss";
// @import "recipe05-05.scss";
   @import "recipe05-06.scss";
// @import "recipe05-07.scss";
// @import "recipe05-08.scss";
```

2. Open `chapter5/start/recipe05-06.scss` and add the following code:

```scss
.navbar-toggleable-md .navbar-nav.small .nav-link {
 border-bottom: none;
 font-size: 0.9rem;
}

@media (min-width: 992px) {
 .navbar-toggleable-md .navbar-nav.small .nav-link:hover {
 border-bottom: none;
 }
}

.navbar-toggleable-md .navbar-nav .nav-link {
 padding-right: 1rem;
 padding-left: 1rem;
 border-bottom: .2rem solid transparent;
 font-size: 1.1rem;
}


@media (min-width: 992px) {
 .navbar-toggleable-md .navbar-nav .nav-link:hover {
 padding-right: 1rem;
 padding-left: 1rem;
 border-bottom: .2rem solid black;
 }
 .navbar {
 padding: 0;
 }
}

.navbar-brand {
 font-size: 1.65rem;
}
```

3. Open the empty file located at `chapter5/start/app/recipe05-06.ejs`, and add the following code:

```ejs
<div class="container">

 <div class="mt-5">
 <h1><%- title %></h1>
 <p><a href="https://v4-alpha.getbootstrap.com/components/buttons/"
 target="_blank">Link to bootstrap buttons docs</a></p>

 </div><!-- /.container -->
```

4. Navigate to the `partial` folder inside the `chapter5/start/app` folder, and add the following code to `_nav6.ejs`:

```
<header class="navbar navbar-light navbar-toggleable-md navbar-
light bg-faded">
 <nav class="container">
 <div class="d-flex justify-content-between">
 <a class="navbar-brand" href="/">
 <span class="fa fa-database"></span>
 Chapter 5
 </a>
 <button class="navbar-toggler collapsed" type="button" data-
  toggle="collapse" data-target="#bd-main-nav" aria-controls="bd-
  main-nav" aria-expanded="false" aria-label="Toggle navigation">
 <span class="navbar-toggler-icon"></span>
 </button>
 </div>
 <div class="navbar-collapse collapse flex-sm-column" id="bd-main-
  nav" aria-expanded="false">
 <ul class="navbar-nav ml-auto small">
 <li class="nav-item active">
 <a class="nav-link hvr-pulse-shrink" href="#"><span class="fa fa-
  shopping-cart text-primary"></span> Cart items: 3</a>
 </li>
 <li class="nav-item">
 <a class="nav-link" href="#"><span class="fa fa-user-circle text-
  primary"></span> Profile</a>
 </li>
 <li class="nav-item">
 <a class="nav-link" href="#"><span class="fa fa-sign-out text-
  primary"></span> Logout</a>
 </li>
 </ul>
 <ul class="nav navbar-nav ml-auto">
 <li class="nav-item dropdown">
 <a class="nav-link dropdown-toggle" href="#" id="dropdown01" data-
  toggle="dropdown" aria-haspopup="true" aria-expanded="false">
 Recipes
 </a>
 <div class="dropdown-menu" aria-labelledby="dropdown01">
 <a class="dropdown-item hvr-wobble-horizontal"
href="recipe05-01">1
  - Adding Font Awesome to Bootstrap navbar</a>
 <a class="dropdown-item hvr-wobble-horizontal"
href="recipe05-02">2
  - Positioning Bootstrap navbar Items to the Right</a>
 <a class="dropdown-item hvr-wobble-horizontal"
href="recipe05-03">3
```

```
  - Centering an Element in the Bootstrap 4 navbar</a>
 <a class="dropdown-item hvr-wobble-horizontal"
href="recipe05-04">4
  - Making a Transparent navbar on a Darker Background</a>
 <a class="dropdown-item hvr-wobble-horizontal"
href="recipe05-05">5
  - Adding Collapsible Content Above the navbar</a>
 <a class="dropdown-item hvr-wobble-horizontal"
href="recipe05-06">6
  - Adding Subnavigation to Bootstrap 4 navbar</a>
 <a class="dropdown-item hvr-wobble-horizontal"
href="recipe05-07">7
  - Bootstrap 4 navbar with 2 Rows at Right</a>
 <a class="dropdown-item hvr-wobble-horizontal"
href="recipe05-08">8
  - Decrease the Height of Bootstrap navbar</a>
 <a class="dropdown-item hvr-wobble-horizontal"
href="recipe05-09">9
  - Adding a Custom Burger Icon</a>
 </div>
 </li>
 <li class="nav-item">
 <a class="nav-item nav-link" href="#">
 Example Link
 </a>
 </li>
 <li class="nav-item">
 <a class="nav-item nav-link" href="#">
 Another Link
 </a>
 </li>
 <li class="nav-item">
 <a class="nav-item nav-link" href="#">
 Example Link
 </a>
 </li>
 <li class="nav-item">
 <a class="nav-item nav-link" href="#">
 Another Link
 </a>
 </li>
 </ul>
 </div>
 </nav>
</header>
```

5. Add the following code to `_layout.ejs`:

```
<!DOCTYPE html>
<html lang="en">

<head>
 <meta charset="utf-8">
 <meta name="viewport" content="width=device-width, initial-
scale=1,
    shrink-to-fit=no">
 <meta name="description" content="">
 <meta name="author" content="">
 <link rel="icon" href="../../favicon.ico">
 <title>
 <%- title %>
 </title>

 <!-- Bootstrap core CSS -->
 <link href="css/main.css" rel="stylesheet">

</head>

<body>

 <%# partial("partial/_nav1") %>
 <%# partial("partial/_nav2") %>
 <%# partial("partial/_nav3") %>
 <%# partial("partial/_nav4") %>
 <%# partial("partial/_nav5") %>
 <%- partial("partial/_nav6") %>
 <%# partial("partial/_nav7") %>
 <%# partial("partial/_nav8") %>

 <%- yield %>

 <%- partial("partial/_js") %>

</body>
</html>
```

6. Run `harp server` to preview the result.

How it works…

In step 1, we import the recipe-specific SCSS file from our `main.scss`. In step 2, we add the SCSS code that will style the navbar. The class is using the `button-outline-variant` mixin to create custom css. First, we specify that we will use no border on `.secondary-nav` and that its font size should be smaller than the font size of the main nav links.

Next, we increase the padding between nav links on the main nav, increase their font size, and add a solid `border-bottom` to each main navigation item on hover. Note that the color of the `border-bottom` for links is initially set to `transparent`. Then, we just change the color on hover. Alternatively, we could have used changes in opacity to achieve the same effect.

In order for the border effect to properly work on hover, we need to remove the padding from the navbar and set it to kick in only above the `min-width` of `992px`. The reason for the media query is that on resolutions smaller than 992 pixels, the hamburger icon will appear, and if we had set `padding: 0` on those small resolutions, the burger menu would be touching the edges of the browser, which is not the effect we want. Finally, in step 2, we increase the `font-size` property of the `navbar-brand` class.

In step 3, we add the structure of the page under the navbar, which lists resources for this recipe.

In step 4, we add the HTML structure. We stack the two groups of links on top of each other using Bootstrap's class of `flex-sm-column`. If you remove this class from the HTML structure, you will see all the links lining up next to one another, on the same line. As you can see if you inspect the code, `.flex-sm-column` sets the `flex-direction` property to `column` for resolutions above 576 pixels.

Finally, we call the recipe-specific nav by setting it as the only uncommented nav partial in `_layout.ejs`.

Adding Yamm3 Megamenu images to a navbar dropdown

In this recipe, we will add a megamenu list of images to a Bootstrap 4 navbar dropdown, using the Yamm3 library. The library is intended for Bootstrap 3, so we will have to make some adjustments to the code. In other words, we will not be able to plug and play this library. Instead, we will have to customize the HTML structure of the provided example in order to make it work in Bootstrap 4.

Getting ready

To get ready for this recipe, take a look at the drop-down component documentation available at `https://v4-alpha.getbootstrap.com/components/dropdowns/`. Also, refer to the navbar component documentation at `https://v4-alpha.getbootstrap.com/components/navbar/`. Finally, visit the address for Yamm3 (yet another megamenu for Bootstrap 3), at `https://github.com/geedmo/yamm3`.

Alternatively, you could install Yamm3 via bower, using the following command in your console:
`bower install yamm3 --save`

How to do it...

1. Open `chapter5/start/main.scss` and comment out all the `@import` statements except the one that pertains to this recipe:

   ```
   @import "./bower_components/bootstrap/scss/bootstrap.scss";
   @import "./bower_components/bootstrap/scss/_mixins.scss";
   @import "./bower_components/font-awesome/scss/font-awesome.scss";
   @import "./bower_components/hover/scss/hover.scss";

   // @import "recipe05-01.scss";
   // @import "recipe05-02.scss";
   // @import "recipe05-03.scss";
   // @import "recipe05-04.scss";
   // @import "recipe05-05.scss";
   // @import "recipe05-06.scss";
      @import "recipe05-07.scss";
   // @import "recipe05-08.scss";
   ```

2. Open `chapter5/start/recipe05-07.scss`, and add the following code:

```scss
/*!
 * Yamm!3 - Yet another megamenu for Bootstrap 3
 * http://geedmo.github.com/yamm3
 *
 * @geedmo - Licensed under the MIT license
 */

//----------------------------
// Yamm Styles
//----------------------------

.yamm {

// reset positions
.nav, .collapse, .dropup, .dropdown {
position: static;
}

// propagate menu position under container for fw navbars
.container {
position: relative;
}

// by default aligns menu to left
.dropdown-menu {
left: auto;
}

// Content with padding
.yamm-content {
padding: 20px 30px;
}

// Fullwidth menu
.dropdown.yamm-fw .dropdown-menu {
left: 0; right: 0;
}
```

3. Open the empty file located at `chapter5/start/app/recipe05-07.ejs`, and add the following code:

```ejs
<div class="container">

<div class="mt-5">
<h1><%- title %></h1>
```

```
<p><a href="https://v4-alpha.getbootstrap.com/components/buttons/"
   target="_blank">Link to bootstrap buttons docs</a></p>

</div><!-- /.container -->
```

4. Navigate to the `partial` folder inside the `chapter5/start/app` folder, and add the following code to `_nav7.ejs`:

```
<header class="navbar yamm navbar-light navbar-toggleable-md
navbar-
 light bg-faded">
<nav class="container">
<div class="d-flex justify-content-between">
<a class="navbar-brand" href="/">
<span class="fa fa-database"></span>
Chapter 5
</a>
<button class="navbar-toggler collapsed" type="button" data-
 toggle="collapse" data-target="#navbar-collapse-1" aria-
 controls="bd-main-nav" aria-expanded="false" aria-label="Toggle
 navigation">
<span class="navbar-toggler-icon"></span>
</button>
</div>

<div class="navbar-collapse collapse" id="navbar-collapse-1" aria-
 expanded="false">
<ul class="nav navbar-nav">
<li class="nav-item dropdown yamm-fw">
<a href="#" data-toggle="dropdown" class="nav-link dropdown-
 toggle"
 aria-haspopup="true" aria-expanded="false">Pictures</a>
<ul class="dropdown-menu">
<li>
<div class="yamm-content">
<div class="row">
<div class="col-xs-6 col-sm-2">
<a href="#" class="thumbnail"><img alt="150x190"
 src="http://placehold.it/150x190"></a>
</div>
<div class="col-xs-6 col-sm-2">
<a href="#" class="thumbnail"><img alt="150x190"
 src="http://placehold.it/150x190"></a>
</div>
<div class="col-xs-6 col-sm-2">
<a href="#" class="thumbnail"><img alt="150x190"
 src="http://placehold.it/150x190"></a>
</div>
```

```
<div class="col-xs-6 col-sm-2">
<a href="#" class="thumbnail"><img alt="150x190"
 src="http://placehold.it/150x190"></a>
</div>
<div class="col-xs-6 col-sm-2">
<a href="#" class="thumbnail"><img alt="150x190"
 src="http://placehold.it/150x190"></a>
</div>
<div class="col-xs-6 col-sm-2">
<a href="#" class="thumbnail"><img alt="150x190"
 src="http://placehold.it/150x190"></a>
</div>
</div>
</div>
</li>
</ul>
</li>
<li class="nav-item dropdown">
<a class="nav-link dropdown-toggle" href="#" id="dropdown01" data-
 toggle="dropdown" aria-haspopup="true" aria-expanded="false">
<span class="fa fa-book"></span>
Recipes
</a>
<div class="dropdown-menu" aria-labelledby="dropdown01">
<a class="dropdown-item" href="recipe05-01">1 - Adding Font
 Awesome to Bootstrap navbar</a>
<a class="dropdown-item" href="recipe05-02">2 - Positioning
 Bootstrap navbar Items to the Right</a>
<a class="dropdown-item" href="recipe05-03">3 - Centering an
 Element in the Bootstrap 4 navbar</a>
<a class="dropdown-item" href="recipe05-04">4 - Making a
 Transparent navbar on a Darker Background</a>
<a class="dropdown-item" href="recipe05-05">5 - Adding Collapsible
 Content Above the navbar</a>
<a class="dropdown-item" href="recipe05-06">6 - Adding
 Subnavigation to Bootstrap 4 navbar</a>
<a class="dropdown-item" href="recipe05-07">7 - Bootstrap 4
 navbar with 2 Rows at Right</a>
<a class="dropdown-item" href="recipe05-08">8 - Decrease the
 Height of Bootstrap navbar</a>
<a class="dropdown-item" href="recipe05-09">9 - Adding a Custom
 Burger Icon</a>
</div>
</li>
<li class="nav-item">
<a class="nav-item nav-link" href="#">
<span class="fa fa-briefcase"></span>
Example Link
```

```
        </a>
        </li>
        <li class="nav-item">
        <a class="nav-item nav-link" href="#">
        Another Link
        <span class="fa fa-bullhorn"></span>
        </a>
        </li>
        </ul>
        </div>
        </nav>
        </header>
```

5. Add the following code to _layout.ejs:

```
        <!DOCTYPE html>
        <html lang="en">

        <head>
         <meta charset="utf-8">
         <meta name="viewport" content="width=device-width, initial-
        scale=1,
          shrink-to-fit=no">
         <meta name="description" content="">
         <meta name="author" content="">
         <link rel="icon" href="../../favicon.ico">
         <title>
         <%- title %>
         </title>

         <!-- Bootstrap core CSS -->
         <link href="css/main.css" rel="stylesheet">

        </head>

        <body>

         <%# partial("partial/_nav1") %>
         <%# partial("partial/_nav2") %>
         <%# partial("partial/_nav3") %>
         <%# partial("partial/_nav4") %>
         <%# partial("partial/_nav5") %>
         <%# partial("partial/_nav6") %>
         <%- partial("partial/_nav7") %>
         <%# partial("partial/_nav8") %>

         <%- yield %>
```

```
<%- partial("partial/_js") %>

</body>
</html>
```

6. Run `harp server` to preview the result.

How it works...

In step 1, we import the recipe-specific SCSS file from our `main.scss`. In step 2, we add the SCSS code that is needed to style Yamm3. The code is copied straight from `https://github.com/geedmo/yamm3/blob/master/yamm/_yamm.scss`.

In step 3 ,we add the usual placeholder information that will go under the navbar, including the `<%- title %>` of the recipe. The title is pulled by harp from the `_data.json` file (which can be found in the `app` folder).

Step 4 includes Yamm3 into our navbar by virtue of including the appropriate Yamm3-specific css classes. It is important here to retain a proper structure of our HTML in accordance with the Bootstrap conventions for this to work.

In step 5, we include the `_nav7.ejs` partial, which will make our site work.

Adding Yamm3 Megamenu list of links to a navbar dropdown

In this recipe, we will add a megamenu list of links to a Bootstrap 4 navbar dropdown, using the Yamm3 library. Again, like in the previous recipe, we will have to customize the HTML structure of the provided example in order to make it work in Bootstrap 4.

Getting ready

To get ready for this recipe, take a look at the drop-down component documentation available at `https://v4-alpha.getbootstrap.com/components/dropdowns/`. Also, refer to the navbar component documentation at `https://v4-alpha.getbootstrap.com/components/navbar/`. Finally, visit the address for Yamm3 (yet another megamenu for Bootstrap 3), at `https://github.com/geedmo/yamm3`.

How to do it...

1. Open `chapter5/start/main.scss` and comment out all the `@import` statements except the one that pertains to this recipe:

```
@import "./bower_components/bootstrap/scss/bootstrap.scss";
@import "./bower_components/bootstrap/scss/_mixins.scss";
@import "./bower_components/font-awesome/scss/font-awesome.scss";
@import "./bower_components/hover/scss/hover.scss";

// @import "recipe05-01.scss";
// @import "recipe05-02.scss";
// @import "recipe05-03.scss";
// @import "recipe05-04.scss";
// @import "recipe05-05.scss";
// @import "recipe05-06.scss";
// @import "recipe05-07.scss";
// @import "recipe05-08.scss";
```

2. Open `chapter5/start/recipe05-08.scss` and copy and paste the code from `chapter5/complete/recipe05-07.scss` into it.

3. Open the empty file located at `chapter5/start/app/recipe05-08.ejs`, and add the following code:

```
<div class="container">

  <div class="mt-5">
  <h1><%- title %></h1>
  <p><a href="https://v4-alpha.getbootstrap.com/components/buttons/"
    target="_blank">Link to bootstrap buttons docs</a></p>

  </div><!-- /.container -->
```

4. Navigate to the `partial` folder inside the `chapter5/start/app` folder, and add the following code to `_nav8.ejs`:

```
<header class="navbar yamm navbar-light navbar-toggleable-md
navbar-light bg-faded">
  <nav class="container">
  <div class="d-flex justify-content-between">
  <a class="navbar-brand" href="/">
  <span class="fa fa-database"></span>
  Chapter 5
  </a>
  <button class="navbar-toggler collapsed" type="button" data-
```

```
toggle="collapse" data-target="#navbar-collapse-1" aria-
controls="bd-main-nav" aria-expanded="false" aria-label="Toggle
navigation">
<span class="navbar-toggler-icon"></span>
</button>
</div>

<div class="navbar-collapse collapse" id="navbar-collapse-1" aria-
expanded="false">
<ul class="nav navbar-nav">
<!-- Classic list -->
<li class="nav-item dropdown yamm-fw"><a href="#" data-
toggle="dropdown" class="nav-link dropdown-toggle" aria-
haspopup="true" aria-expanded="false">List</a>
<ul class="dropdown-menu">
<li>
<!-- Content container to add padding -->
<div class="yamm-content">
<div class="row">
<ul class="col-sm-2 list-unstyled">
<li>
<p><strong>Section Title</strong></p>
</li>
<li>List Item</li>
<li>List Item</li>
<li>List Item</li>
<li>List Item</li>
<li>List Item</li>
<li>List Item</li>
</ul>
<ul class="col-sm-2 list-unstyled">
<li>
<p><strong>Links Title</strong></p>
</li>
<li><a href="#"> Link Item </a></li>
<li><a href="#"> Link Item </a></li>
<li><a href="#"> Link Item </a></li>
<li><a href="#"> Link Item </a></li>
<li><a href="#"> Link Item </a></li>
<li><a href="#"> Link Item </a></li>
</ul>
<ul class="col-sm-2 list-unstyled">
<li>
<p><strong>Section Title</strong></p>
</li>
<li>List Item</li>
<li>List Item</li>
<li>List Item</li>
```

```html
<li>List Item</li>
<li>List Item</li>
<li>List Item</li>
</ul>
<ul class="col-sm-2 list-unstyled">
<li>
<p><strong>Section Title</strong></p>
</li>
<li>List Item</li>
<li>List Item</li>
<li>
<ul>
<li><a href="#"> Link Item </a></li>
<li><a href="#"> Link Item </a></li>
<li><a href="#"> Link Item </a></li>
</ul>
</li>
</ul>
</div>
</div>
</li>
</ul>
</li>
<li class="nav-item dropdown">
<a class="nav-link dropdown-toggle" href="#" id="dropdown01" data-
 toggle="dropdown" aria-haspopup="true" aria-expanded="false">
<span class="fa fa-book"></span>
Recipes
</a>
<div class="dropdown-menu" aria-labelledby="dropdown01">
<a class="dropdown-item" href="recipe05-01">1 - Adding Font
 Awesome to Bootstrap navbar</a>
<a class="dropdown-item" href="recipe05-02">2 - Positioning
 Bootstrap navbar Items to the Right</a>
<a class="dropdown-item" href="recipe05-03">3 - Centering an
 Element in the Bootstrap 4 navbar</a>
<a class="dropdown-item" href="recipe05-04">4 - Making a
 Transparent navbar on a Darker Background</a>
<a class="dropdown-item" href="recipe05-05">5 - Adding Collapsible
 Content Above the navbar</a>
<a class="dropdown-item" href="recipe05-06">6 - Adding
 Subnavigation to Bootstrap 4 navbar</a>
<a class="dropdown-item" href="recipe05-07">7 - Bootstrap 4
 navbar with 2 Rows at Right</a>
<a class="dropdown-item" href="recipe05-08">8 - Decrease the
 Height of Bootstrap navbar</a>
<a class="dropdown-item" href="recipe05-09">9 - Adding a Custom
 Burger Icon</a>
```

```
</div>
</li>
<li class="nav-item">
<a class="nav-item nav-link" href="#">
<span class="fa fa-briefcase"></span>
Example Link
</a>
</li>
<li class="nav-item">
<a class="nav-item nav-link" href="#">
Another Link
<span class="fa fa-bullhorn"></span>
</a>
</li>
</ul>
</div>
</nav>
</header>
```

5. Add the following code to _layout.ejs:

```
<!DOCTYPE html>
<html lang="en">

<head>
 <meta charset="utf-8">
 <meta name="viewport" content="width=device-width, initial-
scale=1,
  shrink-to-fit=no">
 <meta name="description" content="">
 <meta name="author" content="">
 <link rel="icon" href="../../favicon.ico">
 <title>
 <%- title %>
 </title>

 <!-- Bootstrap core CSS -->
 <link href="css/main.css" rel="stylesheet">

</head>

<body>

 <%# partial("partial/_nav1") %>
 <%# partial("partial/_nav2") %>
 <%# partial("partial/_nav3") %>
 <%# partial("partial/_nav4") %>
 <%# partial("partial/_nav5") %>
```

```
<%# partial("partial/_nav6") %>
<%# partial("partial/_nav7") %>
<%- partial("partial/_nav8") %>

<%- yield %>

<%- partial("partial/_js") %>

</body>
</html>
```

6. Run `harp server` to preview the result.

How it works...

This recipe demonstrates the addition of a list of links into the Bootstrap 4 navbar dropdown, using the Yamm3 library. If you look at the dropdown itself, you might note that there is quite a lot of empty space at the right-hand side of the drop-down bubble, enough to either fit another two columns or possibly a promotional image, depending on the situation at hand.

6
Extending Bootstrap 4

In this chapter, we will cover the following topics:

- Converting checkboxes into Toggles with Bootstrap Toggle plugin
- Onboarding users with Shepherd
- Toggling visibility of password fields with custom jQuery code
- Extending the functionality of select elements with Bootstrap Select plugin
- Customizing select boxes with Select2 plugin
- Adding input sliders with Rangeslider.js
- Allowing users to easily add dates to your input fields with jQuery UI Datepicker
- Converting plain tables into sophisticated data tables with Bootgrid
- Navigating easily with simple-sidebar jQuery plugin
- Adding fully customizable notifications with Notify.js
- Integrating a fancy modal using animatedModal.js
- Making pagination dynamic with the jQuery Pagination plugin and simplePagination.js
- Validating forms with svalidate.js
- Adding a rating system using jQuery Bar Rating plugin

Introduction

In this chapter, we will look at a variety of jQuery plugins we can use to extend Bootstrap 4. Some of these plugins are not ready for this iteration of the framework, so we will have to make some adjustments to a few of them. Luckily, not all plugins need to be tweaked. Some are ready for Bootstrap 4 out-of-the-box, and due attention has been paid to giving clarifications on the status of each of the plugins used in this chapter regarding the compatibility issues with Bootstrap 4.

Converting checkboxes into Toggles with Bootstrap Toggle plugin

In this recipe, we will use the Bootstrap Toggle plugin, which has not been updated for over a year at the time of writing this book. The plugin is also intended to be used with Bootstrap 3. Luckily, it will not take us a lot of effort to adjust the behavior of this plugin to work with Bootstrap 4.

Getting ready

To begin this recipe, navigate to the Bootstrap Toggle plugin repository, available at `https ://github.com/minhur/bootstrap-toggle`.

Specifically, we need two files from this repository:

- The plugin's CSS, available at `https://github.com/minhur/bootstrap-toggle /blob/master/css/bootstrap-toggle.css`
- The plugin's JS, available at `https://github.com/minhur/bootstrap-toggle/b lob/master/js/bootstrap-toggle.js`

There is also a Bower installation available for this plugin, by running the `bower install bootstrap-toggle` code (as described in the official plugin website, at `http://www.boots traptoggle.com`).

How to do it...

1. Copy the raw CSS code from the GitHub link at `https://raw.githubuserconten t.com/minhur/bootstrap-toggle/master/css/bootstrap-toggle.css`.

2. Open the currently blank `recipe06-01.scss` and paste the code copied from step 1.

3. Starting on line 58, add the following code to `recipe06-01.scss`:

```scss
// added
.toggle-handle {
 background: #ddd;
}

// added
.btn.active.toggle-off {
 box-shadow: inset 0 3px 5px rgba(0,0,0,.125);
 color: #333;
 background-color: #e6e6e6;
 border-color: #adadad;
}
```

4. Open the currently empty file titled `recipe06-01.ejs`, which can be found inside the `app` folder, and paste the following code:

```html
<div class="container">

 <div class="mt-5">
 <h1><%- title %></h1>
 <p><a href="https://v4-alpha.getbootstrap.com/components/alerts/"
 target="_blank">Link to bootstrap alerts docs</a></p>

 </div><!-- /.container -->

 <div class="col-12 col-md-5">

 <div class="checkbox">
 <label>
 <input type="checkbox" data-toggle="toggle">
 Option one is enabled
 </label>
 </div>
 <div class="checkbox disabled">
 <label>
 <input type="checkbox" disabled data-toggle="toggle">
 Option two is disabled
```

```
    </label>
  </div>

  <div class="form-check mb-2 mr-sm-2 mb-sm-0">
    <label class="form-check-label">
      <input class="form-check-input" type="checkbox"> Remember me
    </label>
  </div>

</div>
```

5. Add the following code to `main.scss`:

```
@import "./bower_components/bootstrap/scss/bootstrap.scss";
@import "./bower_components/bootstrap/scss/_mixins.scss";
@import "./bower_components/font-awesome/scss/font-awesome.scss";
@import "./bower_components/hover/scss/hover.scss";
// @import "./bower_components/bootstrap-toggle/css/bootstrap-
toggle.css";

@import "recipe06-01.scss";
```

6. In `app/partial/_js.ejs`, on line 9, insert the following GitHub CDN link:

```
<script
src="https://gitcdn.github.io/bootstrap-toggle/2.2.2/js/bootstrap-t
oggle.min.js"></script>
```

7. Run the `grunt` and `harp server` commands in separate Bash windows, and preview the result in the browser at `localhost:9000/recipe06-01`.

How it works...

We used an outdated plugin that was built for Bootstrap 3. However, many of these plugins require just a few simple tweaks to make them work on frontend projects other than Bootstrap 3. In the case of using the plugin with Bootstrap 4, we achieved the desired effect with a few changes to our CSS and HTML, as can be seen in `recipe06-01.scss` and `recipe06-01.ejs`. Finally, we referenced the jQuery plugin via GitHub CDN.

Onboarding users with Shepherd

Onboarding is a way to show first-time visitors to your website how to use your site and to showcase its features. It is a great way to get people introduced to what your site offers in a step-by-step fashion.

In this recipe, we will look at using the Shepherd plugin to onboard users. It is available from http://github.hubspot.com/shepherd/docs/welcome/. The official repository is available at https://github.com/HubSpot/shepherd.

Getting ready

To get ready, simply read through the documentation at GitHub. Also, look at the official website for an example of what is possible with this plugin.

How to do it...

1. Open app/partial/_js.ejs and add the following code:

   ```
   <%- partial("_recipe-06-02-js") %>
   ```

2. Open app/recipe06-02.ejs and paste this code:

   ```
   <div class="container">
   <div class="mt-5">
       <h1><%- title %></h1>
     </div>
   </div><!-- /.container -->
   <div class="container">
     <div class="col">
   <div>
       <p class="my-element">Install Shepherd: <code>bower install
   tether-shepherd</code>. Lorem ipsum dolor sit amet consectetur
   adipiscing elit. Lorem ipsum dolor sit amet consectetur adipiscing
   elit. Lorem ipsum dolor sit amet consectetur adipiscing elit. Lorem
   ipsum dolor sit amet consectetur adipiscing elit. Lorem ipsum dolor
   sit amet consectetur adipiscing elit. </p>
     </div>
   <div>
       <p id="my-other-element">Lorem ipsum dolor sit amet consectetur
   adipiscing elit. Lorem ipsum dolor sit amet consectetur adipiscing
   elit. Lorem ipsum dolor sit amet consectetur adipiscing elit. Lorem
   ```

ipsum dolor sit amet consectetur adipiscing elit. Lorem ipsum dolor
sit amet consectetur adipiscing elit. Lorem ipsum dolor sit amet
consectetur adipiscing elit. Lorem ipsum dolor sit amet consectetur
adipiscing elit. Lorem ipsum dolor sit amet consectetur adipiscing
elit. Lorem ipsum dolor sit amet consectetur adipiscing elit. Lorem
ipsum dolor sit amet consectetur adipiscing elit. Lorem ipsum dolor
sit amet consectetur adipiscing elit. Lorem ipsum dolor sit amet
consectetur adipiscing elit. Lorem ipsum dolor sit amet consectetur
adipiscing elit. Lorem ipsum dolor sit amet consectetur adipiscing
elit. </p>
   </div>
  </div>
  </div>

3. Add the following script to app/partial/_recipe-06-02.js.ejs:

```
<script>

var tour;

tour = new Shepherd.Tour({
  defaults: {
    classes: 'shepherd-theme-arrows',
    scrollTo: true
  }
});

tour.addStep('example-step', {
  title: 'Whatever',
  text: 'This step is attached to the bottom of the <code>.my-
element</code> element.',
  attachTo: '.my-element bottom',
  classes: 'example-step-extra-class',
  buttons: [
    {
      text: 'Next',
      action: tour.next
    }
  ]
});

tour.addStep('example-step-2', {
  title: 'Whatever 2',
  text: 'This is step 2',
  attachTo: '#my-other-element bottom',
  classes: 'example-step-extra-class',
  buttons: [
    {
```

```
                text: 'Close',
                action: tour.hide
            }
        ]
    });

    tour.start()

    </script>
```

4. Reference the GitCDN CSS for the plugin in app/_layout.ejs, by adding the following line of code under line 15:

```
<link
href="https://gitcdn.xyz/repo/HubSpot/shepherd/master/dist/css/shep
herd-theme-arrows.css" rel="stylesheet">
```

5. Back in partial/_js.ejs, add the call to Shepherd's JS, just under the line that reads <script src="js/bootstrap.js"></script>:

```
<script
src="https://gitcdn.xyz/repo/HubSpot/shepherd/master/dist/js/shephe
rd.js"></script>
```

6. To style our Shepherd tour, let's add the following SCSS code to recipe06-02.scss:

```
.shepherd-content {
    background: whitesmoke;
    padding: 2rem;
    -webkit-box-shadow: 10px 10px 66px 0px rgba(0,0,0,0.75);
    -moz-box-shadow: 10px 10px 66px 0px rgba(0,0,0,0.75);
    box-shadow: 10px 10px 66px 0px rgba(0,0,0,0.75);
}

ul.shepherd-buttons {
    padding-left: 0;
}
ul.shepherd-buttons li {
    list-style-type: none;
}
ul.shepherd-buttons li a {
    border: 1px solid black;
    padding: .5rem .6rem;
    cursor: pointer;
}
```

7. Compile and run the server. You can preview the Shepherd plugin in action on this recipe's page at `localhost:9000/recipe06-02`.

Toggling visibility of password fields with custom jQuery code

In Bootstrap 3, a very popular plugin for showing passwords, called *Show Password plugin*, is available. However, it has not been updated for some time, and since it is a relatively complex plugin, it would be a bit out of the scope of this recipe to alter the plugin to be used in Bootstrap 4. That is why we will build a custom jQuery functionality in this recipe to use with our Bootstrap 4 input add-on buttons. Specifically, this recipe deals with the input element that has the type attribute of the *password*.

Getting ready

To get ready, we need to be aware of several jQuery functions that we will use in this recipe. They are `on()`, `text()`, `attr()`, and `parent()`. In-depth documentation is available at `https://api.jquery.com/`.

We also need to be aware of how input add-ons and input add-on buttons are used in Bootstrap 4. For information on this subject, visit the *Button add-ons* section on *input-groups* in Bootstrap 4, available at `https://v4-alpha.getbootstrap.com/components/input-group/#button-addons`.

Finally, since we will use Font Awesome icons in this recipe, it might be worthwhile to check out the cheatsheet at `http://fontawesome.io/cheatsheet/`.

How to do it...

1. Let's add the HTML structure for our recipe. We will do it by adding the following code to `app/recipe06-03.ejs`:

```
<div class="container">

 <div class="mt-5">
 <h1><%- title %></h1>
 <p><a href="https://v4-alpha.getbootstrap.com/components/alerts/"
 target="_blank">Link to bootstrap alerts docs</a></p>
```

```
</div><!-- /.container -->

<div class="col-12 col-md-5">

<div>

<form>
 <div class="form-group">
 <label for="exampleInputEmail1">Email address</label>
 <input type="email" class="form-control" id="exampleInputEmail1"
  aria-describedby="emailHelp" placeholder="Enter email">
 <small id="emailHelp" class="form-text text-muted">We'll never
  share your email with anyone else.</small>
 </div>

 <div class="form-group">
 <label for="exampleInputPassword">Password</label>
 <div class="input-group">
 <input type="password" class="form-control"
  id="exampleInputPassword" placeholder="Your Password" aria-
  describedby="basic-addon">
 <span class="input-group-btn">
 <button class="btn btn-danger" id="basic-addon"
type="button"><span
  class="fa fa-lock" id="lock-icon-toggle"></span></button>
 </span>
 </div>
 <small id="emailHelp" class="form-text text-muted">Click on the
  padlock button to view the characters typed into the password
  field.</small>
 </div>
 <button type="submit" class="btn btn-primary">Submit</button>

</form>

</div>
</div>
```

2. The only change to CSS in this recipe involves the change of cursor on the input add-on button, in `recipe06-03.scss`:

```
#basic-addon {
 cursor: pointer;
}
```

3. The main functionality of this recipe revolves around
   `app/partial/_recipe-06-03-js.ejs` since the custom jQuery code in this file
   makes everything work as planned:

```
<script>

var $addonButton = $("#basic-addon");
var $passwordField = $("#exampleInputPassword");

$addonButton.on("click", function() {
  $passwordField.attr("type", function() {
  $("#lock-icon-toggle").attr("class") === 'fa fa-unlock-alt' ?
  $passwordField.attr("type", "password") :
  $passwordField.attr("type", "text")
  });
  $("#lock-icon-toggle").attr("class") === "fa fa-lock" ?
  $("#lock-icon-toggle").attr("class", "fa fa-unlock-alt")
  .parent().attr("class", "btn btn-success") :
  $("#lock-icon-toggle").attr("class", "fa fa-lock")
  .parent().attr("class", "btn btn-danger");
});

</script>
```

4. In `main.scss`, we need to reference the `@import` statement for this recipe:

```
@import "recipe06-03.scss";
```

5. Comment out the rest of the recipe-specific imports in `main.scss` to make sure
   that no styles clash.

6. In `app/partial/_js.ejs`, include the recipe-specific jQuery file we made in
   step 3:

```
<%- partial("_recipe-06-03-js") %>
```

7. While we are still in the aforementioned `_js.ejs` file, comment out other recipe-specific includes.

8. Run `grunt` and `harp`, and preview the completed recipe in your browser at `http://localhost:9000/recipe06-03`.

How it works...

In this recipe, we have a simple form, with two input fields (an `email address` field and a `password` input field) and a `submit` button. The `password` input field has an input add-on button on its right side, with the button styled using the contextual `btn-danger` class. Inside the button, we see an icon of a closed padlock.

The idea is pretty simple, we want to allow the user to click on the input add-on button, on the right edge of the password input field. This click will change the visibility of characters in the password input field. The obscured password characters are made visible via a simple change of the type attribute from `password` to `text`. At the same time, the input add-on button changes its contextual color from `danger` to `success`, and the padlock icon changes from `fa fa-lock` to `fa fa-unlock-alt`.

There are several things happening in our jQuery code. We'll break down the `_recipe-06-03-js.ejs` file by line numbers.

On lines 3 and 4, we cache our jQuery selectors into variables, so as to minimize the number of times we are touching the DOM, which is a good practice to apply, as it improves the performance of our jQuery in general.

On line 6, we target the input add-on button's click event, and pass the click handler to it; this will do several things:

- Using a ternary operator, it will check whether the password input field's class attribute has the value of `fa fa-unlock-alt` (line 9)
- If it does, we'll set the type attribute of the `password` input field to `text` (line 11)
- Otherwise, we'll set the type attribute of the `password` input field to `password` (line 10)

The code thus far deals with the toggling of password visibility on the password input field, and with the toggling of the Font Awesome icon in our input add-on button.

On line 13, we target the icon, and using another ternary operator, verify which kind of padlock icon is displayed--`fa-lock` or `fa-unlock-alt`. Based on the result of this test, we will assign the proper icon and then chain the jQuery's `parent()` method onto the assigned icon. Finally, we will change the class attribute of our `#lock-icon-toggle` parent (that is, the `span` element that wraps the button), to display the appropriate contextual color class on the `btn-danger` button for the closed padlock with hidden password characters, or `btn-success` for the open padlock icon with the password characters displayed as plain text.

Extending the functionality of select elements with Bootstrap Select plugin

In this recipe, we will improve the functionality of select elements with the great Bootstrap Select plugin, available at `https://github.com/silviomoreto/bootstrap-select`. However, since the author of the plugin is intending to update it only after the official release of Bootstrap 4, we need to find a better solution in the meantime. Looking at the plugin's issues on GitHub, a very interesting thread pertaining to making the plugin work with Bootstrap 4 prerelease can be found at `https://github.com/silviomoreto/bootstrap-select/issues/1135`.

A GitHub user, *Rodrigo Martins*, has adapted the plugin to work with Bootstrap v4.0.0-alpha.6. You can check out his fork of the original plugin at `https://github.com/rodrigo-martins/bootstrap-select`.

Using the GitCDN at `https://gitcdn.xyz/`, we can now add this forked repository's customized raw CSS (at `https://raw.githubusercontent.com/rodrigo-martins/bootstrap-select/master/dist/css/bootstrap-select.css`) and raw JS (at `https://raw.githubusercontent.com/rodrigo-martins/bootstrap-select/master/dist/js/bootstrap-select.js`) via this CDN service, as explained in step 1 of this recipe.

How to do it...

1. In our `app/_layout.ejs`, reference the CSS file from the GitCDN with the following line of code:

```
<link
href="https://gitcdn.xyz/repo/rodrigo-martins/bootstrap-select/mast
er/dist/css/bootstrap-select.css" rel="stylesheet">
```

2. Similar to step 1, reference the plugin's js file via GitCDN, in `app/partials/_js.ejs`:

```
<script
src="https://gitcdn.xyz/repo/rodrigo-martins/bootstrap-select/maste
r/dist/js/bootstrap-select.js"></script>
```

3. In `main.scss`, use the `@import` statement on `recipe06-04.scss` and comment out the other recipe-specific styles:

```
@import "recipe06-04.scss";
```

4. Copy the following code and paste it into `app/recipe06-04.ejs`:

```
<div class="container">

 <div class="mt-5">
 <h1><%- title %></h1>
 <p><a href="https://v4-alpha.getbootstrap.com/components/alerts/"
target="_blank">Link to bootstrap alerts docs</a></p>

</div><!-- /.container -->

<div class="col-12 col-md-5">

<div>

<div class="wrapper">

<select class="selectpicker" multiple>
 <option>Mustard</option>
 <option>Ketchup</option>
 <option>Relish</option>
</select>

</div>
```

```
    </div>
```

5. Make a small tweak to the display of our select dropdown, by adding the following simple piece of CSS code to `recipe06-04.scss`:

```
ul.inner {
  padding-left: 0;
}
```

6. Run Grunt and Harp server, and preview the completed recipe at `http://localhost:9000/recipe06-04`.

How it works...

Unfortunately, at the time of writing this book, the plugin was not ready to be used with Bootstrap 4. However, with some research into the issue threads on the plugin's official GitHub repository, we were able to find a developer who had similar requirements and successfully ported the plugin to Bootstrap 4 prerelease.

To make the plugin work with Bootstrap 4 alpha.6, we had to CDN the CSS and JS files from GitCDN. For our HTML structure, we added some minimal markup in `recipe06-04.ejs` using the `select` HTML element. All that was left was to slightly tweak the CSS for the dropdown to make the custom select element fit in perfectly with the rest of the Bootstrap 4 styles.

The end result is a multi-select dropdown that includes Font Awesome icons on each of the selected drop-down items and updates the selection's preview dynamically.

To compare our finished recipe to the original example on the plugin's documentation page, navigate to `http://silviomoreto.github.io/bootstrap-select/examples/` and find the example under the heading **Multiple select boxes**.

 This plugin is very complex. There is a host of options and implementations. This recipe gives you a working multiple select box example to guide you through the process of adapting it for Bootstrap 4. You can use a similar approach to explore other examples available for this plugin. Hopefully, this process should be made even easier once Bootstrap 4 is fully released and the plugin is updated accordingly.

Customizing select boxes with Select2 plugin

In this recipe, we will look into another excellent plugin for customizing select boxes, available at `https://select2.github.io/`. The repository can be found at `https://github.com/select2/select2`.

Getting ready

In this recipe, we will implement Select2 plugin's version of multiple select boxes. That way, we can easily compare the look and feel of this plugin's features with the Bootstrap Select plugin that we covered in the previous chapter.

To get ready, navigate to `https://select2.github.io/examples.html#multiple`and test the functionality in the example.

How to do it...

1. In `app/_layout.ejs`, reference the CSS file from CDNJS:

   ```
   <link
   href="https://cdnjs.cloudflare.com/ajax/libs/select2/4.0.3/css/sele
   ct2.min.css" rel="stylesheet" />
   ```

2. In `app/partials/_js.ejs`, call the JS file from CDNJS:

   ```
   <script
   src="https://cdnjs.cloudflare.com/ajax/libs/select2/4.0.3/js/select
   2.min.js"></script>
   ```

3. Copy the following code and paste it into `app/recipe06-05.ejs`:

   ```
   <div class="container">

    <div class="mt-5">
    <h1><%- title %></h1>
    <p><a href="https://v4-alpha.getbootstrap.com/components/alerts/"
      target="_blank">Link to bootstrap alerts docs</a></p>

    </div><!-- /.container -->
   ```

```html
<div class="col-12 col-md-5">

<div>

<div class="wrapper">

<form>
 <div class="form-group">
 <label>Make one or more selections</label>
 <select class="js-example-basic-multiple form-control"
 multiple="multiple">
 <optgroup label="Alaskan/Hawaiian Time Zone">
 <option value="AK">Alaska</option>
 <option value="HI">Hawaii</option>
 </optgroup>
 <optgroup label="Pacific Time Zone">
 <option value="CA">California</option>
 <option value="NV">Nevada</option>
 <option value="OR">Oregon</option>
 <option value="WA">Washington</option>
 </optgroup>
 <optgroup label="Mountain Time Zone">
 <option value="AZ">Arizona</option>
 <option value="CO">Colorado</option>
 <option value="ID">Idaho</option>
 <option value="MT">Montana</option>
 </optgroup>
 </select>
 </div>
</form>

</div>

</div>
```

4. Target the class of js-example-basic-multiple and call the select2 method on it in app/partial/_recipe06-05-js.ejs:

```html
<script>

$(".js-example-basic-multiple").select2({
 placeholder: "Click to select state(s)",
 allowClear: true
});

</script>
```

5. Run `grunt` and `harp server` and preview the completed recipe at
   `http://localhost:9000/recipe06-05`.

How it works…

This plugin is not specifically intended for Bootstrap, but it fits perfectly. Its setup was really easy, as the plugin can be readily included in some popular CDNs.

To make it work with bootstrap, all we had to do is wrap it in `<div class="form-group">`. For improved styling, we added the class of `form-control` onto the `select` element.

To run the plugin, all we had to do is target its specific class, and then pass in an object of options to the `select2` method. In the options object, we passed in the `placeholder` key and its custom string value, and the `allowClear` key and its Boolean value.

Adding input sliders with Rangeslider.js

At the time of publishing this book, there were only several jQuery plugins specifically intended for Bootstrap 4. However, since jQuery is a stable JavaScript library with a long history, there have been plenty of plugins already made for it. One of those is Rangeslider.js, available at `http://rangeslider.js.org/`.

Although not intended for Bootstrap 4 per se, it is still a great polyfill for the `input` HTML element's `range` type attribute. Bootstrap 4 does not come with its own implementation of the `range` type attribute, so this polyfill is a great solution.

Getting ready

To see the Rangeslider.js files available for use with CDNJS, navigate to `https://cdnjs.com/libraries/rangeslider.js`. Also, to get acquainted with the Rangeslider.js polyfill, visit `http://rangeslider.js.org/` and the GitHub repository at `https://github.com/andreruffert/rangeslider.js`.

How to do it...

1. Reference the CSS file from CDNJS and add it inside the head tag of `app/_layout.ejs`:

```
<link
href="https://cdnjs.cloudflare.com/ajax/libs/rangeslider.js/2.3.0/r
angeslider.css" rel="stylesheet" />
```

2. In `app/partial/_js.ejs`, add the following `script` tag to call the JS file from CDNJS:

```
<script
src="https://cdnjs.cloudflare.com/ajax/libs/rangeslider.js/2.3.0/ra
ngeslider.js"></script>
```

3. Open the `app/recipe06-06.ejs` file in your code editor and paste the following code:

```
<div class="container">

 <div class="mt-5">
 <h1><%- title %></h1>
 <p><a href="https://v4-alpha.getbootstrap.com/components/alerts/"
target="_blank">Link to bootstrap alerts docs</a></p>

</div><!-- /.container -->

<div class="col-12 col-md-5">

<div>

<div class="wrapper">

<input
 type="range"
 min="10"
 max="1000"
 step="10"
 value="300"
 data-orientation="vertical">

</div>

</div>
```

4. Open the partial _recipe-06-06-js.ejs file from the `app/partial` folder, and copy and paste the following code:

```
<script>

$('input[type="range"]').rangeslider({

    // Feature detection the default is `true`.
    // Set this to `false` if you want to use
    // the polyfill also in Browsers which support
    // the native <input type="range"> element.
    polyfill: false,

    // Default CSS classes
    rangeClass: 'rangeslider',
    disabledClass: 'rangeslider--disabled',
    horizontalClass: 'rangeslider--horizontal',
    verticalClass: 'rangeslider--vertical',
    fillClass: 'rangeslider__fill',
    handleClass: 'rangeslider__handle',

    // Callback function
    onInit: function() {},

    // Callback function
    onSlide: function(position, value) {},

    // Callback function
    onSlideEnd: function(position, value) {}
});

</script>
```

5. To override the default colors, add the following code to `recipe06-06.scss`:

```
.wrapper .rangeslider__handle:after {
display: none;
}

.wrapper .rangeslider__handle {
background: #d9edf7;
border: 4px solid rgba(123, 167, 190, 0.3);
background-image: none;
-moz-box-shadow: none;
-webkit-box-shadow: none;
box-shadow: none;
}
```

```
.wrapper .rangeslider__fill {
  background: #bcdff1;
}
```

6. Run the `grunt` and `harp server` commands and preview the completed recipe at `http://localhost:9000/recipe06-06`.

Allowing users to easily add dates to your input fields with jQuery UI Datepicker

In this recipe, we will use jQuery UI and its excellent Datepicker. This is a mature and stable library, but there is one caveat to have in mind, that is, there are no styles compatible with Bootstrap 4.

Thus, the task for this recipe is to make the jQuery UI's Datepicker widget work with Bootstrap 4. This task mostly has to do with CSS. The official jQuery UI documentation for the Datepicker widget is available at `https://jqueryui.com/datepicker/`.

How to do it...

1. Reference the recipe specific SCSS file, `recipe06-07.scss`, on top of `main.scss`. After this addition, `main.scss` should now look as follows:

```
@import "recipe06-07.scss";

@import "./bower_components/bootstrap/scss/bootstrap.scss";
@import "./bower_components/bootstrap/scss/_mixins.scss";
@import "./bower_components/font-awesome/scss/font-awesome.scss";
@import "./bower_components/hover/scss/hover.scss";
```

2. Next, open the SCSS file you imported in the preceding step and paste in the following styles:

```
.ui-datepicker {
  background-color: #fff;
  border: 1px solid #66AFE9;
  border-radius: 4px;
  box-shadow: 0 0 8px rgba(102,175,233,.6);
  display: none;
  margin-top: 4px;
  padding: 10px;
```

```
  width: 240px;
  font-family: "Helvetica Neue",Helvetica,Arial,sans-serif;
  font-size: 14px !important;
}
.ui-datepicker a,
.ui-datepicker a:hover {
  text-decoration: none;
}
.ui-datepicker a:hover,
.ui-datepicker td:hover a {
  color: #2A6496;
  -webkit-transition: color 0.1s ease-in-out;
  -moz-transition: color 0.1s ease-in-out;
  -o-transition: color 0.1s ease-in-out;
  transition: color 0.1s ease-in-out;
}
.ui-datepicker .ui-datepicker-header {
  margin-bottom: 4px;
  text-align: center;
}
.ui-datepicker .ui-datepicker-title {
  font-weight: 700;
}
.ui-datepicker .ui-datepicker-prev,
.ui-datepicker .ui-datepicker-next {
  cursor: default;
  font-family: FontAwesome; // MINE
  -webkit-font-smoothing: antialiased;
  font-style: normal;
  font-weight: normal;
  height: 20px;
  line-height: 1;
  margin-top: 2px;
  width: 20px;
  color: #999;
}
.ui-datepicker .ui-datepicker-prev {
  float: left;
  text-align: left;
}
.ui-datepicker .ui-datepicker-next {
  float: right;
  text-align: right;
}
.ui-datepicker .ui-datepicker-prev:before {
  content: "\f060"; // MINE
}
.ui-datepicker .ui-datepicker-next:before {
```

```
   content: "\f061"; // MINE
 }
.ui-datepicker .ui-icon {
 display: none;
 }
.ui-datepicker .ui-datepicker-calendar {
 table-layout: fixed;
 width: 100%;
 }
.ui-datepicker .ui-datepicker-calendar th,
.ui-datepicker .ui-datepicker-calendar td {
 text-align: center;
 padding: 4px 0;
 color: #000 !important;
 }
.ui-datepicker .ui-datepicker-calendar td {
 border-radius: 4px;
 -webkit-transition: background-color 0.1s ease-in-out, color 0.1s
ease-in-out;
 -moz-transition: background-color 0.1s ease-in-out, color 0.1s
ease-in-out;
 -o-transition: background-color 0.1s ease-in-out, color 0.1s ease-
in-out;
 transition: background-color 0.1s ease-in-out, color 0.1s ease-in-
out;
 }
.ui-datepicker .ui-datepicker-calendar td:hover:not(.ui-datepicker-
current-day) {
 background-color: #eee;
 cursor: pointer;
 }
.ui-datepicker .ui-datepicker-calendar td a {
 text-decoration: none;
 color: #000;
 }
.ui-datepicker .ui-datepicker-current-day {
 background-color: #285e8e;
 /* background-color: #4289cc; */
 }
.ui-datepicker td.ui-datepicker-current-day a {
 color: #fff;
 }
.ui-datepicker .ui-datepicker-calendar .ui-datepicker-
unselectable:hover {
 background-color: #fff;
 cursor: default;
 }
```

```css
.ui-datepicker-month {
 border: 0px;
 color: #000;
}
.ui-datepicker-year {
 border: 0px;
 color: #000;
}
```

3. Navigate to the `app/partial` folder and open the `_js.ejs` file. Add another `script` tag to the bottom of the `script` tags that have been added previously:

```html
<script
src="https://cdnjs.cloudflare.com/ajax/libs/jqueryui/1.12.0/jquery-
ui.min.js"></script>
```

4. At the bottom of `_js.ejs`, add a partial for `_recipe-06-07-js.ejs`, as follows:

```
<%- partial("_recipe-06-07-js") %>
```

5. Copy and paste the following snippet of code into the previously referenced `_recipe-06-07-js.ejs` in the `app/partial` folder:

```html
<script>

$(function () {
$( "#datepicker" ).datepicker();
});

</script>
```

6. Add the following HTML code to `app/recipe06-07.ejs`:

```html
<div class="container">

<div class="mt-5">
<h1><%- title %></h1>
<p><a href="https://v4-alpha.getbootstrap.com/components/alerts/"
target="_blank">Link to bootstrap alerts docs</a></p>

</div><!-- /.container -->

<div class="col-12 col-md-5">

<div>

<div class="wrapper">
```

```
<p>Date: <input type="text" id="datepicker" class="form-
control"></p>


</div>
```

7. Run the `grunt` and `harp server` commands and preview the completed recipe at `localhost:9000/recipe06-07`.

Converting plain tables into sophisticated data tables with Bootgrid

In this chapter, we will significantly improve our tables using the jQuery Bootgrid plugin. The official website of this plugin can be found at `http://www.jquery-bootgrid.com/GettingStarted`. The repository is available at the GitHub page at `https://github.com/rstaib/jquery-bootgrid`.

To use the plugin, inspect the files available via CDNJS on `https://cdnjs.com/libraries/jquery-bootgrid`.

Getting ready

Before we start with the recipe, it could be useful to see the completed example of what happens to a plain table once it gets improved with the use of the Bootgrid plugin. Point your browser to `http://www.jquery-bootgrid.com/Examples`. Locate the **Basic Example** heading, and click on the **Prettify Table** button. This will turn the plugin on and improve the example table on the page, giving it several filters and a search feature, as well as the option of choosing the number of rows visible and a pagination at the bottom of the table.

Now that we have a basic idea of what is possible with jQuery Bootgrid, we can begin to implement it with Bootstrap 4.

How to do it...

1. Add this CDN link just above the closing `head` tag in `app/_layout.ejs`:

```
<link
href="https://cdnjs.cloudflare.com/ajax/libs/jquery-bootgrid/1.3.1/
jquery.bootgrid.css" rel="stylesheet" />
```

2. In `main.scss`, comment out other recipe-specific imports and add the following line to the very bottom of the file:

```
@import "recipe06-08.scss";
```

3. In `app/partial/_js.ejs`, add two `script` tags, referencing the CDN JS files for Bootgrid and to display Font Awesome icons, as follows:

```
<script
src="https://cdnjs.cloudflare.com/ajax/libs/jquery-bootgrid/1.3.1/j
query.bootgrid.js"></script>
<script
src="https://cdnjs.cloudflare.com/ajax/libs/jquery-bootgrid/1.3.1/j
query.bootgrid.fa.js"></script>
```

4. While still in the same file, at the very bottom, add a call to the `_recipe-06-08-js.ejs` partial file:

```
<%- partial("_recipe-06-08-js") %>
```

5. To get the Bootgrid plugin to convert our table with the ID attribute of grid-basic, we need to call it in the partial file, `_recipe-06-08-js.ejs`:

```
<script>

$("#grid-basic").bootgrid();

</script>
```

6. Finally, add the `table` element, together with the rest of the recipe-specific code, in `app/recipe06-08.ejs`:

```
<div class="container">

 <div class="mt-5">
 <h1><%- title %></h1>
 <p><a href="https://v4-alpha.getbootstrap.com/components/alerts/"
```

```
target="_blank">Link to bootstrap alerts docs</a></p>

</div><!-- /.container -->

<div class="col-12">

<div>

<div class="wrapper">

<table id="grid-basic" class="table table-condensed table-hover
table-striped">
 <thead>
 <tr>
 <th data-column-id="id" data-type="numeric">ID</th>
 <th data-column-id="sender">Sender</th>
 <th data-column-id="received" data-order="desc">Received</th>
 </tr>
 </thead>
 <tbody>
 <tr>
 <td>12345</td>
 <td>eduardo@pingpong.com</td>
 <td>14.10.2013</td>
 </tr>
 <tr>
 <td>67890</td>
 <td>asdf@pingpong.com</td>
 <td>11.10.2013</td>
 </tr>
 <tr>
 <td>13579</td>
 <td>qwerty@pingpong.com</td>
 <td>11.10.2017</td>
 </tr>
 </tbody>
</table>

</div>
```

7. Run the `grunt` and `harp` server commands and preview the result at
   `localhost:9000/recipe06-08`.

How it works…

To integrate this plugin with Bootstrap was really easy. We simply had to give our `table` element an `id` attribute with the `grid-basic` value.

Then, all we had to do to make it work was to run the following code:

```
$("#grid-basic").bootgrid();
```

What this code does is look for the HTML element that has the `grid-basic` ID on our web page and then runs the jQuery `bootgrid()` method on it. The dynamics of how this works behind the scenes are discussed in `Chapter 7`, *Make Your Own jQuery Plugins in Bootstrap 4*.

Navigating easily with simple-sidebar jQuery plugin

In this chapter, we will utilize the jQuery simple-sidebar plugin to achieve a mobile menu that appears as a sidebar. The plugin is The plugin website can be accessed via `https://simple-sidebar.github.io/simpler-sidebar/`.

To make things easier, we will use GitCDN for this plugin's files.

Getting ready

To get ready, look at the setup instructions. These instructions are available at the official website for the plugin.

How to do it…

1. Since we are showcasing a different navbar, we need to change the structure of our project a bit. First, we will alter the `_data.json` file inside the `app` folder. Specifically, we need to alter the entry that starts with `recipe06-09`, beginning on line 29:

   ```
   // below code starts at line 29 of _data.json:
   "recipe06-09": {
   "title": "Recipe 06-09: Navigate Easily with a Custom Offcanvas
   Navbar",
   ```

```
  "layout": "_layout06-09" // newly added line - specifies an
  alternate layout for this page only
},
```

2. Now we can add the layout referenced in the preceding step. Open the currently empty _layout06-09.ejs in the app folder and paste in the following code:

```html
<!DOCTYPE html>
<html lang="en">
  <head>
    <meta charset="utf-8">
    <meta name="viewport" content="width=device-width, initial-
    scale=1, shrink-to-fit=no">
    <meta name="description" content="">
    <meta name="author" content="">
    <link rel="icon" href="../../favicon.ico">
    <title>
      <%- title %>
    </title>
    <!-- Bootstrap core CSS -->
    <link href="css/main.css" rel="stylesheet">
    <link href="https://fonts.googleapis.com/css?family=Pacifico"
    rel="stylesheet">
  </head>
  <body class="">
    <%- partial("partial/_nav2") %> <!-- CUSTOM NAVBAR INCLUDE -->
    <%- yield %>
    <%- partial("partial/_js") %>
  </body>
</html>
```

3. In app/partial, add the following code to _nav2.ejs:

```html
<div id="navbar">
  <!--
    #navbar is positioned fixed.
    It does not matter what kind of element #toggle-sidebar is.
    -->
  <div class="d-flex justify-content-center mt-5">
    <h1 style="font-family: 'Pacifico', cursive; color: #8a9">Our
    Website Name</h1>
  </div>
  <div class="d-flex justify-content-center">
    <button id="toggle-sidebar" class="btn btn-primary btn-large
mt-
    5">MENU</button>
  </div>
</div>
```

```
<div id="sidebar">
  <!--
    simpler-sidebar will handle #sidebar's position.
    To let the content of your sidebar overflow, especially when
you
    have a lot of content in it, you have to add a "wrapper" that
    wraps all content.
    TIP: provide a background color.
  -->
  <div id="sidebar-wrapper" class="sidebar-wrapper">
    <!--
      Links below are just an example. Give each clickable element,
      for example links, a class to trigger the closing animation.
    -->
    <div class="col sidebar-offcanvas mt-5 pr-5" id="sidebar">
      <div class="list-group">
        <a href="#" class="list-group-item active">Link</a>
        <a href="#" class="list-group-item">Link</a>
        <a href="#" class="list-group-item">Link</a>
        <a href="#" class="list-group-item">Link</a>
        <a href="#" class="list-group-item">Link</a>
        <a href="#" class="list-group-item">Link</a>
        <a href="#" class="list-group-item">Link</a>
        <a href="#" class="list-group-item">Link</a>
        <a href="#" class="list-group-item">Link</a>
        <a href="#" class="list-group-item">Link</a>
      </div>
    </div>
  </div>
</div>
```

4. In app/partial/_js.ejs, append the following code to the very bottom of the file:

```
<%- partial("_recipe-06-09-js") %>
```

5. While still in the same file, under all the other `script` tags, add another `script` element and pass the recipe-specific GitCDN's JavaScript file URL in the `src` attribute:

```
<script
src="https://gitcdn.xyz/repo/simple-sidebar/simpler-sidebar/master/
dist/jquery.simpler-sidebar.js"></script>
```

6. In `app/recipe06-09.ejs`, add the following code:

```
<div class="container">
  <div class="mt-5">
    <h1><%- title %></h1>
    <p>
      <a
href="https://v4-alpha.getbootstrap.com/components/navbar/"
        target="_blank">
          Link to bootstrap navbar docs
      </a>
    </p>
</div> <!-- /.container -->
<div class="col-12">
<div>
  <div class="wrapper">
    <p class="h2">
      This recipe showcases the use of simpler-sidebar, integrated
      with Bootstrap 4.
    </p>
    <p>
      The code for the plugin is available at
      <a href="https://github.com/simple-sidebar/simpler-sidebar"
       target="_blank">
        https://github.com/simple-sidebar/simpler-sidebar
      </a>.
    </p>
</div>
```

7. To make the plugin work, copy and paste the following code into the
   `_recipe-06-09-js.ejs`, inside the `app/partial` folder:

```
<script>
    $( document ).ready( function() {
        $( "#sidebar" ).simplerSidebar( {
            selectors: {
                trigger: "#toggle-sidebar",
                quitter: ".close-sidebar"
            }
        } );
    } );
</script>
```

8. Run the `grunt` and `harp server` commands and preview the result at
   `localhost:9000/recipe06-09`.

How it works...

The implementation of the plugin is simple; we set a button to trigger the appearance of the
sidebar navigation. The navigation itself is just a list group with a number of list group
items. Combining Bootstrap 4 with the simple-sidebar plugin like this creates an interesting
effect, without too much effort.

Adding fully customizable notifications with Notify.js

In this recipe, we will show how to use the Notify.js plugin. To begin using it, we will install
it via `GitCDN.xyz`. After that, we'll explore some of its many options.

To get acquainted with this plugin, navigate to `https://notifyjs.com/` and `https://gith
ub.com/jpillora/notifyjs/tree/master/dist`.

Getting ready

Let's navigate to the raw Notify.js file on its GitHub repository and copy and paste it to the `GitCDN.xyz` interface. The link that we get back is `https://gitcdn.xyz/repo/jpillora/notifyjs/master/dist/notify.js`. We will use it in our recipe to reference this library.

How to do it...

1. Add the Notify.js to the `_js.ejs` partial in the `app/partial` folder:

   ```
   <script
   src="https://gitcdn.xyz/repo/jpillora/notifyjs/master/dist/notify.j
   s"></script>
   ```

2. Add the following code to `app/partial/_recipe-06-10-js.ejs`:

   ```
   <script>
   // Basic Example
   $.notify("Click to hide or wait 20 seconds…");
   </script>
   ```

   This should give us the Notify.js default styling, as shown on the projects, website.

3. While still in the same file, let's add Bootstrap 4 success alert CSS:

   ```
   $.notify.addStyle('bs4success', {
   html: '<div><span class="fa fa-spinner fa-spin fa-2x"></span>
   <span
     data-notify-text/></div>',
   classes: {
   base: {
   "background-color": "#dff0db",
   "border-color": "#d0e9c6",
   "color": "#3c763d",
   "padding": ".75rem 1.25rem",
   "margin-bottom": "1rem",
   "border": "1px solid transparent",
   "border-radius": ".25rem"
   },
   }
   });
   ```

4. Finally, let's add some options to our custom Notify.js alert:

```
$.notify(
" Click to hide or wait 20 seconds…",
{
  autoHideDelay: 20000,
  clickToHide: true,
  style: 'bs4success'
}
);
```

5. Run the `grunt` and `harp server` commands and preview the recipe at `localhost:9000/recipe06-10`.

How it works…

To achieve Bootstrap 4 alert look, we used the `addStyle()` method by passing it two parameters. The first one was a made-up name of `bs4success`. The second parameter was an object. We passed certain key-value pairs to the object, and thus determined the HTML structure and the base classes to use in CSS. Then, finally, when we called the plugin, we passed it two arguments to the function call. The first one was a string with the message we want to show in our alert, and the second one was an object with key-value pairs to use to override the default behavior of the plugin. Note the third key-value pair, where we gave the value of `bs4success`, our made-up name of the first parameter of the plugin function definition, to the `style` key in our function call's second argument's third key-value pair.

Integrating a fancy modal using animatedModal.js

In this recipe, we will combine the already great Bootstrap 4 card elements with the animatedModal.js jQuery plugin to create an awesome fullscreen modal with CSS3 transitions. We will use the ready-made transitions from `animate.css`, but we could create our own as well.

Getting ready

To get an idea of what `animatedModal.js` offers, navigate to its official website at `http://joaopereirawd.github.io/animatedModal.js/`. Also, make sure that you check out the GitHub repository at `https://github.com/joaopereirawd/animatedModal.js`. To reference `animatedModal.js` and `animate.css`, we will use `GitCDN.xyz` and `cdnjs`, respectively, as detailed in the following recipe.

How to do it...

1. Include `animate.css` inside the head tag in `app/_layout.ejs`:

    ```
    <link rel="stylesheet"
    href="//cdnjs.cloudflare.com/ajax/libs/animate.css/3.2.0/animate.min.css">
    ```

2. In `app/recipe06-10.ejs`, add the following code in between the HTML body tags:

    ```
    <!--Call your modal-->
    <a id="demo01" href="#animatedModal">DEMO01</a>

    <!--DEMO01-->
    <div id="animatedModal">
     <!--THIS IS IMPORTANT! to close the modal, the class name has to
      match the name given on the ID class="close-animatedModal" -->
     <div class="close-animatedModal">
     CLOSE MODAL
     </div>

     <div class="modal-content">
     <!--Your modal content goes here-->
     </div>
    </div>
    ```

3. Add the address of the raw `animatedModal.js` file from the plugin's GitHub repository into the `GitCDN.xyz` input field. Copy the link that gets generated in the output field and paste it into `app/partial/_js.ejs`, under the other `script` tags:

```
<script
src="https://gitcdn.xyz/repo/joaopereirawd/animatedModal.js/master/
animatedModal.js"></script>
```

4. While still in the same file, add the recipe-specific partial:

```
<%- partial("_recipe-06-11-js") %>
```

5. Now that we have got the modal working, let's add the cards. Locate the bit of code from step 2, with the HTML comment:

```
<!--Your modal content goes here-->
```

Replace the comment with the following code:

```
<!--
<div class="modal-content">
-->
<!--Your modal content goes here-->
<!--
</div>
-->
<div class="container container-narrow">
<div class="row">
<div class="col-xs-4">
<div class="col-sm-6">
<div class="card">
<div class="card-block">
<h3 class="card-title">Special title treatment</h3>
<p class="card-text">With supporting text below as a natural
 lead-in to additional content.</p>
<a href="#" class="btn btn-primary">Go somewhere</a>
</div>
</div>
</div>
<div class="col-sm-6">
<div class="card">
<div class="card-block">
<h3 class="card-title">Special title treatment</h3>
<p class="card-text">With supporting text below as a natural
 lead-in to additional content.</p>
<a href="#" class="btn btn-primary">Go somewhere</a>
```

```
            </div>
          </div>
        </div>
      </div>
    </div>
  </div>
df
```

6. In `recipe06-10.scss`, add the following code:

```
.container-narrow {
  width: 500px;
  max-width: 500px;
}
```

7. In `main.scss`, make the `@import` statement to include the code from the preceding step:

```
@import "recipe06-11.scss";
```

8. Run the `grunt` and `harp server` commands and preview the completed recipe at `localhost:9000/recipe06-11`.

How it works...

The way this works is simpler than most other recipes in this chapter, as the animatedModal plugin takes care of everything for us. The modal is triggered when an anchor element is clicked. The anchor element that triggers the modal looks like this:

```
<a id="demo01" href="#animatedModal">DEMO01</a>
```

The click will find `div` with the `id` attribute of animatedModal. This `div` holds the code for the two Bootstrap 4 card components, copied from the official docs.

The following snippet of code, taken from step 5, shows what needs to be done to set up the modal's close button:

```
<!--THIS IS IMPORTANT! to close the modal, the class name has to match
  the name given on the ID class="close-animatedModal" -->
<div class="close-animatedModal">
<span class="btn btn-primary text-center fa fa-close fa4x"></span>
</div>
```

Making pagination dynamic with the jQuery Pagination plugin and simplePagination.js

In this recipe, we will look at the truly amazing jQuery Pagination plugin. The official website can be found at `https://esimakin.github.io/twbs-pagination/`. The project can be found on GitHub and at: `https://github.com/esimakin/twbs-pagination`.

To further customize our pagination, we will utilize a second plugin, the wonderful `simplePagination.js`, at `http://flaviusmatis.github.io/simplePagination.js/`.

One of the nice things about the first plugin is that it is fully compliant with Bootstrap 4 prerelease, which will make it a lot easier for us to integrate it.

Getting ready

To get started, we will reference the unminified raw JS files on the plugins' respective repositories. We will then copy and paste the addresses of the raw files into the `GitCDN.xyz` interface, and that will give us the links to use in the script tags in our recipe. The links that `GitCDN.xyz` produces are the following:

- `https://gitcdn.xyz/repo/esimakin/twbs-pagination/master/jquery.twbsPagination.js`
- `https://gitcdn.xyz/repo/flaviusmatis/simplePagination.js/master/jquery.simplePagination.js`

How to do it...

1. In `app/partial/_js.ejs`, at the bottom of the other script tags already present in the file, add the following two `script` tags :

    ```
    <script
    src="https://gitcdn.xyz/repo/esimakin/twbs-pagination/master/jquery
    .twbsPagination.js"></script>
     <script
    src="https://gitcdn.xyz/repo/flaviusmatis/simplePagination.js/maste
    r/jquery.simplePagination.js"></script>
    ```

2. While still in the same file, at the very bottom, add the following line of code:

```
<%- partial("_recipe-06-12-js") %>
```

3. Next, in `recipe06-12.ejs`, add the HTML for the recipe:

```html
<div class="container">

<div class="mt-5">
<h1><%- title %></h1>
<p><a href="https://v4-alpha.getbootstrap.com/components/alerts/"
target="_blank">Link to bootstrap alerts docs</a></p>

</div><!-- /.container -->

<div class="col-12">

<div>

<div class="wrapper">


<nav aria-label="Page navigation">
<ul class="pagination" id="pagination"></ul>
</nav>

</div>

</div>
```

4. Add the recipe-specific JavaScript code in `app/partial/_recipe-06-12-js.ejs`:

```javascript
<script>

$('#pagination').pagination({
items: 20,
itemOnPage: 8,
currentPage: 1,
cssStyle: '',
prevText: '<span aria-hidden="true">&laquo;</span>',
nextText: '<span aria-hidden="true">&raquo;</span>',
onInit: function () {
// fire first page loading
},
onPageClick: function (page, evt) {
```

```
$('#alt-style-pagination-content').text('Page ' + page);
    }
});
```

```
</script>
```

5. In `recipe06-12.scss`, add the CSS code to give it the needed Bootstrap 4 styling:

```css
.pagination>.active>a,
.pagination>.active>a:focus,
.pagination>.active>a:hover,
.pagination>.active>span,
.pagination>.active>span:focus,
.pagination>.active>span:hover {
  z-index: 3;
  color: #fff;
  cursor: default;
  background-color: #337ab7;
  border-color: #337ab7;
}

.pagination>li>a, .pagination>li>span {
  position: relative;
  float: left;
  padding: 6px 12px;
  margin-left: -1px;
  line-height: 1.42857143;
  color: #337ab7;
  text-decoration: none;
  background-color: #fff;
  border: 1px solid #ddd;
}
```

6. In `main.scss`, reference the file mentioned in step 5:

```
@import "recipe06-12.scss";
```

7. Run `grunt` and `harp server` and preview the improved pagination functionality at `localhost:9000/recipe06-12`.

How it works...

This recipe is a bit different from the others in this chapter, because we are actually combining two separate plugins to get quite an interesting effect to use on our sites. The end result is that we get a fully dynamic pagination, styled to be used with Bootstrap 4.

Validating forms with svalidate.js

In this recipe, we will utilize a small and useful jQuery plugin called svalidate.js. A demo of this plugin is available at `http://s-validate.ipatieff.me`. The GitHub repository can be found at `https://github.com/SergeIpatyev/svalidatejs`.

Getting ready

To get ready, let's grab the raw `svd.js` available at `https://raw.githubusercontent.com/SergeIpatyev/svalidatejs/master/svd.js`. Next, we will put `GitCDN.xyz` to work and obtain the link to use in our script tag:
`https://gitcdn.xyz/repo/SergeIpatyev/svalidatejs/master/svd.js`.

How to do it...

1. Let's begin by adding the `script` tag to `app/partial/_js.ejs`:

   ```
   <script
   src="https://gitcdn.xyz/repo/SergeIpatyev/svalidatejs/master/svd.js
   "></script>
   ```

2. Next, let's add another line of code to the bottom of `_js.ejs`:

   ```
   <%- partial("_recipe-06-13-js") %>
   ```

3. Open the file titled `recipe06-13.ejs` and add the following code on line 15:

   ```
   <form method="post">
   <div class="form-group row">
   <label for="inputCustom" class="col-sm-2 col-form-
     label">Custom</label>
   <div class="col-sm-10">
   <input type="text" class="form-control" id="inputCustom"
     placeholder="Custom input">
   ```

```
<small class="text-muted"></small>
</div>
</div>
<div class="form-group row">
<label for="inputEmail" class="col-sm-2 col-form-
label">Email</label>
<div class="col-sm-10">
<input type="email" class="form-control" id="inputEmail"
placeholder="Email">
<small class="text-muted"></small>
</div>
</div>
<div class="form-group row">
<label for="inputPassword" class="col-sm-2 col-form-
label">Password</label>
<div class="col-sm-10">
<input type="password" class="form-control" id="inputPassword"
placeholder="Password">
<small class="text-muted"></small>
</div>
</div>
<div class="form-group row">
<label class="col-sm-2">Checkbox</label>
<div class="col-sm-10">
<div class="form-check">
<label class="form-check-label">
<input class="form-check-input" type="checkbox"> Check me out
</label>
</div>
</div>
</div>
<div class="form-group row">
<div class="offset-sm-2 col-sm-10">
<button type="button" id="submit" class="btn btn-primary">Sign in
or Send</button>
</div>
</div>
</form>
```

4. Copy the following code and paste it into the file titled _recipe-06-13-js.ejs, in app/partial:

```
var settings = {
// set #id for validation email
emailID: '#inputEmail',
// set text for validation email
ErrorTextEmail: 'Enter valid email',
// set #id for validation password
```

```
passwordID: '#inputPassword',
// set text for validation password
ErrorTextPassword: 'Must be minimum 7 characters long.',
// set value required chars for validation password
MinCharsPass: '7',
// set #id for validation custom
Custom: '#inputCustom',
// set text for validation password
ErrorTextCustom: 'Must be minimum 5 characters long custom.',
// set value required chars for validation custom form
MinCharsCustom: '5'
}
```

5. Run the `grunt` and `harp server` commands and preview the form with the validation at `localhost:9000/recipe06-13`.

How it works...

The basics of how the plugin works can be gleaned from step 5, with all the options in the settings object copied from the plugin's docs. We basically have an object with a number of key-value pairs, where each of them is responsible for a specific task inside the plugin, such as, for example, setting the required characters for the validation custom form with the `MinCharsCustom` key.

Adding a rating system using jQuery Bar Rating plugin

In this recipe, we'll add a rating system using the jQuery Bar Rating plugin. The plugin documentation can be accessed via `http://antenna.io/demo/jquery-bar-rating/exampl es/`. The GitHub repository is available at `https://github.com/antennaio/jquery-bar-r ating`.

Getting ready

To get ready, let's grab the raw JS, available at `https://raw.githubusercontent.com/ante nnaio/jquery-bar-rating/master/dist/jquery.barrating.min.js`. Next, we will put `GitCDN.xyz` to work and obtain the `https://gitcdn.xyz/repo/antennaio/jquery-bar-rating/master/dist/jquery.barrating.min.js` link to use in our `script` tag.

Similarly, let's grab the raw CSS available at `https://raw.githubusercontent.com/anten naio/jquery-bar-rating/master/dist/themes/fontawesome-stars.css`. Now, let's process it via `GitCDN.xyz`, and copy the processed link, `https://gitcdn.xyz/repo/antennaio/jquery-bar-rating/master/dist/themes/fontawesome-stars.css`.

How to do it...

1. First, in `app/partial/_js.ejs`, add the following `script` tag:

   ```
   <script src="../../bower_components/jquery-bar-
   rating/dist/jquery.barrating.min.js"></script>
   ```

2. While still in the same file, append the following line of code at the very bottom:

   ```
   <%- partial("_recipe-06-14-js") %>
   ```

3. In `recipe06-14.ejs`, add the following code inside the `div` tag with the class of wrapper:

   ```
   <select id="example">
   <option value="1">1</option>
   <option value="2">2</option>
   <option value="3">3</option>
   <option value="4">4</option>
   <option value="5">5</option>
   </select>
   ```

4. In `app/partial/_recipe-06-14-js.ejs`, add the DOM ready event handler:

   ```
   $(function() {
   $('#example').barrating({
   theme: 'fontawesome-stars'
   });
   });
   ```

5. Just above the closing `head` tag in `app/_layout.ejs`, add the following `link` tag:

```
<link rel="stylesheet" href="../bower_components/jquery-bar-
rating/dist/themes/fontawesome-stars.css">
```

6. Run the `grunt` and `harp server` commands and preview the result at `localhost:9000/recipe06-14`.

How it works...

The way this works is similar to other plugins used in this chapter. As we can see in step 4, when the document ready event fires, we target the HTML element with an ID of `example`, and then we call the `barrating()` method on it. We pass an object to this method, and in this case, we give it a key-value pair of `theme: 'fontawesome-stars'`. This will override the default behavior of the `barrating()` plugin. It is a simple way to allow us as plugin users to customize the plugin behavior. For a detailed explanation of how this works, check out the second recipe in `Chapter 7`, *Make Your Own jQuery Plugins in Bootstrap 4*.

7

Make Your Own jQuery Plugins in Bootstrap 4

In this chapter, we will cover the following topics:

- Making the simplest possible jQuery plugin
- Making the plugin customizable with the extend() and each() methods
- Integrating a simple CSS Class Replacement plugin with Bootstrap 4

Introduction

Making jQuery plugins can be a very rewarding learning experience. It is good for understanding both jQuery and the inner workings of JavaScript. With so many jQuery plugins available online, and with so many used to extend Bootstrap's capabilities, it is an invaluable piece of knowledge for any frontend developer. In this chapter, we will look at creating the simplest possible jQuery plugin, then we'll build on the foundations and add more options to tweak and extend our plugins.

Making the simplest possible jQuery plugin

In this recipe, we will create the simplest possible Bootstrap plugin, with just the most basic functionality. The intention of having such a recipe in this book is to clarify the core principles of extending Bootstrap 4 via jQuery plugins as a starting point for more complex code.

Getting ready

To get ready, you can review the completed recipe by running harp server in the `chapter7/complete` folder, and navigate to `localhost:9000/recipe07-01`. The result you see should be a simple web page, with a navbar, a heading, and a paragraph.

After previewing the result we are trying to achieve, navigate to the `chapter7/start` folder and open the `_js.ejs, _nav.ejs, _recipe-07-01-js.ejs` files in the app/partial folder. Also, one level up, in the root of the `app` folder, open the file titled `recipe07-01.ejs`.

How to do it...

1. Open the currently blank `_recipe07-01-js.ejs` and paste the code as follows:

   ```
   // Step 1: Add an IIFE
   (function($) {
     // step 2 code goes here
   })(jQuery);
   ```

2. Continue by deleting the `// step 2 code goes here` comment from the preceding step and replacing it with this code:

   ```
   // Step 2: Attach the plugin onto jQuery.fn
   $.fn.canYouFindIt = function() {
     // the actual plugin code goes here (step 3)
   }
   ```

3. Similar to the preceding step, delete the second comment from step 2 and add the following code in its place:

   ```
   // Step 3: Chain an existing jQuery method onto 'this'
   this.css("background-color", "gold");
   ```

4. If we run the code now, it will not work. The reason for this is simple--we need to add a return keyword, like this:

   ```
   // Step 4: You MUST return 'this'
   return this.css("background-color", "gold");
   ```

5. The preceding steps have defined our plugin. Now we need to call it. For the sake of simplicity, we'll do it in the very same file we worked on in the previous steps. This time, we have to get to the very bottom of the file and add the following lines:

```
// calling the plugin
$('body').canYouFindIt();
```

6. To make sure that you have correctly performed all the steps, the following is the full code added to _recipe07-01-js.ejs, with the only difference being that only two comments are left, to make things more obvious.

```
// the actual plugin
(function() {
$.fn.canYouFindIt = function() {
return this.css("background-color", "gold");
};
})(jQuery);

// calling the plugin
$('body').canYouFindIt();
```

7. Now all that is left is to add the HTML for the recipe. Open app/recipe07-01.ejs and paste in the following code:

```
<div class="container">

<div class="mt-5">

<h1><%- title %></h1>

<p class="mt-4">The following steps deal with the very basics: How to create the simplest possible jQuery plugin.</p>

</div><!-- /.container -->

</div>
```

8. Run the harp server command and preview the result at localhost:9000/recipe07-01.

How it works…

In step 1, we added an **Immediately-Invoked Function Expression (IIFE)**. This is what every plugin should start with. The only parameter passed into the function declaration is the $, and the argument passed to the function call is jQuery. Doing this solves several problems, such as using the IIFE will make our code self-contained. Passing it the $ as the parameter will ensure that this $ is indeed referring to jQuery and not some other library that might also potentially use the $ and clash with our code. That's why we invoke the IIFE by passing jQuery as its argument.

In step 2, we attach our plugin, called canYouFindIt, onto jQuery.fn (or $.fn for short). This is crucial to make the plugin work. Without going into too much depth, suffice it to say that it helps us extend jQuery and make our method available to all the other jQuery methods. If you are curious about what jQuery.fn actually is, you might want to look at functions, objects, and prototypes in JavaScript. However, even without going into all of the complexity that hides behind $.fn, it is crucial to know that appending our plugin onto it is simply something we must do to make it work.

In step 3, we run the actual plugin-specific jQuery code. This is the heart of our plugin. Here, we are just highlighting DOM node(s), using the jQuery css() method. In the css() method, we can pass any key-value pair that reflects a CSS property-value combination, as used in regular CSS. In our example, we are passing the background-color as the first parameter, and the color of gold as the second parameter. This will result in the DOM node(s) getting the value of gold for their background-color css property . However, how does the browser know which DOM node(s) to color? It knows which node(s) to color because the this keyword refers to the so-called jQuery wrapped set, which is just a collection of DOM node(s) extracted from a web page's HTML structure (plus the jQuery methods that we can chain onto the nodes themselves). This collection is determined by the jQuery selector syntax, such as $('h1'), $(':focus'), and so on.

In step 4, we add the return keyword in front of the code from step 3. This return keyword is very important, as it returns a jQuery object that can then be manipulated with other jQuery methods. In other words, we must use the return keyword in order to preserve jQuery's method-chaining functionality.

Steps 1 through 4 dealt with plugin creation. Now that our most basic plugin is ready, in step 5, we finally put it to work by calling it on a jQuery selector. In our example, we are targeting the HTML body element, as follows:

```
$('body').canYouFindIt();
```

However, one great thing about jQuery plugins is that they are versatile. In other words, we can target anything that comes to mind, as follows:

```
$('h1').canYouFindIt();
$('p').canYouFindIt();
$('li a').canYouFindIt();
```

We can even target multiple selectors at once:

```
$('h1, p, li a').canYouFindIt();
```

Making the plugin customizable with the extend() and each() methods

In this recipe, we will build on the concepts discussed in the preceding recipe. The plugin we make in this recipe will have an additional functionality, using jQuery's extend() method. This will allow us to both specify defaults and to allow plugin users to override those defaults if they need to. This makes our plugin easier to use and allows us to cater for many more use-case scenarios.

Getting ready

To get ready, you can review the completed recipe by running harp server in the chapter7/complete/recipe2 folder and navigating to localhost:9000/recipe07-02. The result you see should be a simple web page with a navbar, a heading, and a paragraph.

After previewing the result we are trying to achieve, navigate to the chapter7/start folder and open the _js.ejs, _nav.ejs, _recipe-07-02-js.ejs files in the app/partial folder. Also, one level up, in the root of the app folder, open the file titled recipe07-02.ejs.

How to do it...

1. Open the currently blank _recipe07-02-js.ejs and paste the following code:

```
<script>

// the plugin itself
(function ($) {
```

```
$.fn.canYouFindIt2 = function() {
return this.css("background-color", "lightsalmon");
}
})(jQuery);

// calling the plugin
$('a').canYouFindIt2();

</script>
```

2. Let's abstract away the hardcoded values using the `extend()` method and passing in the options object:

```
$.fn.canYouFindIt2 = function( options ) {
  var defaults = $.extend({
    cssProperty: 'background-color',
    cssValue: 'lightsalmon'
  }, options);
  // step 3 will be added here
}
```

3. Find the commented line that reads `step 3 will be added here`, and in its place, add the following code:

```
return this.each(function(i, elem) {
  var $currentIndex = $(elem);
  $currentIndex.css(defaults.cssProperty, defaults.cssValue);
});
```

4. Now we can override the defaults by specifying either one or two parameters in the plugin call:

```
// calling the plugin
$('a').canYouFindIt2({
 cssValue: 'yellow'
});
```

5. Let's add the recipe-specific HTML to `recipe07-02.ejs`:

```
<div class="container">

<div class="mt-5">

<h1><%- title %></h1>

<p class="mt-4">This recipe helps us understand how to add default
options and how to override them, with the help of the extend()
```

```
method.</p>

</div><!-- /.container -->

</div>
```

6. Finally, in `app/partial/_js.ejs`, let's add the partial for recipe-specific JavaScript:

   ```
   <%- partial("_recipe-07-02-js") %>
   ```

7. Run the `harp server` command and preview the result at `localhost:9000/recipe07-02`.

How it works...

The core of this recipe can be found in `_recipe-07-02-js.ejs`. This code is relatively complex if you are new to it; thus, to make sure that we have the correct code, let's list the completed file after all the steps that pertain to it are inserted as described:

```
<script>
// the plugin itself
(function ($) {
$.fn.canYouFindIt2 = function( options ) {

var defaults = $.extend({
cssProperty: 'background-color',
cssValue: 'lightsalmon'
}, options);

return this.each(function (i, elem) {
var $currentIndex = $(elem);

$currentIndex.css(defaults.cssProperty, defaults.cssValue);
});
};
})(jQuery);

// calling the plugin
$('a').canYouFindIt2({
cssValue: 'yellow'
});

</script>
```

There are quite a few things happening here, so let's go through each of the steps in the recipe.

In step 1, we add the starting code that works as is. However, there are issues with the code in this step. First of all, the values returned are hardcoded. It is not possible to make it any easier to use this plugin as is. Even though this plugin is only several lines of code in length, this is never the case for any serious project.

If we want to make our plugin versatile and user-friendly, we need to allow for a few things:

1. We need to make it possible to pass one or more parameters to the plugin.
2. We need to make it easy to work with these parameters.
3. We need to make it possible for our users to override the default plugin parameters if they want to.

We address all these requirements in step 2. We pass an `options` parameter to the `plugin` function. The options parameter is actually an object that we assign to a variable so that we can access its members as needed.

The options are then placed as the second parameter of the jQuery `extend()` function. The `extend()` function takes in two parameters. The first one is an object literal that holds key-value pairs that will be used as the plugin's default values. The second parameter, named `options`, can be omitted when we call the plugin. In other words, we can call the plugin like this:

```
$('a').canYouFindIt2();
```

We can, for example, call this code from our browser's console. In that case, jQuery selector will return its wrapped set of the targeted nodes (all the anchor tags on the page). Then, we run the `canYouFindIt2()` function. The code will get executed and the `plugin` function definition will provide the built-in default attributes of `cssProperty` and `cssValue`, which are `background-color` and `lightsalmon`, respectively. These built-in default attributes in the function call are parameters of the object literal that we provided in the `extend()` method's first parameter.

However, these default parameters in the function definition can be easily overridden in the function call by passing either one, or both, as arguments, as we saw in step 4.

There is one more piece of the puzzle that we haven't discussed, and that is the code in step 3, which has to do with the `each()` method.

The official jQuery documentation has a description of what the each() method does, at ht tps://api.jquery.com/each/. As we can see in the official docs, the description of what the each() method does is as follows:

Iterate over a jQuery object, executing a function for each matched element.

So, the each() method takes a function. This function will iterate over the jQuery object (in our example, the jQuery-wrapped set of anchor tags). So, the function will do something for each anchor element it finds.

As any other function, this function can take in arguments, and as we specified in the function definition, the arguments it takes when it is called are based on the parameters provided in the function definition. Specifically, it takes the index and the element. We then assign each iterated element, wrapped into jQuery, to the $currentIndex variable so that we have an easily accessible handle to reach the currently iterated element.

Then, we run the following code:

```
$currentIndex.css(defaults.cssProperty, defaults.cssValue);
```

This code takes cssProperty and cssValue that were either provided by the plugin, or, if passed as members of the options object, as user-specified overrides. Of course, both the cssProperty and the cssValue are members of the defaults variable that we set earlier. Then, we call the css() method with these parameters passed in. Depending on whether the user passes none, one, or both arguments to our canYouFindIt2 jQuery plugin, the behavior of the plugin will be altered.

Up until this point in the explanation of this recipe, we have only briefly looked at the value of abstraction that this plugin has; now is the time to discuss it.

In all the previous paragraphs of this section, we have looked at the example where we specified the cssProperty of background-color and the cssValue of the actual color. However, the possibilities for users to implement this plugin do not stop there. For example, a user could do this when calling the plugin:

```
// calling the plugin
$('a').canYouFindIt2({
  cssProperty: 'border',
  cssValue: '3px dotted orange'
});
```

So, now, we can basically alter any CSS property of any element or group of elements by simply passing a few arguments to the options object literal upon calling our jQuery plugin.

Of course, this chapter only scratches the surface of what is possible with jQuery in Bootstrap. However, having this solid understanding of the very basics of how jQuery plugins work will arm us with the necessary conceptual background to inspect, understand, learn, and expand on the many existing jQuery plugins that can be used in Bootstrap. With this solid foundation, creating our own plugins (or tweaking the ones that we find online) will become that much easier.

Integrating a simple CSS Class Replacement plugin with Bootstrap 4

In this recipe, we will build on the concepts discussed in the preceding recipe. The plugin we make in this recipe will be used to help us showcase Flexbox layout options in the next chapter. For now, we will focus on making the plugin itself. The goal of the plugin is very simple--we want to have a plugin that we can pass two classes to. Then, in our HTML, we will add a button, and it will serve as a toggle. On clicking it, it will find the first css class and replace it with the second one. On another click, it will do the opposite.

Getting ready

To get ready, you can review the completed recipe by running harp server in the `chapter7/complete` folder and navigating to `localhost:9000/recipe07-03`. To see the simple effect we can achieve with this plugin, click on the button that reads **Toggle Navbar Color**.

After previewing the result we are trying to achieve, navigate to the `chapter7/start` folder and open the `_js.ejs, _nav.ejs, _recipe-07-03-js.ejs` files in the `app/partial` folder. Also, one level up, in the root of the `app` folder, open the file titled `recipe07-03.ejs`.

How to do it...

1. Open the currently blank `_recipe07-03-js.ejs` and paste the code as follows:

```
<script>
// plugin definition

(function ($) {
```

```
$.fn.classToggler = function (oldClass, newClass) {
return this.each(function(i, elem) {
var $currentIndex = $(elem);

$currentIndex.toggleClass(oldClass + " " + newClass);
});
};
})(jQuery);

// calling the plugin
$('#switchNavbar').click(function() {
$('.navbar')
.classToggler("bg-faded", "bg-info")
});
</script>
```

2. Now, open `recipe07-03.ejs` and paste the following code:

```
<div class="container">

<div class="mt-5">
<h1><%- title %></h1>
<p>A Simple CSS Class Replacement jQuery Plugin.</p>

</div><!-- /.container -->

<button type="button" class="btn btn-default" id="switchNavbar"
style="cursor: pointer"><span class="fa fa-eyedropper"></span>
Toggle Navbar Color</button>
```

3. Run the `harp server` command in the console and preview the recipe at `localhost:9000/recipe07-03`. Click on the button and note the change of background color on the navbar.

4. Let's change the text color too to have a better contrast between the navbar background and the navbar text. To do that, we need to replace the class of `navbar-dark` with the class of `navbar-inverse`. There are many ways to do this, but for the sake of simplicity, let's chain the `classToggler()` function onto itself when calling the plugin. The complete code of the file titled `_recipe-07-03-js.ejs` will now look like this:

```
<script>
// plugin definition

(function ($) {
$.fn.classToggler = function (oldClass, newClass) {
return this.each(function(i, elem) {
```

```
        var $currentIndex = $(elem);

        $currentIndex.toggleClass(oldClass + " " + newClass);
        });
    };
    })(jQuery);

    // calling the plugin
    $('#switchNavbar').click(function() {
    $('.navbar')
    .classToggler("bg-faded", "bg-success")
    .classToggler("navbar-dark", "navbar-inverse");
    });
    </script>
```

5. Preview the result once again to confirm that both the background and the text color of the navbar are toggled on the button click.

How it works…

The plugin is called `classToggler`. It has a simple role, that is, to swap one CSS class with a different one. Integrating it with Bootstrap 4 was really simple; we just needed to know which Bootstrap 4 CSS class needed to be replaced, and what that class would be replaced with.

An interesting line of code could be this one:

```
    $currentIndex.toggleClass(oldClass + " " + newClass);
```

Here, we are concatenating the two parameters passed to the `toggleClass()` method with a space character. The reason is simple--the `toggleClass()` method takes two classes in quotes, separated by a space. Thus, to make it work, we had to add a space character, as shown in the preceding code.

Another interesting piece of code is the duplicate call to the `classToggler()` function. Of course, this could have been handled differently. We could have created a plugin that would take any number of CSS classes and toggle them with other CSS classes as specified. However, this simple plugin still does the job, and it does it well.

8
Bootstrap 4 Flexbox and Layouts

In this chapter, we will cover the following topics:

- Breakpoint-dependent switching of flex direction on card components
- Letting cards take up space with the .flex-wrap and .col classes
- Adding any number of columns with Flexbox
- Combining numbered .col classes with plain .col classes
- Working with the card component and the Flexbox grid
- Center-aligning cards on wider viewports only
- Positioning nav-tabs with Flexbox

Introduction

In this chapter, we will take a look at the brand new Flexbox--enabled grid in Bootstrap. We will also look at practical examples of using the Flexbox grid and the ways in which this CSS specification allows us to make layouts in an alternative way, by stepping away from float-based layouts. By including Flexbox in its new version, Bootstrap 4 really brings a whole new way to build websites. We will look at some of the new approaches in this chapter.

Breakpoint-dependent switching of flex direction on card components

In this recipe, we will ease into using the flexbox grid in Bootstrap 4 with a simple example of switching the flex-direction property. To achieve this effect, we will use a few helper classes to enable the use of Flexbox in our recipe. To get acquainted with the way Flexbox works in Bootstrap, check out the official documentation at `https://v4-alpha.getbootstr ap.com/utilities/flexbox/`.

Getting ready

To get started with the recipe, let's first get an idea of what we will make. Navigate to `chapter8complete/app/` and run `harp server`. Then, preview the completed recipe at `localhost:9000/recipe08-01`. You should see a simple layout with four card components lined up horizontally.

Now, resize the browser, either by changing the browser's window width or by pressing *F12* (which will open developer tools and allow you to narrow down the viewport by adjusting the size of developer tools). At a certain breakpoint (md, i.e. the medium breakpoint), you should see the cards stacked on top of one another. That is the effect that we will achieve in this recipe.

How to do it...

1. Open the folder titled `chapter8/start` inside this book's source code. Open the currently empty file titled `recipe08-01.ejs` inside the `app` folder; copy the below code and paste it into `recipe08-01.ejs`:

   ```
   <div class="container">

   <h2 class="mt-5">Recipe 08-01: Breakpoint-dependent Switching of
   Flex Direction on Card Components</h2>

   <p>In this recipe we'll switch DIRECTION, between a vertical
   (.flex-{breakpoint}column), and a horizontal (.flex-{breakpoint}-
   row) stacking of cards.</p>

   <p>This recipe will introduce us to the flexbox grid in Bootstrap
   4.</p>
   ```

```
</div><!-- /.container -->
<div class="container">
<%- partial("partial/_card0") %>
 <%- partial("partial/_card0") %>
 <%- partial("partial/_card0") %>
 <%- partial("partial/_card0") %>
</div>
```

2. While still in the same file, find the second `div` with the class of `container` and add more classes to it, as follows:

```
<div class="container d-flex flex-column flex-lg-row">
```

3. Now, open the `app/partial` folder and copy and paste the following code into the file titled `_card0.ejs`:

```
<div class="p-3" id="card0">
 <div class="card">
 <div class="card-block">
 <h3 class="card-title">Special title treatment</h3>
 <p class="card-text">With supporting text below as a natural lead-
in to additional content.</p>
 <a href="#" class="btn btn-primary">Go somewhere</a>
 </div>
 </div>
</div>
```

4. Now, run the `harp server` command and preview the result at `localhost:9000/recipe08-01`, inside the `chapter8start` folder. Resize the browser window to see the stacking of card components on smaller resolutions.

How it works...

To start discussing how this recipe works, let's first do a little exercise. In the file titled `recipe08-01`, inside the `chapter8start` folder, locate the first `div` with the `container` class. Add the class of `d-flex` to this `div`, so that this section of code now looks like this:

```
<div class="container d-flex">
```

Save the file and refresh the page in your browser. You should see that adding the helper class of d-flex to our first container has completely changed the way that this container is displayed. What has happened is that our recipe's heading and the two paragraphs (which are all inside the first container div) are now sitting on the same flex row. The reason for this behavior is the addition of Bootstrap's utility class of d-flex, which sets our container to display: flex. With display: flex, the default behavior is to set the flex container to flex-direction: row. This flex direction is implicit, meaning that we don't have to specify it.

However, if we want to specify a different value to the flex-direction property, we can use another Bootstrap 4 helper class, for example, flex-row-reverse. So, let's add it to the first div, like this:

```
<div class="container d-flex flex-row-reverse">
```

Now, if we save and refresh our page, we will see that the heading and the two paragraphs still show on the flex row, but now the last paragraph comes first, on the left edge of the container. It is then followed by the first paragraph, and finally, by the heading itself.

There are four ways to specify flex-direction in Bootstrap, that is, by adding one of the following four classes to our wrapping HTML element: flex-row, flex-row-reverse, flex-column, and flex-column-reverse. The first two classes align our flex items horizontally, and the last two classes align our flex items vertically.

Back to our recipe, we can see that on the second container, we added the following three classes on the original div (that had only the class of container in step 1): d-flex, flex-column, and flex-lg-row.

Now we can understand what each of these classes does. The d-flex class sets our second container to display: flex. The flex-column class stacks our flex items (the four card components) vertically, with each card taking up the width of the container.

Since Bootstrap is a mobile first framework, the classes we provide also take effect mobile first. If we want to override a class, by convention, we need to provide a breakpoint at which the initial class behavior will be overridden. In this recipe, we want to specify a class, with a specific breakpoint, at which this class will make our cards line up horizontally, rather than stacking them vertically.

Because of the number of cards inside our second container, and because of the minimum width that each of these cards takes up, the most obvious solution was to have the cards line up horizontally on resolutions of `lg` and up. That is why we provide the third class of `flex-lg-row` to our second container. We could have used any other helper class, such as `flex-row`, `flex-sm-row`, `flex-md-row`, or `flex-xl-row`, but the one that was actually used made the most sense.

Letting cards take up space with the .flex-wrap and .col classes

In this recipe, we will look at the power of applying helper classes to flex containers in combination with using the Flexbox grid on the flex items, in order to create a fully responsive Flexbox grid of Bootstrap components. This grid is very versatile and allows us to create wonderful responsive designs on the fly. Bootstrap now delivers even more on its promise of the fast layout of web pages with the simple use of predefined classes in its HTML markup. In this recipe, we will see how easy it is to set up a Flexbox-enabled layout.

Getting ready

To get started with the recipe, we will first inspect a completed recipe. Navigate to `chapter8complete/app/` and run `harp server`. Then, preview the completed recipe at `localhost:9000/recipe08-02`. You should see a simple layout with eight card components, lined up in rows as per the available screen size.

If you resize the browser, you will be able to see that the cards always take up the full space of the container. There are no gaps on different screen sizes. Regardless of how many cards fit inside the first row, the remaining cards will take up the rest of the available screen space on the second, third, or fourth row, depending on the width of the screen. That is Bootstrap's Flexbox grid in practice.

How to do it...

1. Open the file titled `recipe08-02.ejs` in `chapter8/start/app` folder, and add the following code:

   ```
   <div class="container">
   ```

```
<h2 class="mt-5">Recipe 08-02: <br>Letting Cards Take Up Space with
the <code>.flex-wrap</code> and <code>.col</code> Classes</h2>

<p class="mt-4">In this recipe we'll switch DIRECTION, between a
vertical (.flex-{breakpoint}column), and a horizontal (.flex-
{breakpoint}-row) stacking of cards.</p>

<p class="mt-4">This recipe will introduce us to the flexbox grid
in Bootstrap 4.</p>


</div><!-- /.container -->

<div class="container">

 <%- partial("partial/_card1") %>
 <%- partial("partial/_card1") %>
 <%- partial("partial/_card1") %>
 <%- partial("partial/_card1") %>
 <%- partial("partial/_card1") %>
 <%- partial("partial/_card1") %>
 <%- partial("partial/_card1") %>
 <%- partial("partial/_card1") %>

</div>
```

2. On the second `div` with the class of container, change the opening `div` by adding additional values to the `class` attribute, as follows:

```
<div class="container d-flex flex-wrap">
```

3. Open the `_card1.ejs` file inside the `app/partial` folder and copy and paste the following code:

```
<div class="p-3">
 <div class="card">
 <div class="card-block">
 <h3 class="card-title">Special title treatment</h3>
 <p class="card-text">With supporting text below as a natural lead-
in to additional content.</p>
 <a href="#" class="btn btn-primary">Go somewhere</a>
 </div>
 </div>
</div>
```

4. While still in the same file, add the `.col` class to the wrapping `div`:

```
<div class="col p-3">
```

5. Run the `harp server` command and preview the result in your browser.

How it works...

The code in this recipe is really simple. A lot of the complexity has been resolved by Bootstrap giving us proper classes to use. This was made even easier by the careful class naming by Bootstrap developers. All the Flexbox-related class names reflect the underlying Flexbox properties and values, so it is easy to guess what each class will do once you know how Flexbox works.

In this specific recipe, the way this layout was achieved is as follows: in step 1, the first `div` holds the introductory heading for the recipe, as well as the two paragraphs with text. The second `div` initially only has the `container` class. In step 2, we add two additional classes to this `div`: `d-flex` and `flex-wrap`.

As explained earlier, the `d-flex` class sets the `display` property of our `div` to `flex`. The `flex-wrap` class allows the flex items to wrap in multiple lines; if they are too wide to fit on a single flex line, then it is done by setting the `flex-wrap` CSS property to the value of `flex`, or, in other words:

```
flex-wrap: wrap !important;
```

 For more information about flex-wrap in CSS, check out `https://develop er.mozilla.org/en/docs/Web/CSS/flex-wrap?v=control`.

In step 3, we add the code to make a simple card component. This card component is saved as a partial, which we can include as many times as we need to. By including our `_card1` partial eight times (inside the `recipe08-02` code), we ensure that there will be too many flex items to fit on a single flex line, which in turn makes the use of the `flex-wrap` class appropriate.

Finally, in step 4 of the recipe, we add the class of `col` to the card-wrapping `div` element. The `col` class is a part of Bootstrap's Flexbox grid, which will ensure that the `flex-wrap` class will indeed affect the behavior of the present card components. To drive this point home, try to remove the `col` class from the `_card1` partial file. Save the file and run it. Inspect the result in your browser--the layout will be broken.

The class of col will add the following CSS to a `div` that it is applied to:

```
.col {
  flex-basis: 0;
  flex-grow: 1;
  max-width: 100%;
}
```

The `flex-basis` property sets the size for a flex item. The `flex-grow` property sets the flex grow factor for a flex item. The `max-width` of 100% makes the flex item stretch to 100% of the available space.

To find out more about these properties, check out the following links:

- https://developer.mozilla.org/en/docs/Web/CSS/flex-grow

- https://developer.mozilla.org/en/docs/Web/CSS/flex-basis

Adding any number of columns with Flexbox

In this recipe, we will see how to add an arbitrary number of columns with Flexbox. This means we no longer have to stick to the 12-column grid. This simple recipe will show the fundamental paradigm shift that the Flexbox model brings to front-end development.

Getting ready

Before you start with this recipe, preview the completed page by running the `harp server` command inside the `chapter8/completed/app` folder. To see the recipe itself, point your browser to `localhost:9000/recipe08-03`. Try resizing the browser to see the behavior of the completed Flexbox grid.

How to do it...

1. Open the file titled `recipe08-03.ejs` add the following code in it:

```
<style>
.col {
flex-grow: 0;
}
</style>
<div class="container">
 <h2 class="mt-5">Recipe 08-03: Adding Any Number of Columns with
Flexbox</h2>
 <p class="mt-4">In this recipe we will look at using the flexbox
grid to create layouts that were not possible in earlier versions
of Bootstrap.</p>
 <p class="mt-4">With the flexbox grid, you can add any arbitrary
number of columns to your rows.</p>
</div>
<!-- /.container -->
<div class="container-fluid d-flex flex-column">
<div class="row bg-faded justify-content-center">
 <%- partial("partial/_five-cols") %>
</div>
<div class="row bg-warning justify-content-start">
 <%- partial("partial/_seven-cols") %>
</div>
<div class="row bg-info justify-content-between">
 <%- partial("partial/_eight-cols") %>
</div>
```

2. Open the partial folder, and navigate to the `_col1.ejs` partial file, and paste in the following code:

```
<div class="col p-1">
 <div class="card">
 <div class="card-block">
 <h3 class="card-title">Special title treatment</h3>
 <p class="card-text">With supporting text below as a natural lead-
in to additional content.</p>
 <a href="#" class="btn btn-primary">Go somewhere</a>
 </div>
 </div>
</div>
```

3. Open another partial file in the same folder, the one titled `_five-cols.ejs`, and paste the following code into it:

```
<%- partial("_col1") %>
<%- partial("_col1") %>
<%- partial("_col1") %>
<%- partial("_col1") %>
<%- partial("_col1") %>
```

4. Similar to the preceding step, open the files titled `_seven-cols.ejs` and `_eight-cols.ejs`, and paste in the appropriate number of lines to include the `_col1` partial file.

5. Preview the completed website in your browser.

How it works...

There are several simple, yet important concepts to mention in this recipe. For example, it is worth mentioning that we have used partials within partials in this recipe, in order to make our code more modular and to stick to the principle of DRY development.

Also, we have used the `d-flex` utility class to display the wrapping `div` as the flex container (which will in turn make the wrapped rows into flex items). To control the positioning of these rows as flex items, we use the `justify-content-*` helper classes. However, the effect of applying these classes might not be visible for two reasons. The first reason is the size of the viewport. If you preview the web page we made on a larger viewport, the `justify-content-*` helper will not affect the display because there will be enough room for the flex items to stay on a single row.

The second reason requires us searching the compiled CSS for the `col` class, which is as follows:

```
.col {
  flex-basis: 0;
  flex-grow: 1;
  max-width: 100%;
}
```

The third line of the preceding code reads `flex-grow: 1`. It determines the factor by which each flex item will grow (take up the available space). If we set its value to zero, so that we get `flex-grow: 0`, the flex item will not be resized to take up the flex container's available space on the main axis. In other words, it will retain its original width.

So, if you indeed change the `flex-grow` property on the `col` class in your CSS, as described in the previous paragraph, flex items will obey the `justify-content-*` classes and align to `start`, `center`, `end`, and so on, depending on what utility class you provided in the specific example.

The above points would be more obvious if we changed the class of the wrapper div that holds our rows in `recipe08-03.ejs` from container-fluid to container. Because of the content of our cards, our columns would not be able to fit on one line in their respective rows (except for the first row). Thus, they would wrap onto the next line, and we would be able to see the effect described above, in the previous paragraph. If our CSS is set up so that our `col` class has the line that reads `flex-grow: 1`, the cards will take up the available space on each of their lines. If, on the other hand, the same line reads `flex-grow: 0`, the cards will not take up the available space of their flex container, but rather align themselves in accordance with the `justify-content-*` helper classes we assign to each of the rows.

However, the most important takeaway from this recipe is the idea that we can indeed fit as many arbitrary columns on a single row, which will work on wider resolutions. On smaller resolutions, the columns will behave in accordance with the principles of responsive web design. That is not to say that we have to refrain from using numbers with `col` classes, for example, using `col-9`. We can even combine the simply named `col` class with other column classes that follow the `col-*number*` pattern, as we will see in the next recipe.

Combining numbered .col classes with plain .col classes

In this recipe, we will combine plain `col` classes with numbered `col` classes. This will allow us to create some wonderful combinations of columns that were previously not possible in Bootstrap. Even though this recipe is quite simple, having a firm understanding of these basic concepts will help us with more advanced recipes later in the chapter.

Getting ready

To begin the recipe, preview the completed one by navigating to `chapter8/complete/app`. Inside the folder, run the `harp server` commands from your console. Next, open the browser at `localhost:9000/recipe08-04`. You should see a row with three columns, a simple demonstration of important concepts we will discuss in this recipe.

How to do it...

1. Open the folder with the starter code at `chapter8/start/app`.
2. Open the file titled `recipe08-04.ejs` and add the code as follows:

```
<div class="container">
 <h2 class="mt-5">Recipe 08-04: Combining Numbered <code>col</code>
Classes with Plain <code>col</code> Classes</h2>
 <p class="mt-4">In this recipe we will look at combining the
numbered <code>col</code> classes with plain <code>col</code>
classes to create layouts that were not possible in earlier
versions of Bootstrap.</p>
 <p class="mt-4">For example, setting the middle div to the width
of seven columns, with the left and right divs taking up the rest
of the space.</p>
</div>
<!-- /.container -->
<div class="container">
<div class="row bg-faded">
 <%- partial("partial/_seven-cols-in-the-center") %>
</div>
```

3. Open the file titled _seven-cols-in-the-center.ejs (in the `partial` folder) and paste in the following code:

```
<div class="col m-1 bg-info">This div spans the remaining space on
the left.</div>
 <div class="col-7 m-1 bg-warning">This div spans seven
columns.</div>
 <div class="col m-1 bg-info">This div spans the remaining space on
the right.</div>
```

4. Look at the second `div` in the preceding code. The code works perfectly on larger viewports, but at smaller resolutions, the flex items (namely, the third `div`), start wrapping onto the next flex line (the next *row*). Also, the second `div` still takes up only seven cols of the available screen width. To rectify this, we need to add more classes to our second `div`, like this:

```
<div class="col-12 col-sm-7 m-1 bg-warning">This div spans seven
columns.</div>
```

5. Finally, save everything and preview the result in the browser.

How it works...

This simple recipe showcases several important concepts. For example, we can add a `div` with an arbitrary number of columns by adding it a class of `col-*`, where the asterisk can be replaced with any number we desire. In our example, it was 7, but it can be anything from 1 to 12.

Secondly, to overcome weird flex-wrapping on smaller resolutions, we added a breakpoint to our seven-column div so that it kicks in at the `sm` resolutions, and, consequently, since Bootstrap is mobile first, works the same on all the higher resolutions.

However, on resolutions smaller than `sm`, we added another class, the class of `col-12`. This class allows our `div` to span the full width of the available screen on these narrow viewports.

At resolutions between 576 and 768 pixels, you will still note the flex-wrapping effect, which works quite well. However, if you want to avoid this flex-wrapping, you could try changing the second class on the second div from `col-sm-7` to `col-md-7`, which would make all the divs stack vertically on resolutions under 768 pixels wide.

Working with card layouts and the Flexbox grid

In this recipe, we will make layouts using the cards component with the help of Bootstrap 4 Flexbox grid to align them and look at some new CSS properties that will make the use of images in our cards easier by retaining their proper aspect ratio and preventing image stretching. We will also look at using `lorempixel.com` to create more believable mock-ups of our layouts.

Getting ready

To begin, open the completed page in your browser by navigating to the `chapter8/complete/app` folder and running the harp server command through the console. Point your browser to the completed recipe by visiting `localhost:9000/chapter08-05`. Observe the changes in the layout of the cards, components on different viewport resolutions.

How to do it...

1. Open the `chapter8/start` folder. Inside that folder, open the `app` folder, and then open the file titled `recipe08-05.ejs` and paste in the code that follows:

```
<div class="container">
 <h2 class="mt-5 pb-3">Recipe 08-05: Working with Card Layouts and
the Flexbox Grid</h2>
 <p class="mt-4">In this recipe we will look at two ways of using
card components with the flexbox grid.</p>
 <p class="mt-4">In the first example (the first three cards on a
gray background), we will take a more traditional approach of
adding several <code>col-*</code> classes to control the layout of
elements on the page.</p>
 <p class="mt-4 mb-5">In the second example, we will wrap all the
cards in a div with just a simple <code>col</code> class. Then we
```

will set the min-width on the `<code>col</code>` class to prevent it from getting too narrow. After that, flexbox will take care of controlling the layout of elements on the page.</p>

```
</div>
<!-- /.container -->
<style>
 .card img {
 max-height: 300px;
 /* object-fit: contain; */
 object-fit: cover;
 object-position: 35% 25%;
 /* http://caniuse.com/#search=object-fit */
 /* https://css-tricks.com/almanac/properties/o/object-position/ */
 }
 .col {
 min-width: 282px;
 }
 .card-white {
 background-color: white !important;
 }
</style>
<%- partial("partial/_the-first-container") %>
<%- partial("partial/_the-second-container") %>
```

2. Next, open the partial folder, and inside it, open the currently empty _the-first-container.ejs file and copy and paste the following code:

```
<div class="container-fluid bg-faded pt-5 pb-5">
 <div class="container">
 <h2 class="h3 text-center">With "old-school" <code>col-*</code>
classes:</h2>
 <div class="row">
 <div class="col-12 col-sm-6 col-lg-4 mt-3 mb-3">
 <div class="card card-outline-success card-white">
 <img class="card-img-top img-responsive"
src="http://lorempixel.com/400/800/food/" alt="A sports image">
 <%- partial("_a-card-in-both-containers") %>
 </div>
 </div>
 <div class="col-12 col-sm-6 col-lg-4 mt-3 mb-3">
 <div class="card card-outline-success card-white">
 <img class="card-img-top img-responsive"
src="http://lorempixel.com/400/800/nature/" alt="A sports image">
 <%- partial("_a-card-in-both-containers") %>
 </div>
 </div>
 <div class="col-12 col-sm-6 col-lg-4 mt-3 mb-3">
 <div class="card card-outline-success card-white">
```

```
<img class="card-img-top img-responsive"
src="http://lorempixel.com/400/800/animals/" alt="A sports image">
<%- partial("_a-card-in-both-containers") %>
</div>
</div>
</div>
</div>
</div>
```

3. While still in the partial folder, open the file titled `_the-second-container` and add the following snippet of code:

```
<div class="container-fluid pt-5 pb-5">
<div class="container">
<h2 class="h3 text-center">With css-customized <code>col</code>
class:</h2>
<div class="row">
<div class="col mt-3 mb-3">
<div class="card card-block">
<img class="card-img-top img-fluid"
src="http://lorempixel.com/400/800/food/" alt="A sports image">
<%- partial("_a-card-in-both-containers") %>
</div>
</div>
<div class="col mt-3 mb-3">
<div class="card card-block">
<img class="card-img-top img-fluid"
src="http://lorempixel.com/400/800/nature/" alt="A sports image">
<%- partial("_a-card-in-both-containers") %>
</div>
</div>
<div class="col mt-3 mb-3">
<div class="card card-block">
<img class="card-img-top img-fluid"
src="http://lorempixel.com/400/800/animals/" alt="A sports image">
<%- partial("_a-card-in-both-containers") %>
</div>
</div>
<!-- -->
<div class="col mt-3 mb-3">
<div class="card card-block">
<img class="card-img-top img-fluid"
src="http://lorempixel.com/400/800/technics/" alt="A sports image">
<%- partial("_a-card-in-both-containers") %>
</div>
</div>
<div class="col mt-3 mb-3">
<div class="card card-block">
```

```
  <img class="card-img-top img-fluid"
src="http://lorempixel.com/400/800/transport/" alt="A sports
image">
  <%- partial("_a-card-in-both-containers") %>
  </div>
  </div>
  <div class="col mt-3 mb-3">
  <div class="card card-block">
  <img class="card-img-top img-fluid"
src="http://lorempixel.com/400/800/city/" alt="A sports image">
  <%- partial("_a-card-in-both-containers") %>
  </div>
  </div>
  <div class="col mt-3 mb-3">
  <div class="card card-block">
  <img class="card-img-top img-fluid"
src="http://lorempixel.com/400/800/business/" alt="A sports image">
  <%- partial("_a-card-in-both-containers") %>
  </div>
  </div>
  </div>
  -->
  </div>
</div>
```

4. Open another file in the partial folder; this time, open the _a-card-in-both-
   containers.ejs file and paste in the following code:

```
<div class="card-block">
  <h4 class="card-title text-success">A Blog Post</h4>
  <p class="text-muted">2 days ago</p>
  <p class="card-text text-justify">Lorem ipsum dolor sit amet,
consectetur adipisicing elit. Maxime aspernatur voluptatem quia ab,
quae ad excepturi voluptate laboriosam temporibus nostrum.</p>
  <a href="#" class="btn btn-outline-success mt-2">Read the
post...</a>
</div>
```

5. Preview the recipe in the browser by navigating to `chapter8/start/app`, running harp server, and pointing the browser to `localhost:9000/recipe08-05`.

6. Read the explanations on the page. Resize the browser window to see the difference in the behavior between the two containers.

7. Open the partial file titled `_the-second-container.ejs` and comment out the last four cards by deleting the greater than character (>) on line 25. Doing this will turn on the HTML comment on the rest of the cards in the file.

8. Preview the recipe again. This time, you should have three cards in the first container and three cards in the second container, which should help compare the two containers while they have the same number of cards. Resize the browser window to inspect this behavior.

How it works...

There are several things happening in this recipe, which is why the end result is a great design that shows all the styling improvements brought about by the newest version of Bootstrap. To understand how exactly this layout was achieved, we need to go through each of the steps in this recipe.

In step 1, we added the usual container on top, with the heading that shows the recipe title, and the paragraphs under it that give some short explanation of the recipe. On this first container, we only used the margin and padding utility classes to space out the elements nicely.

The middle section of the code added in step 1 is a `style` tag, with a few CSS declarations that will be explained later in this section. The last few lines of the code are calls to the two partials; they are in fact containers that hold the card components we will lay out in this recipe.

In step 2, we added the code to the `_the-first-container.ejs` partial file. The file begins with the wrapping container, followed up with a regular container. The reason to do this is that, since the first wrapping container is fluid, we can add the `bg-faded` class to it, thereby adding the grayed background stripe across this section of our page. The next container is regular, and since it is inside the `container-fluid` div, it will contain our cards in the middle of the screen, while still retaining its parent's background color.

While still in step 2, further down in our code, we see a div with a class of row, which wraps three `div`s with their columns specified in their `class` attribute, as follows:

```
<div class="col-12 col-sm-6 col-lg-4 mt-3 mb-3">
```

By adding these layout columns to our divs, we say that they should perform the following:

- Span 100% of the parent container on lower resolutions (`col-12`)
- Override the previous class with the width spanning 50% of the parent on `sm` and larger resolutions (`col-sm-6`)
- Override the previous class with the width spanning 33% of the parent on `lg` and larger resolutions (`col-lg-4`)

Still in step 2, inside each of the divs referenced above, we add the code as follows:

```
<div class="card card-outline-success card-white">
 <img class="card-img-top img-fluid"
src="http://lorempixel.com/400/800/food/" alt="A sports image">
 <%- partial("_a-card-in-both-containers") %>
</div>
```

This is what we achieve with the preceding code:

- We turn the `div` into a card by adding the `card` class to the div's `class` attribute
- We add the green outline to the card
- We add our own custom class of `card-white`, which gives a white background to each card component
- We add an image at the top of our card with `card-img` and make it responsive with `img-fluid`
- We add a random food-related image from `lorempixel.com`
- We include the inner card code

It is important to note that the reason why we did not include the preceding code in the card partial also has to do with the simple necessity to serve different pictures in each of the cards. That is pretty much the reason why the code is slightly more complicated. If all the images were the same, we could have simply added everything inside the partial; there would be no need to split our card code and the inner card partial code.

It is also important to mention the use of the empty HTML comment on line 25 of step 2 of this recipe, namely <!-- -->. This line of code, and the additional closing HTML comment tag near the bottom of the file, was added for convenience for readers, who can turn the comment on and off by simply erasing the greater than sign (>) on line 25 to comment out the last four cards in the second container. It is still useful to have all seven cards in the second container and inspect their behavior on various resolutions. Still, to make the differences (between the three cards in the first container and the three cards in the second container) more obvious, an option to preview those differences with a handy HTML comment was needed.

In step 3, the code for the second container partial was added. The code is quite similar to the one used in the first container, with the important difference that the wrapping div has the class of card-block, in addition to the class of card (which exists in both container partials). The addition to card-block in the second container partial changes the look of the cards in the second container by adding a significant white space around the card image. This is an example of how a simple addition of card-block significantly changes the styling of our card images. It is also worth mentioning here that in the code from step 4, the rest of the card content (besides the image) is shared by the cards in both containers (because they both reference the same partial).

Finally, it is time to discuss the styling. There are several things achieved with the styles added inside the recipe08-05.ejs file.

Let's look at the styles added inside the style tags (with the CSS comments removed):

```
.card img {
max-height: 300px;
object-fit: cover;
object-position: 35% 25%;
}

.col {
min-width: 282px;
}

.card-white {
background-color: white !important;
}
```

The first CSS declaration, `.card img`, sets the maximum height of the image to 300 pixels. The reason for this is to control images that are tall and narrow. In our recipe's code, all the images were made to be tall and narrow by passing in the appropriate width/height dimensions to the lorempixel URL. Next, to retain the aspect ratio of the images, a CSS property of `object-fit` was used, and the value of `cover` was assigned to it. There is another, commented-out line of code just above this line that sets the value to `contain`. Changing the value from `cover` to `contain` will produce an interesting result.

We follow up the declaration of the `object-fit` property with the declaration of `object-position`, which basically receives two values that describe the distance from the upper edge (35%), and the distance from the left edge (25%) when fitting the object. Obviously, the two properties go hand in hand, and the CSS comments in this section of `recipe08-05.ejs` provide links to more information on these properties, including a link to `http://.caniuse.com`, which shows that this CSS property is still in early adoption. Next, we extend the Bootstrap class of `col` by setting its `min-width` property. This is what prevents our cards from going below a specified width, which in turn sets the flex-wrapping in motion and allows the nice responsive effect that we can see in the recipe.

The use of the custom class of `card-white` was already discussed earlier in this recipe.

Center-aligning cards on wider viewports only

In this recipe, we will look at how we can center align cards' content. We will have varying amounts of content in cards inside the same row. We will see how easy it is to align this content with the use of Flexbox.

Getting ready

To get ready for this recipe, we will first preview the end result that we are trying to achieve. In your console, locate the `chapter8/complete/app` folder run the `harp server` command on it. Preview the completed recipe by visiting `localhost:9000/recipe08-06` in your browser.

How to do it...

1. Open the folder titled `chapter8/start/app`, search the file named `recipe08-06.ejs` and paste in the following code:

```
<div class="container">
 <h2 class="mt-5 pb-3">Recipe 08-06: Center-Aligning Cards on Wider
Viewports Only</h2>
 <p class="mt-4">In this recipe we will look at centering the card
content with flexbox.</p>
</div>
<!-- /.container -->
<style>
 .col {
 min-width: 280px;
 }
 .card img {
 max-height: 320px;
 /* height: 300px; */
 object-fit: cover;
 object-position: 50% 10%; /* object-position:
 <from-left>
 <from-top>
 */
 }
</style>
<div class="container-fluid bg-faded pt-5 pb-5">
 <div class="container">
 <div class="row align-items-lg-center">
 <div class="col mt-3 mb-3">
 <%- partial("partial/_card-0806-01") %>
 </div>
 <div class="col mt-3 mb-3">
 <%- partial("partial/_card-0806-02") %>
 </div>
 <div class="col mt-3 mb-3">
 <%- partial("partial/_card-0806-03") %>
 </div>
 </div>
 </div>
</div>
```

2. Open the `partial` folder and paste the following code into the `_card-0806-01.ejs` partial:

```
<div class="card h-100">
```

```
<img class="card-img-top"
src="http://lorempixel.com/400/270/city/">
 <div class="card-block d-flex flex-column">
 <h4 class="card-title">Card title</h4>
 <p class="card-text">Some quick example text to build on the card
title and make up the bulk of the card's content. Some quick
example text to build on the card title.</p>
 <a href="#" class="btn btn-primary btn-block mt-auto">Go
somewhere</a>
 </div>
 </div>
```

3. Still in the `partial` folder, add the following code to the file titled `_card-0806-02.ejs`:

```
<div class="card h-100">
 <img class="card-img-top"
src="http://lorempixel.com/400/320/sports/">
 <div class="card-block">
 <h4 class="card-title">Card title</h4>
 <p class="card-text">Some quick example text to build on the card
title and make up the bulk of the card's content. Some quick
example text to build on the card title and make up the bulk of the
card's content. Some quick example text to build on the card title
and make up the bulk of the card's content.</p>
 <a href="#" class="btn btn-primary btn-block">Go somewhere</a>
 </div>
 </div>
```

4. There is another partial file, titled `_card-0806-3.ejs`, to which we will add the following code:

```
<div class="card h-100">
 <img class="card-img-top"
src="http://lorempixel.com/400/280/business/">
 <div class="card-block">
 <h4 class="card-title">Card title</h4>
 <p class="card-text">Some quick example text to build on the card
title and make up the bulk of the card's content.Some quick example
text to build on the card title and make up the bulk of the card's
content.</p>
 <a href="#" class="btn btn-primary btn-block">Go somewhere</a>
 </div>
 </div>
```

5. Run the `harp server` command from the `chapter8/start/app` folder, point your browser to `localhost:9000/recipe08-06`, and preview the completed file. Try resizing the viewport and see the way that the three cards align on narrow resolutions versus the way they align on wider resolutions.

How it works...

In step 1 of this recipe, we added the HTML structure, which has two divs and a `style` tag in between. As usual, the first `div` has the class of container and holds the heading and a paragraph that succinctly explain the recipe.

Inside the `style` tag, we had a couple of CSS declarations, similar to the previous recipe. We set the `min-width` property on the `col` class and specified the behavior of `img` elements inside cards with the use of `object-fit` and `object-position` properties, as well as setting the `max-height` property on the image.

In the second `div` in step 1, we specified the wrapping fluid container with the background. Inside of this wrapping container, we have a regular container, and inside of it, we have a `div` with a class of `row`, and another class of `align-items-lg-center`. This class is responsible for aligning the three cards along the center of the flex line. The effect is made more obvious by setting different heights on each of the containers. The heights are determined by both the varying heights of the images used in each card and the varying length of text inside the cards, with the second card having the most text. This gives a sense of balance to our layout, with the emphasis on the second card.

However, there is also a problem. If we just add three cards of varying heights, they would look great on large screen widths, but the layout would break on smaller widths. To get the idea of how that broken layout would look, try removing any of the classes we will mention next.

In step 2, we add the code for the first card. The most important classes used on this card are `h-100`, `d-flex`, `flex-column`, and `mt-auto`. What follows is an explanation of what each of these classes achieve.

The class of `h-100` gives our cards equal height on smaller resolutions, that is, it stretches the first card to have the same height as the second card, which leaves the first card with a lot of white spaces and a button that awkwardly hangs somewhere around the middle of the card.

The classes of `d-flex` and `flex-column` make our `card-block` div behave as a flex-container with the direction of flex-column, which, as described in previous recipes, makes the flex items (the `h4`, the `p` tag, and the `a` tag) stack on top of each other.

Finally, adding the class of `mt-auto` to the anchor tag button makes the button stick to the lower bottom of the card, regardless of the fact that there is not nearly enough text to push the button to the bottom. This way, on narrow screens, the buttons on the first and on the second cards are in alignment.

In step 3, we added the second card. Note the absence of `d-flex`, `flex-column`, and `mt-auto` in the card's code. The code in card three is similar to the code in card two, with the difference being in the `img` tag's `src` attribute, since we are referencing different images from `lorempixel.com`.

Positioning nav-tabs with Flexbox

In this recipe, we will look into using Flexbox utility classes to easily align nav-tabs. Doing this is a simple task. However, to extend the recipe and make it more useful, we have also included a lot of content in each of the nav-tabs. Thus, in this recipe, besides demonstrating how to align nav-tabs, we will look into splitting a complex layout into several partials, dealing with different heights on tabs, and using a few simple CSS declarations to modify the look of our nav-tab items.

Getting ready

To preview the completed recipe, navigate to `chapter8/complete/app` through your console. Run the `harp server` command. Open your browser and visit `localhost:9000/recipe08-07`. Click on different tabs and try resizing the viewport. Look at the way that tab content responds to changes in viewport size.

How to do it...

1. In the `chapter8/start/app` folder, open the file titled `recipe08-07.ejs` and paste the following code in it:

```
<%- partial("partial/_0807-01-recipe-intro") %>
<%- partial("partial/_0807-02-style-tag") %>
<%- partial("partial/_0807-03-nav-tabs-menu") %>
<%- partial("partial/_0807-04-the-actual-tabs-content") %>
```

2. Next, open the `partial` folder, then open the file titled `_0807-01-recipe-intro` and paste the following code in it:

```
<!-- _0807-01-recipe intro -->
<div class="container">
 <h2 class="mt-5 pb-3">Recipe 08-07: Positioning Nav-tabs with
Flexbox</h2>
 <p class="mt-4">In this recipe we will look at positioning nav-
tabs with flexbox.</p>
 <p class="mt-4">We will also utilize several partials to create a
complex nav-tabs menu.</p>
</div>
```

3. Open the next partial file referenced in step 1, the file named `_0807-02-style-tag.ejs`, and add this snippet of code to it:

```
<!-- _0807-02-style-tag -->
<style>
 .card img {
   object-fit: cover;
 }
 .nav-tabs .nav-link {
   border-top-right-radius: .5rem;
   border-top-left-radius: .5rem;
 }
 #wrapper-for-tab-content {
   min-height: 1200px;
 }
</style>
```

4. The third partial file we are referencing is `_0807-03-navbar-tabs-menu.ejs`; open it, and paste the following code:

```
<!-- 0807-03-nav-tabs-menu -->
<div class="container">
 <div class="row">
 <div class="col">
 <ul class="nav nav-tabs justify-content-start justify-content-sm-
center justify-content-md-end justify-content-lg-between justify-
content-xl-around" role="tablist">
 <!-- first tab link -->
 <li class="nav-item">
 <a class="nav-link active" href="#first" id="the-first-tab"
role="tab" data-toggle="tab" aria-controls="First" aria-
expanded="true">First</a>
 </li>
 <!-- second tab link -->
 <li class="nav-item">
 <a class="nav-link" href="#second" role="tab" id="the-second-tab"
data-toggle="tab" aria-controls="Second">Second</a>
 </li>
 <!-- third tab link -->
 <li class="nav-item">
 <a class="nav-link" href="#third" role="tab" id="the-third-tab"
data-toggle="tab" aria-controls="Third">Third</a>
 </li>
 <!-- fourth tab link (dropdown) -->
 <li class="nav-item dropdown">
 <a class="nav-link dropdown-toggle" data-toggle="dropdown"
href="#" role="button" aria-haspopup="true" aria-
expanded="false">Fourth</a>
 <div class="dropdown-menu">
 <!-- the first dropdown link -->
 <a class="dropdown-item" href="#fourth-a-dropdown" role="tab"
id="the-fourth-a-tab" data-toggle="tab" aria-controls="Fourth
A">Fourth A</a>
 <!-- the second dropdown link -->
 <a class="dropdown-item" href="#fourth-b-dropdown" role="tab"
id="the-fourth-b-tab" data-toggle="tab" aria-controls="Fourth
B">Fourth B</a>
 <!-- the third dropdown link -->
 <a class="dropdown-item" href="#fourth-c-dropdown" role="tab"
id="the-fourth-c-tab" data-toggle="tab" aria-controls="Fourth
C">Fourth C</a>
 </div>
 </li>
 </ul>
 </div>
```

```
    </div>
  </div>
```

5. Next, open the partial file named `_0807-04-the-actual-tabs-content.ejs` and paste the following code in it:

```
<!-- _0807-04-the-actual-tabs-content -->
<div class="container p-5"id="wrapper-for-tab-content">
  <div class="tab-content">
  <!-- first tab content -->
  <div role="tabpanel" class="tab-pane fade show active" id="first"
aria-labelledby="the-first-tab">
  <h2>First Tab Content</h2>
  <%- partial("_tab-pane-container") %>
  </div>
  <!-- second tab content -->
  <div role="tabpanel" class="tab-pane fade" id="second" aria-
labelledby="the-second-tab">
  <h2>Second Tab Content</h2>
  <p>Lorem ipsum dolor sit amet, consectetur adipisicing elit.
Commodi, aperiam.</p>
  </div>
  <!-- third tab content -->
  <div role="tabpanel" class="tab-pane fade" id="third" aria-
labelledby="the-third-tab">
  <h2>Third Tab Content</h2>
  <%- partial("_tab-pane-container") %>
  </div>
  <!-- fourth tab, first dropdown content -->
  <div role="tabpanel" class="tab-pane fade" id="fourth-a-dropdown"
aria-labelledby="the-fourth-a-tab">
  <h2>Fourth Tab, First Dropdown Content</h2>
  <p>Lorem ipsum dolor sit amet, consectetur adipisicing elit.
Commodi, aperiam.</p>
  </div>
  <!-- fourth tab, second dropdown content -->
  <div role="tabpanel" class="tab-pane fade" id="fourth-b-dropdown"
aria-labelledby="the-fourth-b-tab">
  <h2 class="bg-success text-white">Fourth Tab, Second Dropdown
Content</h2>
  <p>Lorem ipsum dolor sit amet, consectetur adipisicing elit.
Commodi, aperiam.</p>
  </div>
  <!-- fourth tab, third dropdown content -->
  <div role="tabpanel" class="tab-pane fade" id="fourth-c-dropdown"
aria-labelledby="the-fourth-c-tab">
  <h2>Fourth Tab, Third Dropdown Content</h2>
  <p class="bg-danger text-white">Lorem ipsum dolor sit amet,
```

```
consectetur adipisicing elit. Commodi, aperiam.</p>
</div>
</div>
</div>
```

6. The previous partial file references another partial file, titled _tab-pane-container. Open this file, and paste the code as follows:

```
<div class="container">
<div class="row align-content-center">
<%- partial("_card-0807-01") %>
<%- partial("_card-0807-01") %>
<%- partial("_card-0807-01") %>
<%- partial("_card-0807-01") %>
</div>
</div>
```

7. The previous partial file also references another partial file. Find the file titled _card-0807-01.ejs, and add the following code to it:

```
<div class="col col-md-6 col-xl-4 mt-3 mb-4">
<div class="card">
<img class="card-img-top"
src="http://lorempixel.com/400/320/city/">
<div class="card-block">
<h4 class="card-title">Card title</h4>
<p class="card-text">Some quick example text to build on the card
title and make up the bulk of the card's content. Some quick
example text to build on the card title.</p>
<a href="#" class="btn btn-primary btn-block mt-auto">Go
somewhere</a>
</div>
</div>
</div>
```

8. Save all the files and run the harp server command from chapter8/start/app in your console. Preview the result in your browser at localhost:9000/recipe08-07.

How it works...

There is a lot of code in this recipe. Some of this code is repetitive. To make the code both easier to understand (since there is so much of it) and easier to work with (for example, we could decide later on to alter or replace the cards in the recipe), we have separated our code into partials.

Step 1 started with the main recipe file, which consists of four sections--four partial files:

- The top-most section of the recipe, which holds the recipe title and a short explanation in a couple of paragraphs
- The `style` tag partial, which holds our recipe-specific CSS
- The third partial file holds the markup for the actual nav-tabs, that is, the nav tab menu itself
- The fourth partial file has the actual content for each of the tabs

In step 2, we added the code to the first partial file. All the code in this partial is self-explanatory.

In step 3, we added the `style` tag as a separate partial. The `style` tag declares the `object-fit` property for the card image. It also adds some additional rounding on nav-tab borders and sets the `min-height` on the `#wrapper-for-tab-content` div. We set this height to 1200 pixels so that all the content in all the nav-tabs is high enough for the browser to display a scroll bar on its right edge. Without this CSS declaration, there would be an awkward *jump* between short tabs and tall tabs, which simply does not look good. Adding the `min-height` property is a simple solution for this issue.

In step 4, we added the actual `nav-tab` links. Each of the first three links follows the same pattern:

```
<!-- first tab link -->
 <li class="nav-item">
 <a class="nav-link active" href="#first" id="the-first-tab" role="tab"
data-toggle="tab" aria-controls="First" aria-expanded="true">First</a>
 </li>
```

Looking at the preceding code more closely, we can see that each tab link needs to have a unique `href` attribute. This `href` attribute is the one that we will use as the `id` attribute (only without the hash sign), on the actual content of each of our tabs. We will add this content in step 5. To make the tab link work, we also need the `data-toggle` attribute. To complete the structure, several other accessibility-related attributes are added.

In step 5, we added the actual content for our tabs. To make the mock-up more realistic, some tabs contain card components, whereas others just have some headings and paragraphs. Each tab's content follows the same pattern:

```
<!-- first tab content -->
<div role="tabpanel" class="tab-pane fade show active" id="first" aria-
labelledby="the-first-tab">
 <h2>First Tab Content</h2>
 <%- partial("_tab-pane-container") %>
</div>
```

The most important thing in the preceding code is the `id` attribute, as it hooks our the nav-tab menu links with their actual content. Each `div` also shares the same `role` attribute and the `tab-pane` and `fade` classes.

The first and the third tab content `divs` also wrap EJS calls to partial files. The reason for using the partials was explained earlier. Steps 6 and 7 simply separate these partials in a meaningful way, so as to avoid repetition as much as possible.

However, how was the positioning of nav-link menu items achieved with Flexbox? This was achieved by simply adding the existing `justify-content-*` Bootstrap 4 classes to the `ul` element inside the partial file titled `_0807-03-navbar-tabs-menu.ejs`. By adding these five classes, we positioned the nav-tab links differently, based on the viewport width. We started with justifying content to `start` (left) on all the resolutions under the `xs` breakpoint; next, we positioned the content to `center` between the `xs` and `sm` widths. Between the `sm` and `md` widths, the nav-tab items were set to `end` (right). Starting with the `lg` breakpoint, the `justify-content` CSS property was set to `between`, and finally, at the `xl` breakpoint, the property was set to `around`.

9
Workflow Boosters

In this chapter, we will cover the following topics:

- Customizing Bootstrap builds by cherry-picking Sass partials
- Cleaning up unused CSS with UnCSS and Grunt
- Removing CSS comments with grunt-strip-CSS-comments

Introduction

In this chapter, we will look at ways to optimize our code and to boost our workflow. This topic is fairly wide, as there are many ways of accomplishing similar tasks. Some of these tasks include the use of, for example, task runners, such as Grunt, Gulp, or Webpack. There is no single best approach or tool to accomplish this. Thus, several different approaches are discussed in this chapter, without giving preference to any particular one.

Customizing Bootstrap builds by cherry-picking Sass partials

In this recipe, we will look at tweaking the process of compilation of CSS from Bootstrap 4 Sass partials. The recipe will be made much easier to complete because we already have our Grunt task runner in place, as described in Chapter 1, *Installing Bootstrap 4 and Comparing Its Versions* and Chapter 2, *Layout Like a Boss with the Grid System*.

Since Grunt is already compiling our CSS, we will focus on cherry-picking the Sass partials that the framework provides. The point of this is to understand the process of compilation better, as well as to see one possible approach of elegantly removing the code that will not be used in production. For example, if we know that the alert component will not be used in our site, we can simply not include the alert `scss` file in our CSS compilation process. As we will see in this recipe, this leads to some interesting results.

Getting ready

To preview the result of this recipe, navigate to the `chapter9/complete/app` folder from your command line. Then, run the `harp server` command and preview the result in your browser. Pay close attention to the button under the recipe description. Note that the styling is not as you would expect in Bootstrap 4. In this recipe, we will explain the reasons for this, as well as how to add the styles to make any component work when needed.

How to do it...

1. Open a new command-line window and, using it, navigate to `chapter9/start/grunt`. Run the `grunt` command.

2. Open the `chapter9/start` folder. Locate the file titled `main.scss`, open it in your code editor, and paste in the following code:

```scss
// Core variables and mixins
@import "./bower_components/bootstrap/scss/_variables";
@import "./bower_components/bootstrap/scss/_mixins";
@import "./bower_components/bootstrap/scss/_custom";

// Reset and dependencies
@import "./bower_components/bootstrap/scss/_normalize";
@import "./bower_components/bootstrap/scss/_print";

// Core CSS
@import "./bower_components/bootstrap/scss/_reboot";
@import "./bower_components/bootstrap/scss/_type";
@import "./bower_components/bootstrap/scss/_images";
@import "./bower_components/bootstrap/scss/_code";
@import "./bower_components/bootstrap/scss/_grid";
@import "./bower_components/bootstrap/scss/_tables";
@import "./bower_components/bootstrap/scss/_forms";
@import "./bower_components/bootstrap/scss/_buttons";
```

```scss
// Components
@import "./bower_components/bootstrap/scss/_transitions";
@import "./bower_components/bootstrap/scss/_dropdown";
@import "./bower_components/bootstrap/scss/_button-group";
@import "./bower_components/bootstrap/scss/_input-group";
@import "./bower_components/bootstrap/scss/_custom-forms";
@import "./bower_components/bootstrap/scss/_nav";
@import "./bower_components/bootstrap/scss/_navbar";
@import "./bower_components/bootstrap/scss/_card";
@import "./bower_components/bootstrap/scss/_breadcrumb";
@import "./bower_components/bootstrap/scss/_pagination";
@import "./bower_components/bootstrap/scss/_badge";
@import "./bower_components/bootstrap/scss/_jumbotron";
@import "./bower_components/bootstrap/scss/_alert";
@import "./bower_components/bootstrap/scss/_progress";
@import "./bower_components/bootstrap/scss/_media";
@import "./bower_components/bootstrap/scss/_list-group";
@import "./bower_components/bootstrap/scss/_responsive-embed";
@import "./bower_components/bootstrap/scss/_close";

// Components w/ JavaScript
@import "./bower_components/bootstrap/scss/_modal";
@import "./bower_components/bootstrap/scss/_tooltip";
@import "./bower_components/bootstrap/scss/_popover";
@import "./bower_components/bootstrap/scss/_carousel";

// Utility classes
@import "./bower_components/bootstrap/scss/_utilities";
```

3. Save the above file, and note that the `grunt` command, which was set to watch for changes on `main.scss`, has initialized the `sass:dist` task, which will lead to the `main.css` file being compiled in the `chapter9/start/app/css` folder.

4. Using your operating system's file explorer, navigate to the `chapter9/start/app/css` folder and look at the information regarding the size of the compiled `main.css` file; it should be 151 kilobytes.

5. It is time to make changes to `main.scss` by commenting out a lot of redundant `scss` includes. The simplest way to do this is to comment out everything inside `main.scss`. Then, at the bottom, call the include for recipe09-01.scss: `@import "recipe09-01.scss";` and finally, open `recipe09-01.scss` and then paste in the following code:

```scss
// Core variables and mixins
@import "./bower_components/bootstrap/scss/_variables";
@import "./bower_components/bootstrap/scss/_mixins";
@import "./bower_components/bootstrap/scss/_custom";
```

```scss
// Reset and dependencies
@import "./bower_components/bootstrap/scss/_normalize";
// @import "./bower_components/bootstrap/scss/_print";

// Core CSS
@import "./bower_components/bootstrap/scss/_reboot";
@import "./bower_components/bootstrap/scss/_type";
// @import "./bower_components/bootstrap/scss/_images";
@import "./bower_components/bootstrap/scss/_code";
@import "./bower_components/bootstrap/scss/_grid";
// @import "./bower_components/bootstrap/scss/_tables";
// @import "./bower_components/bootstrap/scss/_forms";
// @import "./bower_components/bootstrap/scss/_buttons";

// Components
@import "./bower_components/bootstrap/scss/_transitions";
@import "./bower_components/bootstrap/scss/_dropdown";
// @import "./bower_components/bootstrap/scss/_button-group";
// @import "./bower_components/bootstrap/scss/_input-group";
// @import "./bower_components/bootstrap/scss/_custom-forms";
@import "./bower_components/bootstrap/scss/_nav";
@import "./bower_components/bootstrap/scss/_navbar";
// @import "./bower_components/bootstrap/scss/_card";
// @import "./bower_components/bootstrap/scss/_breadcrumb";
// @import "./bower_components/bootstrap/scss/_pagination";
// @import "./bower_components/bootstrap/scss/_badge";
// @import "./bower_components/bootstrap/scss/_jumbotron";
// @import "./bower_components/bootstrap/scss/_alert";
// @import "./bower_components/bootstrap/scss/_progress";
// @import "./bower_components/bootstrap/scss/_media";
// @import "./bower_components/bootstrap/scss/_list-group";
// @import "./bower_components/bootstrap/scss/_responsive-embed";
// @import "./bower_components/bootstrap/scss/_close";

// Components w/ JavaScript
// @import "./bower_components/bootstrap/scss/_modal";
// @import "./bower_components/bootstrap/scss/_tooltip";
// @import "./bower_components/bootstrap/scss/_popover";
// @import "./bower_components/bootstrap/scss/_carousel";

// Utility classes
@import "./bower_components/bootstrap/scss/_utilities";
```

6. Now, save the file, which will make `grunt` run the compilation to `main.css` again.

7. Inspect the size of the newly compiled `main.css` file inside `chapter9/start/app/css`. This time, the size of the file is 98 kilobytes. We have just saved 35 percent of our file size, without even minifying the compiled CSS. We will do that next.

8. Navigate to the `chapter9/start/grunt` folder, open the file titled `Gruntfile.js`, and add another option inside the `sass:dist:options` JavaScript object on line 12, like this:

```
sass: { // Begin Sass Plugin
 dist: {
 options: {
 sourcemap: 'inline',
 style: 'compressed' // this is the newly added line
 },
```

Previously, we did not have the `style` option specified, so it defaulted to the value of `nested`.

9. Inspect the file size of `main.css` - now it's only 65 kilobytes, which is much less than half of the initial file size of the compiled CSS file.

10. Finally, inspect the completed website by navigating to `chapter9/start/app` in your console, running the `harp server` command, and visiting `localhost:9000/recipe09-01` in your browser. You should see that the `navbar` looks and behaves as expected. However, the button is unstyled, or, to be more precise, it uses the default browser styles instead of the button styles of Bootstrap 4.

11. To rectify this issue, simply uncomment line 18 of the `main.scss` file and, once the `main.css` file has finished recompiling, refresh the web page. Now the button is back to its regular Bootstrap 4 style.

How it works...

Different from most of the `main.scss` files used throughout the recipes in this book, in this recipe, we are directly referencing multiple Sass partials. This allows us to turn them on and off by simply commenting out their respective includes. When we combine the addition or removal of specific `scss` partials with changes to the way that grunt compiles Sass to CSS, using the available options, we can significantly reduce the file size of the compiled CSS file.

However, even though this is useful for experiments, it is important to note that since the Bootstrap framework is so popular, it is probable that your browser has already cached the complete minified Bootstrap 4 code from some other web page. However, it is rarely the case that the production code on websites will contain only the out-of-the-box, vanilla Bootstrap 4 CSS. Most likely, the styles will have been heavily changed and added to. With that in mind, it becomes obvious that making our production CSS code lean by removing unused Sass partials makes perfect sense in our production code. The only time CDN could be a preferred approach is if we did not alter our CSS in any way, or if we do not mind overriding the regular CDN-served Bootstrap 4 styles from another custom CSS stylesheet, which is possible, even though not optimal.

To see other available options in the `grunt-sass` plugin, visit `https://github.com/gruntjs/grunt-contrib-sass`.

Cleaning up unused CSS with UnCSS and Grunt

In this recipe, we will continue with CSS optimization. In the preceding recipe, we cherry-picked `scss` partials by simply commenting out those that were not used. For example, we did not use the alert component, so we commented out its Sass `@include` command in `main.scss`.

This time, the approach is different. We will use pretty much the same code in our `main.scss` file in this recipe; however, this time, we will not comment out anything. In other words, we will include all the partials. Then, we'll set up our Grunt task runner with another Grunt plugin, namely, the `grunt-uncss` plugin. Running the plugin command through our console, we will then take the compiled CSS file and clean it up by removing the unused CSS declarations from it, which will significantly reduce its file size.

Getting ready

To begin with, let's preview the completed recipe. Navigate to `chapter9/complete/app/` and run `harp server` in your console. Next, open your browser and point it to `localhost:9000/recipe09-02`. Then, view the page source (in Chrome, you can use the *CTRL + u* shortcut keys and the page source will appear in a new tab).

Locate the call to the `main.css` style sheet and right-click on the style sheet link. Finally, click on the **open in new tab** command in the right-clicked contextual menu, and the style sheet will open in a new tab. Note that the file is minified.

Also, in your file explorer, you can navigate to `chapter9/complete/app/www/css/main.css` and verify the file size for this minified file--it should be around 35 kilobytes.

Now that we know what the result we are trying to achieve is, it's time to go through our recipe.

How to do it...

1. This recipe requires us to add an additional Grunt plugin. Thus, open your console, navigate to `chapter9/start/grunt/`, and run the `npm install grunt-uncss --save-dev` command.

2. Next, from your text editor, navigate to `chapter9/start/grunt` and open the `package.json` file. Verify that the command issued in the first step of this recipe has added this line of code at the bottom of the `devDependencies` section:

   ```
   "grunt-uncss": "^0.6.1"
   ```

3. While still in the `grunt` folder, we will add a new task to our `Gruntfile.js` starting from line 45:

   ```
   // Remove CSS that is not used
   uncss: {
   dist: {
   files: [
   { src: '../app/www/*.html', dest: '../app/www/css/main.css'}
   ]
   },
   options: {
   compress: true
   }
   },
   ```

4. We also need to load the `grunt-uncss` plugin, so go to line 66 of `Gruntfile.js`, and add the following line of code:

   ```
   grunt.loadNpmTasks('grunt-uncss');
   ```

5. Now, open your Bash or its equivalent, and `cd` into `chapter9/start/grunt`. Run the following command:

```
grunt uncss
```

6. Open the file titled `main.css` inside the `chapter9/start/app/www/css` folder, and note the reduced file size. Open the file to confirm that the file is minified. You should also note a lot of comments for different sections of the libraries used (Bootstrap 4, `Hover.css`, Font Awesome), but there should be no code. Stripping CSS comments will be discussed in the next recipe.

How it works...

This process is quite simple. You just add `grunt-uncss` to other Grunt plugins you are already using in your build process. In step 3, we specified options related to UnCSS in our `Gruntfile.js`. We specified the source folder to look at HTML files (and, thus, the CSS classes and ID's that these HTML files reference), and then the destination folder, where we will output the minified CSS files, stripped from unused declarations.

There are multiple ways to work with Grunt plugins in your workflow, but it is important to note one thing when working with preprocessors, or, in the case of Bootstrap 4, when working with Sass. All the Grunt tasks related to processing `scss` files can be thought of as the preprocessing step of our workflow.

Running the `grunt-uncss` command can be thought of as the postprocessing step.

To see the benefits of using UnCSS, let's add a new component to our HTML. Open the file titled `recipe09-02.ejs`, inside the `chapter9/start/app` folder, and add another Bootstrap 4 component, for example, a table. You can simply copy and paste the code straight from the `http://getbootstrap.com` website.

Now, run the `grunt uncss` command via console and inspect the produced `main.css` file. Note that the table-related styles have been added, which has increased the file size a bit. It is this dynamic nature of UnCSS that truly helps when making production-ready code.

Removing CSS comments with the grunt-strip-CSS-comments plugin

In this recipe, we will further decrease the file size of our `main.css` file by stripping comments from it. To this end, we will incorporate another Grunt plugin, `grunt-strip-css-comments`, into our workflow.

Getting ready

To get ready, open the `main.css` file from the `chapter9/start/app/www` folder in your text editor. Note the difference in both file size and content between the two files--the file from this recipe, and the file from the preceding recipe. Obviously, removing comments can add significant improvements to our CSS file size, and ultimately to our page speed.

 Page speed is important. You should always inspect your code with tools such as Google's PageSpeed Insights, available at:
`developers.google.com/speed/pagespeed/insights/`.

How to do it...

1. To begin, open Bash or a similar program and navigate to `chapter9/start/grunt`. Add the plugin by running the following command:

   ```
   npm install grunt-strip-css-comments --save-dev
   ```

2. Open your `Gruntfile.js` and add another Grunt task by inserting the following code on line 56:

   ```
   stripCssComments: {
   dist: {
   files: {
   '../app/www/css/main.css': '../app/www/css/main.css'
   }
   }
   },
   ```

3. On line 74 of your `Gruntfile.js`, add the following line of code:

   ```
   grunt.loadNpmTasks('grunt-strip-css-comments');
   ```

4. Navigate your console to `chapter9/start/grunt` and run the following command:

   ```
   grunt stripCssComments
   ```

5. Preview the file size and contents of `main.scss`.

How it works...

By now, you should be pretty familiar with how the setup of Grunt plugins works, and how they are run. In this recipe, we simply add another Grunt plugin through our Bash console, using npm. This results in the plugin being added as another `devDependency` inside our `Package.json` file. Then, all we have to do is to add it as a task inside `Gruntfile.js`, and finally, toward the bottom of the same file, register the task in question.

Finally, when needed, we simply run the appropriate task in our console. To make this process even smoother, a possible next step for improving this workflow could be to automate all these plugins by adding them to the watch task.

10
Creating a Blog with Jekyll and Bootstrap 4

In this chapter, we will cover the following topics:

- Making Jekyll work with Bootstrap 4
- Splitting Jekyll files into partials
- Making Jekyll blog-aware
- Deploying your blog to the web with GitHub

Making Jekyll work with Bootstrap 4

In this recipe, we will start making a static blog-aware system in Jekyll. Specifically, we will set up its basic structure and make it work with Bootstrap 4 Sass files, which will be compiled into CSS. We will also look at how to override Bootstrap's Sass variables with Jekyll.

Getting ready

This recipe will show you how to create a simple layout in Bootstrap 4 using Jekyll. The recipe deals with the whole setup, that is, creation of folders, running commands via console, and adding partial files in Jekyll. Thus, this recipe deals with a lot of other tasks than just working with Bootstrap 4. The result of this recipe is a working Jekyll blog, running on Bootstrap 4 and Sass.

Before we begin, we need to install Bootstrap 4 (via Bower), as well as having Ruby and Jekyll installed on our machine.

To install Bootstrap, we'll simply run the following command inside our `chapter10/start` folder:

```
bower install bootstrap#v4.0.0-alpha.6
```

To check if you have Ruby and Jekyll installed, run the following command in your console:

```
which Ruby; which Jekyll
```

With prerequisites out of the way, let's set up our blog with Jekyll.

 If you are having issues setting up any of the above on your system, you can alternatively use Cloud9 IDE, which comes with node, npm, and Ruby preinstalled. All that is left to do is install Bower (with `npm install bower`) and install Jekyll, with `gem install jekyll`. The details of how this is done have already been covered in Chapter 1.

How to do it...

1. Navigate to the `chapter10/start` folder using your console.
2. Run the `gem install jekyll` command. Verify the installation with `jekyll -v`, which will inform you which Jekyll version has been installed.
3. Next, type another command, `jekyll new recipe1 --blank`, in Bash to add a blank Jekyll installation. A new folder will be created, with the following structure:

```
jekyll
├── _drafts
├── _layouts
├── _posts
└── index.html
```

4. CD into the `recipe1` folder. Add a new folder; we will call it `assets`. Inside of this assets folder, we will add three subfolders, `css`, `js`, and `scss`, by running the following command:

```
mkdir assets assets/js assets/css assets/scss
```

5. Now, let's copy and paste the SCSS, JS, and jQuery files we need for Bootstrap 4 to run properly. We will copy them from Bower into the assets folder. We will start with the SCSS files:

```
cp -rv ../bower_components/bootstrap/scss ./assets/
```

6. Next, we will copy the JavaScript files:

```
cp -rv ../bower_components/bootstrap/dist/js/ ./assets/
```

7. Finally, we will add the jQuery files:

```
cp -rv ../bower_components/jquery/dist/jQuery.js ./assets/js/
```

8. Create a simple config file in the root of the `recipe1` folder by running this command:

```
touch _config.yml
```

9. Open the file we just made and paste in the following code:

```
# Site settings
title: Your Bootstrap 4 Blog Title
email: your-email@domain.com
description: Just a simple site description here.
baseurl: "" # the subpath for your Jekyll, for example
the"/subpath" bit in the url: http://yourdomain.com/subpath
url: "http://yourdomain.com" # your site's url

# Build settings
markdown: kramdown

# Excerpts
excerpt_separator: "<!-- more -->"

# Pretty URL
permalink: pretty

# Assets
#
# Enable the use of @imports in Jekyll:
sass:
  sass_dir: assets/scss
  style: :nested
```

10. Let's also create the `main.scss` file, inside `assets/css`:

```
touch assets/css/main.scss
```

11. Now, let's open the newly created file and paste in the code to include Bootstrap 4 Sass partials:

```
---
# This front matter comment makes Jekyll read the file correctly.
---
// Imports
@import "customstyles";
@import "bootstrap";
```

12. The first imported file, `bootstrap.scss`, was copied over earlier. However, we still need to make the other imported file, which we will do with this command:

```
touch assets/scss/customstyles.scss
```

13. Let's override a variable in `customstyles.scss` to check whether it will compile correctly. We will add something that will be obvious, like this:

```
$white:    lightskyblue;
```

14. Now it's time to add the most basic code to `index.html`, straight from the docs, with the only difference being the referencing of CSS and JS:

```
<!DOCTYPE html>
<html lang="en">
 <head>
 <!-- Required meta tags -->
 <meta charset="utf-8">
 <meta name="viewport" content="width=device-width, initial-
scale=1, shrink-to-fit=no">

 <!-- Bootstrap CSS -->
 <link rel="stylesheet" href="assets/css/main.css">
 </head>
 <body>
 <h1 class="bg-primary text-white display-4">Hello, world!</h1>

 <!-- jQuery first, then Tether, then Bootstrap JS. -->
 <script src="assets/js/jQuery.js"></script>
 <script src="assets/js/bootstrap.js"></script>
 </body>
</html>
```

15. Now we will build our blog with `jekyll build`, and we can follow it up with `jekyll serve`.

At this point, you have a Jekyll blog, with Sass set up to compile with CSS, and the ability to override any variable. There is still more work to be done, such as adding the actual blog functionality and Jekyll partials, but for now, let's preview the result of this recipe by pointing our browser to `http://127.0.0.1:4000`.

How it works...

This recipe is easy, although it involves quite a few steps. After the unavoidable preparations in steps 1 and 2, in step 3 we created the actual Jekyll serverless blog by running the `jekyll new recipe1 --blank` command. The command in plain English, could be read as something like this: "Create a new Jekyll blog system in a new folder called *recipe 1*, but do not install all the regular Jekyll blog assets; rather, just create a barebones installation, so that we can add our own custom implementation".

 We could have done a simple `jekyll new recipe1` command, without passing the `--blank` flag, but that would prevent us from adding our own custom Bootstrap 4 build. Instead, we would get a complete blog, with a predefined `_config.yml` file, and setting up Bootstrap 4 with it would be much harder.

In step 4, we prepared folders for all the assets that we will use--Sass, CSS, and JS. It might seem redundant to create `assets/css` and `assets/scss` when all we do in the `assets/css` folder is add the `main.scss` file. However, there are many benefits to this approach. Jekyll comes with its own Sass-to-CSS compiler and, by default, it will look for an SCSS file in the `assets/css` folder. Furthermore, adding the `assets/scss` folder allowed us to copy over the full contents of the `bower_components/bootstrap/scss` folder into it. This makes our Bootstrap installation easy to manage, because we can follow up with the most recent updates to the Bootstrap framework, when they happen, by simply running the following command:

```
bower install bootstrap#4.0 --force-latest --save
```

Alternatively, we could run some of the commands used in `Chapter 1`, *Installing Bootstrap 4 and Comparing Its Versions* to achieve the same effect.

Then, the only thing we need to do is copy over the updated SCSS from `bower_components/bootstrap/scss` to `assets/scss`. To make this approach even more automatic, we could create a Grunt task to automatically make such a copy, as discussed in previous chapters.

In steps 8 and 9, we added the `_config.yml` file, with the sole purpose of guiding Jekyll to the correct location of our Sass partials, and the way to compile them to CSS.

In steps 10 through 13, we set up both the Sass includes and the overrides, using the `assets/scss/bootstrap.scss` and `asstes/scss/customstyles.scss` files.

There is a little caveat in step 14 that we need to understand. The assets that we referenced are actually located in the `recipe1/_site` folder. This is the folder that is compiled once we run the `jekyll build` command. This is the core of how Jekyll works--it takes all the files we provide it, and then compiles them into the `_site` folder. The end product is just a bunch of static files, which gives Jekyll the popular description of a *serverless blog-aware system*.

In the next recipe, we will look at separating Jekyll files into partials, similar to what we did with Harp in previous chapters.

Splitting Jekyll files into partials

In this recipe, we will look at observing the don't repeat yourself principle. By separating our code into partials, and using Jekyll's front matter, we will achieve just that.

Getting ready

To start off, navigate to `chapter10/complete/recipe2` and run the console from this folder. Start the Jekyll server by running the `jekyll serve --watch` console command. Open your browser, point it to `localhost:4000` and preview the result. Click on some of the links on the navbar to see how it behaves.

How to do it...

1. Open the folder titled `chapter10/start/recipe2` in Bash.

2. Create a new file inside the `_layouts` folder by typing the following command:

   ```
   touch _layouts/default-layout.html
   ```

3. Cut the first 11 lines from `index.html` and paste them inside `_layouts/default-layout.html`. Your `_layouts/default-layout.html` file should now look like this:

   ```
   <!DOCTYPE html>
   <html lang="en">
    <head>
    <!-- Required meta tags -->
    <meta charset="utf-8">
    <meta name="viewport" content="width=device-width, initial-
    scale=1, shrink-to-fit=no">

    <!-- Bootstrap CSS -->
    <link rel="stylesheet" href="assets/css/main.css">
    </head>
    <body>
   ```

4. Cut the five lines from the bottom of `index.html` and paste them into `default-layout.html`. The snippet of code to be copied and pasted is this:

   ```
    <!-- jQuery first, then Tether, then Bootstrap JS. -->
    <script src="assets/js/jQuery.js"></script>
    <script src="assets/js/bootstrap.js"></script>
    </body>
   </html>
   ```

5. Now, our `index.html` file should only have one line of code:

   ```
    <h1 class="bg-primary text-white display-4">Hello, world!
    </h1>
   ```

6. Back inside the `default-layout.html` file, point your cursor one line above the jQuery HTML comment and add the following line of code:

   ```
    {{ content }}
   ```

7. Now the bottom section of `default-layout.html` should look like this:

```
<body>

{{ content }}

<!-- jQuery first, then Tether, then Bootstrap JS. -->
<script src="assets/js/jQuery.js"></script>
<script src="assets/js/bootstrap.js"></script>
</body>
</html>
```

8. For Jekyll to be able to compile the `index.html` file back to what it was, we need to specify the layout file that we are using. Since there is only one layout file right now, we simply reference this one file, using front matter, like this:

```
---
layout: default-layout
---

<h1 class="bg-primary text-white display-4">Hello, world!</h1>
```

9. It's time to add another folder for partial files. We'll call it _includes. This folder will hold partial files, such as `nav.html`; so let's create them:

mkdir _includes; touch _includes/nav.html

10. Now, we can add the navbar code:

```
<nav class="navbar navbar-toggleable-md navbar-light fixed-top bg-
faded">
  <button class="navbar-toggler navbar-toggler-right" type="button"
data-toggle="collapse" data-target="#navbarNav" aria-
controls="navbarNav" aria-expanded="false" aria-label="Toggle
navigation">
  <span class="navbar-toggler-icon"></span>
  </button>
  <a class="navbar-brand" href="#">Navbar</a>
  <div class="collapse navbar-collapse" id="navbarNav">
  <ul class="navbar-nav">
  <li class="nav-item active">
  <a class="nav-link" href="/our-blog">Our Blog</a>
  </li>
  <li class="nav-item">
  <a class="nav-link" href="/about-us">About Us</a>
  </li>
  <li class="nav-item">
```

```
<a class="nav-link" href="/contact-us">Contact Us</a>
</li>
</ul>
</div>
</nav>
```

11. To have the navbar appear, we need to add it to _includes/default-layout.html, on line 12, just after the opening body tag:

    ```
    {% include nav.html %}
    ```

12. Let's erase the override for the $white variable by simply commenting out the content of customstyles.scss, in recipe2/assets/scss:

    ```
    // $white:  lightskyblue;
    ```

13. While customstyles.scss is open, we can add some additional CSS to it:

    ```
    /* Sticky footer styles
    -------------------------------------------------- */
    html {
     position: relative;
     min-height: 100%;
    }

    body {
     /* padding-top set for fixed navbar */
     padding-top: 54px;
     /* margin-bottom by footer height (72px), and then some */
     margin-bottom: 100px !important;
    }

    .footer {
     position: absolute !important;
     width: 100%;
     bottom: 0;

     p {
     margin-bottom: 0;
     }
    }
    ```

14. Let's create another include; this time, it will be a simple footer:

```
touch _includes/footer.html
```

15. Open the new footer include in your code editor and paste in the following code:

```
<footer class="footer bg-info ">
<p class="text-center text-white p-4">(c) {{ site.title }},
2017</p>
</footer>
```

16. Add the footer include to `default-layout.html` by inserting the following code just above the jQuery HTML comment:

```
{% include footer.html %}
```

17. Back in the root of our blog, we will make a new file and call it `02-about.html`. Then, we will paste in the following code:

```
---
layout: page
title: About Us
permalink: /about-us/
---

This is the about page.
```

18. Similarly, we will add the contact page by creating a new file, calling it 03-contact.html, and adding the following code to it:

```
---
layout: page
title: Contact Us
permalink: /contact-us/
---

This is the contact page.
```

19. Next, we will add another file, `page.html`, inside the _layouts folder and add the following code to this file:

```
---
layout: default-layout
---

<div class="container-fluid bg-info pt-3 pb-3">
 <div class="container">
```

```
    <h1 class="display-3 pt-5 pb-5 text-white">{{ page.title }}</h1>
    </div>
</div>
<div class="container mt-5">
 {{ content }}
</div>
```

20. Save all the files, run `jekyll server` from the console, and preview the result in your browser at `localhost:4000`. Click on the about link in the navbar and click back on the navbar brand.

How it works...

This recipe is pretty straightforward; we separate our `index.html` file in a meaningful way, so as to be able to reuse it with any other file. That is exactly what we do when we add the `about.html` page. Besides using the _layout file of `default-layout.html`, we also address the use of _includes, namely the `nav.html` and `footer.html` files. Although we could have added the includes to our `default-layout.html`, this setup is much better, as it caters for greater modularity and gives us options that we would not have otherwise. For example, we could add a different layout, and inside that layout, we could add a different nav and a different footer, which would be great for A/B testing.

Making Jekyll blog-aware

In this recipe, we will make Jekyll blog-aware. To do this, we need to set up our posts. The way that Jekyll works is, it allows us to add posts inside a partial folder titled _posts. This folder was automatically created for us when we ran the `jekyll new` command.

Next, we need to create our files, using either the markdown or the HTML file extension. While markdown can be described as a simplified HTML format, one wonderful thing about using it is that the code inside can be HTML, at least in Jekyll. Jekyll will compile markdown files that have HTML inside of them without issues. That is why we will be using markdown files for our posts.

Jekyll posts also need to follow another convention--a naming convention. This naming convention is what allows Jekyll to be blog-aware. Each post in Jekyll needs to have the `YYYY-MM-DD-title-of-post.markdown` structure. Alternatively, you can use `YYYY-MM-DD-title-of-post.html`, but as already explained, we will use the first option.

Getting ready

To start off, navigate to `chapter10/complete/recipe3` and run the console from this folder. Start the Jekyll server by running the `jekyll serve --watch` console command. Open your browser, point it to `localhost:4000`, and preview the result. Click on the **Our Blog** button in the navbar and look through a few posts.

How to do it...

1. Open the folder titled `chapter10/start/recipe3` in your Bash.
2. Some of the files have been added in advance to make the recipe simpler to follow. These files are the four files in the `_posts` folder. Feel free to copy and paste some of them or alter the contents of the posts in any way you like.
3. Create a new file inside the `_layouts` folder called `post.html`. To do this, type the following command with your console pointing to the root of `recipe3` folder:

   ```
   touch _layouts/post.html
   ```

4. Inside the `post.html` file, add the following code:

   ```
   ---
   layout: default-layout
   ---

   <div class="container">
    <div>
    <h2 class="display-4 mt-5 mb-4">{{ page.title }}</h2>
    <p class="h3 text-muted mb-4">
    By: <em>{{ page.author }}</em>, Published: <em>{{ page.date |
   date_to_long_string}}</em>
    </p>
    <div>{{ content }}</div>
    </div>
   </div>
   ```

5. Make a new page in the root of `recipe3`:

```
touch 01-our-blog.html
```

6. Add the following code to it:

```
---
layout: page
title: Our Blog
permalink: /our-blog/
---

<div class="row">
 {% for post in site.posts %}
 <div class="col-6 p-2">
 <div class="card h-100">
 <div class="card-header">
 {{ post.category }}
 </div>
 <div class="card-block">
 <h3 class="card-title"><a class="text-info" href="{{ post.url |
prepend: site.baseurl }}">{{ post.title }}</a></h3>
 <p class="card-text">{{ post.excerpt }}</p>
 <a href="{{ post.url | prepend: site.baseurl }}" class="btn btn-
info">Read more</a>
 </div>
 <div class="card-footer text-muted">
 {% if post.date %}
 Published: <em>{{ post.date | date_to_long_string}}</em>
 {% endif %}
 </div>
 </div>
 </div>
 {% endfor %}
</div>
```

7. Still in the root of your project, open the `index.html` file and erase everything. Paste in the following code:

```
---
layout: default-layout
---

<div class="container mt-5 pt-5">
 <div class="row">
 <div class="col-sm-6">
 <h1 class="display-1 mt-5 pt-5 ">Welcome to my Blog</h1>
```

```
</div>
<div class="col-sm-6">
<img src="http://placehold.it/500x500" class="img-fluid rounded-
circle img-thumbnail">
</div>
</div>
<div class="row mt-5">
<div class="col-sm-6">
<img src="http://placehold.it/500x500" class="img-fluid img-
thumbnail">
</div>
<div class="col-sm-6">
<h2 class="display-2 mt-5 pt-5">Lorem Ipsum Dolor Sit</h2>
</div>
</div>
</div>
```

8. Open the `nav.html` include and delete everything under the closing `</button>` tag. Click on the return key, then paste in the following code:

```
 <a class="navbar-brand" href="{{ site.baseurl }}/">{{ site.title
 }}</a>
</div>
<div class="collapse navbar-collapse" id="navbarNav">
<ul class="navbar-nav ml-auto">
{% for page in site.pages %}
{% if page.title %}
<li class="nav-item">
<a class="btn btn-info btn-block" href="{{ page.url | prepend:
site.baseurl }}">{{ page.title }}</a>
</li>
{% endif %}
{% endfor %}
</ul>
</div>
</div>
</nav>
```

9. Separate `default-layout.html` into partials by replacing the code inside with includes only, like this:

```
{% include head.html %}

{% include nav.html %}

 {{ content }}

{% include footer.html %}
```

10. Replace the code inside `_includes/head.html` with this code:

```
<!DOCTYPE html>
<html lang="en">
 <head>
 <meta charset="utf-8">
 <meta name="viewport" content="width=device-width, height=device-
height, user-scalable=yes, initial-scale=1">

 <title>
 {% if page.title %}
 {{ page.title }}
 {% else %}
 {{ site.title }}
 {% endif %}
 </title>

 <meta name="description" content="{% if page.excerpt %}{{
page.excerpt | strip_html | strip_newlines | truncatewords: 20 }}{%
else %}{{ site.description }}{% endif %}">

 <link rel="canonical" href="{{ page.url | replace:'index.html',''
| prepend: site.baseurl | prepend: site.url }}">

 <link rel="stylesheet" href="{{ "/assets/css/main.css" | prepend:
site.baseurl }}">
 </head>

 <body>
```

11. Open the `_includes/footer.html` file and change its code so that it looks like this:

```
<footer class="footer bg-info ">
<p class="text-center text-white p-4">(c) {{ site.title }},
2017</p>
</footer>

<script src="/assets/js/jQuery.js"></script>
<script src="/assets/js/bootstrap.min.js"></script>

</body>
</html>
```

12. Open the `_includes/postcontent.html` file and paste in the following code:

```
<div class="container">
<div class="row">
<div class="col-md-4">
 <img class="img-fluid img-round"
src="http://placehold.it/400x400/add100">
</div>
<div class="col-md-8">
 <p>Lorem ipsum Lorem ipsum Lorem ipsum dolor sit amet. Lorem ipsum
Lorem ipsum Lorem ipsum dolor sit amet. Lorem ipsum Lorem ipsum
Lorem ipsum dolor sit amet. Lorem ipsum Lorem ipsum Lorem ipsum
dolor sit amet. Lorem ipsum Lorem ipsum Lorem ipsum dolor sit amet.
Lorem ipsum Lorem ipsum Lorem ipsum dolor sit amet. Lorem ipsum
Lorem ipsum Lorem ipsum dolor sit amet.</p>
</div>
```

13. Open `customstyles.scss` from the `assets/scss` folder and add this code to the bottom of the file:

```
nav .btn-block {
 width: 95%;
}

.display-4 {
 font-size: 2.8rem !important;
}

.col {
 min-width: 320px;
}
```

14. Save all the files, point your browser to `localhost:5000` and preview the result.

> You can have multiple instances of Jekyll running from multiple console windows. All you have to do, when serving a Jekyll installation, is to issue the `jekyll s --port 5555` command. Note that the "s" is an alias of "serve" and that the port number is arbitrary.

How it works...

There are a lot of things happening in this recipe. In steps 2 through 4, we added the posts layout. This layout in turn called the default layout, so this is a practical example of an excellent possibility in Jekyll to include layouts within layouts. Inspecting the code inside post.html, you might notice snippets of code such as this one:

```
{{ page.title }}
```

The preceding code comes from a templating language called Liquid, created by Shopify and also used by Jekyll.

> To find out more about the Liquid templating language, navigate to `https://shopify.github.io/liquid/`. Using Liquid in Jekyll is sort of a separate skill. To find out more about Jekyll in general, visit the official website at `https://jekyllrb.com/docs/home/`.

If you have had experience with other scripting languages, such as, for example, PHP, you will understand and appreciate the power of using conditional statements (if statements) and different kinds of loops.

Both looping and conditional statements are possible in Liquid. We can see an example of an `if` statement in step 6 and an example of a for loop in step 8.

> The mentioned abilities of the Liquid templating language are quite powerful, but it will take some time for you to grasp it. If you are in a hurry to put together your static website, you can do it by either simply copying the recipe, or by even skipping the blog bit completely. With Jekyll, it is entirely possible to make a completely static website, consisting only of posts and partial files.

In steps 9 through 11, we separated our `default-layout.html` into includes so that they are easier to manage. We have already discussed the advantages of modular code. An example of the advantages of such an approach can be seen in step 12, where we added the code that each of our four example posts use, after the `<!-- more -->` tag. The tag itself is quite interesting. A similar concept appears in WordPress. It's an elegant way to distinguish a post's introductory text (the text that will be displayed in the `div` with the class of `card-text`) and the rest of the post's body. This is achieved by specifying the way that our Jekyll installation will deal with excerpts, which was already done in recipe 1 of this chapter, specifically, in the file titled `_config.yml`. The `yml` extension is used for YAML format, which is just another simple, human-friendly format (because of its readability). Jekyll uses this file to allow us to make our own configurations, which can be very versatile.

This recipe also includes a special navigation that we did not employ in other recipes of this book. Namely, it is a navbar with buttons instead of default navbar links, as added in step 8. In order to not lose too much time on styling these buttons, the most minimal possible Sass code was provided to deal with them, at the bottom of the `customstyles.scss` file. There is a lot more that could have been done with this code, but this is a starting point.

Deploying your blog to the web with GitHub

In this recipe, we will take the blog that we completed in the previous recipe and publish it on GitHub. There are many other popular pages being hosted on GitHub, or more specifically being hosted on GitHub Pages.

 To get acquainted with what GitHub Pages is all about, check out their website at `https://pages.github.com/`.

Among some of the more popular sites hosted on GitHub Pages is the official Bootstrap website itself, which can be found at `http://getbootstrap.com`.

Getting ready

In order to complete this recipe, you need to have a GitHub account, which you can register for free at `https://github.com`. Once you have registered your account, you will need to create a new repository. The simplest explanation of a repository is that it is a copy of your code on a remote server. It is much more than that, but for our purposes, that definition is good enough.

How to do it...

1. Make a new repository by visiting `https://github.com/new`.

2. Enter the name of your repository, for example "jekblog". Leave all the other options as is, and click on the button at the bottom that says "Create repository".

3. A new window will open. Find the section that has the title with the following text:

   ...or push an existing repository from the command line

   Do not close the browser, we will need the two commands under this title soon.

4. Open the `chapter10/complete/recipe3` folder in your Bash.

5. Add a new file to the folder; this will be a dotfile, titled `.gitignore`. To add it, type the following command with your console pointing to the root of recipe 3:

   ```
   touch .gitignore
   ```

6. Open the preceding file in your code editor and add the following code:

   ```
   _site
   .sass-cache
   ```

7. Then, save the file.

8. Now is the time to initialize our local repository (to start tracking our code with Git). Open Git Bash in your project's root and type the following code:

```
git init
```

9. Add all our code to the Git staging index:

```
git add --all
```

10. Now, commit it to the local repository:

```
git commit -m "The first commit"
```

11. Now, copy the first line from the new repository tab, under the heading described in step 3. If you called your new repository `jekblog`, the line should follow this pattern:

```
git remote add origin https://github.com/yourusername/jekblog.git
```

12. Paste in the preceding command into your Bash (replacing the `yourusername` section with whatever you chose as your username), and click on *return*.

13. Copy the next line from the browser and paste it into Bash as is:

```
git push -u origin master
```

14. GitHub will ask for your credentials, that is, username and password. Provide them as prompted. If done successfully, the push command will copy your local repository into the remote repository on GitHub.

15. Refresh the repository web page in your browser, and note that all your code is now on GitHub.

16. GitHub pages are served from a special branch in your repository, called `gh-pages`. We need to add the branch to our local repository. The following command will both create a new branch called `gh-pages`, and switch to it from the master branch:

```
git checkout -b gh-pages
```

17. Run the following command in your Bash:

```
git push -u origin gh-pages
```

18. Back in the repository web page, in the branches view, click on the `gh-pages` link. It should be the left-most button under the text that reads **1 commit**. The button should have the text of **Branch: master**, and a little drop-down icon. Click on the button to select the `gh-pages` branch.

19. Once you are inside the `gh-pages` branch, click on the **Settings** tab, and scroll down to the *GitHub Pages* section. Click on the link to preview your website. It should be served from a URL with the following pattern:

```
https://<yourusername>.github.io/jekblog/
```

How it works...

We started off the recipe with initial preparations--making a new repository on GitHub in steps 1 through 3. In steps 4 and 5, we added the `.gitignore` file. This file will tell Git which files not to track. Files that we do not want to track are most often dynamic files that are created as Jekyll compiles. In this case, the files that need to be ignored are located in the `_site` and the `.sass-cache` folders.

 Git itself has a system of the so-called "three trees". It is the way that repositories work. To read up more on the subject, check out Packt Publishing's title "Git Version Control Cookbook", available to subscribers at `https://www.packtpub.com/application-development/git-version-control-cookbook`.

In steps 7 through 9, we set up the local git repository--we started tracking our files locally. In steps 10 through 12, we set up a remote repository on GitHub.

The steps 13 through 18 involve the setup of the `gh-pages` branch and describe how to preview our site online.

11
Bootstrap 4 with ASP.NET Core

In this chapter, we will cover the following topics:

- Starting a project in ASP.NET Core and Bootstrap 4 in Visual Studio 2017
- Migrating the default web page of a .NET Core project from Bootstrap 3 to Bootstrap 4
- Working with Bower, Sass, and Grunt in our .NET Core project

Starting a project in ASP.NET Core and Bootstrap 4 in Visual Studio 2017

In this recipe, we will make a new project in ASP.NET Core and Bootstrap 4. We will use Visual Studio 2017 Community Edition.

Getting ready

To get ready for this recipe, you need to have Visual Studio 2017 installed on your computer. You also need to have .NET Core installed.

 To make sure that you have all the needed installations, check out `https://www.microsoft.com/net/core#windowsvs2017`.

Visual Studio 2017 is installed via Visual Studio Installer. In order to install the .NET Core workload, you need to run the Visual Studio Installer as an administrator (with administrator privileges). Once the Installer starts, click on the **Modify** button on the Visual Studio 2017 Community Edition section of the installer. Under Workloads, scroll down to the very bottom and locate the **.NET Core cross-platform development**, which can be found in the **Other Toolsets** section. Click on it, and your download should start. Note that the installation size is quite big (several gigabytes), so, depending on your connection, it could take some time.

Once the installation is complete, you will be ready to start working with .NET Core in Visual Studio 2017.

How to do it...

1. On Visual Studio's main menu, click on **File > New > Project**, then choose **ASP.NET Core Web Application (.NET Core)**, as shown in the following screenshot:

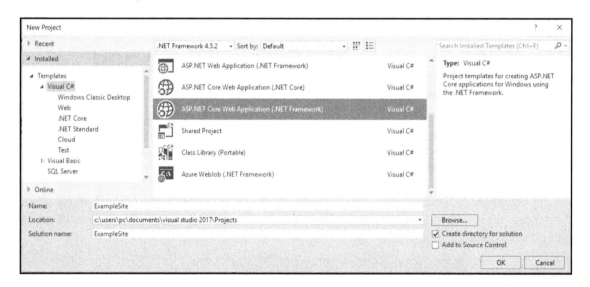

Starting a new .NET Core project in Visual Studio 2017

2. A new window will pop up with **Empty project** preselected. Click on the Web Application icon, then click on the **OK** button to create your project.

3. Verify the currently installed version of Bootstrap in the Solution Explorer, by searching for it. Using the shortcut keys of *Ctrl + ;* will bring the Solution Explorer's search bar into focus. Type bootstrap, and you will get two sets of results--the first one lists Bootstrap as a Bower dependency and the second lists it in the lib folder.

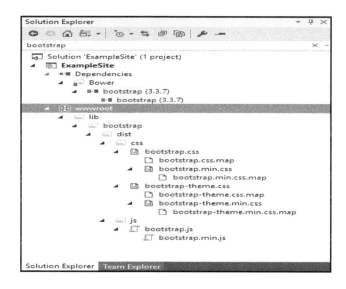

Searching through the Solution Explorer

4. In the Solution Explorer, all the occurrences found of the searched term (in our case, bootstrap), are highlighted in yellow. Look at the very first highlighted result. The word bootstrap is listed as a dependency in the Bower folder. The version of Bootstrap used as a dependency is shown in round brackets--it is version 3.3.7. To update the current version of Bootstrap in use, go to the main menu and click on **Project > Manage Bower Packages...**

5. In the window that appears, locate bootstrap and click on the **Update** button. Make sure that **v4.0.0-alpha.6** is preselected, and that the **Options** checkbox is checked:

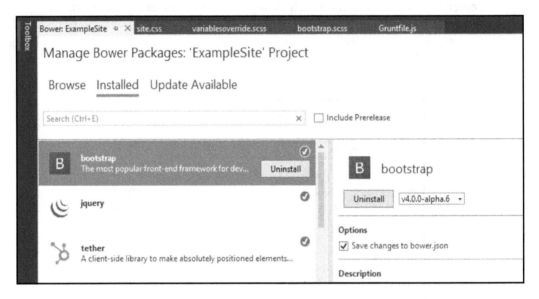

Updating Bower components in Visual Studio 2017

6. Update **jQuery** as well, by selecting it in the list of installed Bower packages and clicking on the **Update** button.

How it works...

In this recipe, we saw how simple it is in Visual Studio 2017 to verify the current Bootstrap installation. We were using .NET Core version 1.1 in our project. Using the Solution Explorer search, we saw how easy it is to check the installed Bootstrap version on the fly. We also saw how to manage bower packages for finer control over the installed dependencies and their updates.

Migrating the default web page of a .NET Core project from Bootstrap 3 to Bootstrap 4

In this recipe, we will fix the default web page of a .NET Core project. Why do we need to fix it? The reason is simple: after updating our Bootstrap to version 4 (instead of the default version 3), the HTML structure needs to be changed as well. We will do it in this recipe.

Getting ready

To begin, it would be worthwhile to digress from our current project and open a new .NET Core web application in Visual Studio 2017. Next, to preview the way the default web application should look out of the box (using Bootstrap 3), we will utilize *Shift + Ctrl + W*. This is the **View in Browser** command, which will, by default, open our project in the Edge browser.

The website should look like this:

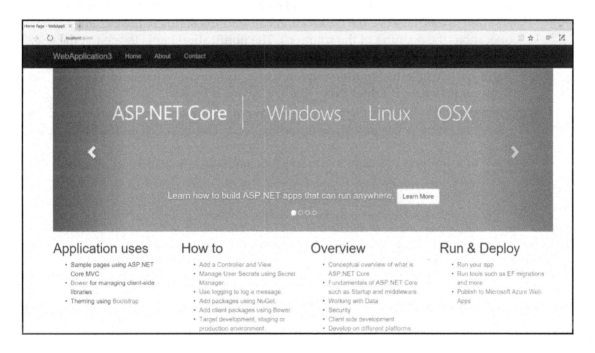

Previewing the default web application in the browser

So, we have the navbar, a carousel component, four columns with some headings and lists, and finally, a footer.

Now that we know what the desired result should be, it's time to fix our web application (the one using Bootstrap 4 as a Bower dependency).

In order to be able to better track changes made to the navbar and other components used in the View of our .NET Core web application, it is worth tracking our code with some version control system, such as Git. Doing this will make it a lot easier to compare changes between Bootstrap 3 and Bootstrap 4 for the same components we work with.

How to do it...

1. Open the solution with the Bootstrap 4 installation (the one titled **ExampleSite**) by navigating to **File > Open Project/Solution** on the main menu.
2. In the pop-up window that appears, double-click on the ExampleSite folder, select the ExampleSite.sln file, and click on the **Open** button. While the solution opens, observe the notification bar with the status of the current operation (the opening of the solution). The notification bar is located at the very bottom of the Visual Studio window.
3. Right-click inside the Solution Explorer, and click on the command **View in Browser (MicroSoft Edge)**. Note that the layout is broken.
4. Press the *Ctrl + ;* shortcut key and type **_layout**. The search result will point to the _Layout.cshtml file in your Solution Explorer. Double-click on the file to open it.
5. First, we will fix the navbar. You can locate it between lines 22 and 41 of the _Layout.cshtml file:

```
<1nav class="navbar navbar-inverse navbar-fixed-top">
  <div class="container">
    <div class="navbar-header">
      <button type="button" class="navbar-toggle" data-
        toggle="collapse" data-target=".navbar-collapse">
        <span class="sr-only">Toggle navigation</span>
        <span class="icon-bar"></span>
        <span class="icon-bar"></span>
        <span class="icon-bar"></span>
      </button>
      <a asp-area="" asp-controller="Home" asp-action="Index"
        class="navbar-brand">ExampleSite</a>
```

```
        </div>
        <div class="navbar-collapse collapse">
          <ul class="nav navbar-nav">
            <li><a asp-area="" asp-controller="Home" asp-
                action="Index">Home</a>
            </li>
            <li><a asp-area="" asp-controller="Home" asp-
                action="About">About</a>
            </li>
            <li><a asp-area="" asp-controller="Home" asp-
                action="Contact">Contact</a>
            </li>
          </ul>
        </div>
      </div>
    </nav>
```

6. Cut the navbar code referenced in the preceding step and paste the following in its place:

```
<nav class="navbar navbar-toggleable-md navbar-light bg-faded
fixed-top">
<button class="navbar-toggler navbar-toggler-right" type="button"
data-toggle="collapse" data-target="#navbarSupportedContent" aria-
controls="navbarSupportedContent" aria-expanded="false" aria-
label="Toggle navigation">
<span class="navbar-toggler-icon"></span>
</button>
<a asp-area="" asp-controller="Home" asp-action="Index"
class="navbar-brand">ExampleSite</a>
<div class="collapse navbar-collapse" id="navbarSupportedContent">
    <ul class="navbar-nav mr-auto">
        <li class="nav-item active">
            <a class="nav-link" asp-area="" asp-controller="Home" asp-
              action="Index">Home</a>
        </li>
        <li class="nav-item">
            <a class="nav-link" asp-area="" asp-controller="Home" asp-
              action="About">About</a>
        </li>
        <li class="nav-item">
            <a class="nav-link" asp-area="" asp-controller="Home" asp-
              action="Contact">Contact</a>
        </li>
    </ul>
</div>
</nav>
```

7. Next, we will replace the carousel with a jumbotron section. Open the `index.cshtml` file, and erase all the carousel code (lines 5 through 66).

8. Paste in the following code for the `jumbotron`:

```
<div class="jumbotron mt-5 mb-4">
    <h1 class="display-3">Hello, world!</h1>
    <p class="lead">This is a simple hero unit, a simple jumbotron-
    style component for calling extra attention to featured
content
    or information.</p>
    <hr class="my-4">
    <p>It uses utility classes for typography and spacing to space
        content out within the larger container.</p>
    <p class="lead">
        <a class="btn btn-primary btn-lg" href="#"
            role="button">Learn more</a>
    </p>
</div>
```

9. Let's also adjust the positioning of the About page using the utility class of `mt-5`. Open the `About.cshtml` file, which can be found inside the `Views/Home` folder. Add changes to `About.cshtml` file by making line 4 of the file look like this:

```
<h2 class="mt-5">@ViewData["Title"].</h2>
```

10. Make a similar change in the *Contact* page, by changing line number 4 to this:

```
<h2 class="mt-5">@ViewData["Title"].</h2>
```

11. Right-click on `wwwroot` inside the Solution Explorer. Click on the **View in Browser...** command, and browse your brand new Bootstrap 4 layout in .NET Core.

How it works...

The changes made both to the navbar and the carousel are to do mostly with CSS classes that changed their names between the two versions of Bootstrap, with minor changes in their HTML structure.

 The way that we changed the components in this recipe highlights the reason why Bootstrap is so popular. We have not once had to open a style sheet. All we had to do to make the recipe work was to change the values of class attributes used in our HTML. This distinction between having to dig into CSS files and being able to simply work with class attributes to alter our layouts is a huge part of the initial success of Bootstrap and the reason why it became such a success.

Working with Bower, Sass, and Grunt in our .NET Core project

There is a major difference between NuGet and Bower. NuGet, as the package manager used to control .NET libraries, cannot deal with static frontend libraries, such as Bootstrap or Tether. However, when working on .NET Core web applications, we need to include these libraries. That is where Bower comes into play, and it is the reason why we had to use Bower in our previous recipes, when we set up our simple app.

In other chapters of this book, we used to install Bower using **Node Package Manager (NPM)**. In this recipe, we will let Visual Studio manage Bower for us, as it comes preinstalled with .NET Core and can be accessed via the **Manage Bower Packages** command. However, contrary to the previous chapters, in this chapter we will also use the bower.json file, which is used to list dependencies we use in our project. The way that bower.json file works is quite similar to the way that the package.json file is used by Grunt--it simply lists dependencies. While in the case of Grunt, these dependencies are Grunt plugins, in the case of Bower, the bower.json file lists the actual frontend libraries as dependencies.

To locate bower.json, simply use the Solution Explorer's search box, accessing it quickly by pressing the *Ctrl +;* shortcut key. There will be multiple results; open the one that sits at the root of ExampleSite.

Getting ready

In the Visual Studio .NET Core project, there is no `bower_components` folder, like you might expect based on the previous chapters. Visual Studio has its own way of doing things. Search for `bowerrc` in the Solution Explorer, and open the file you found. The file should have the following code:

```
{
    "directory": "wwwroot/lib"
}
```

What this means is that the `wwwroot/lib` is the `bower_components` folder. Twirl it open to see that this is indeed the case. Once you do this, it should be easy to find the `lib/bootstrap/scss` path, with all the Bootstrap 4 SCSS partial files present.

How to do it...

1. In `www.root/lib/bootstrap/scss`, copy the `bootstrap.scss` and `_variables.scss` files.
2. In Solution Explorer, right-click on `www.root` and click on; **Add > New Folder**.
3. Right-click on `New Folder` and click on `Rename`. Type `sass` as the new name for the folder.
4. Paste in the files copied in step 1, into the `sass` folder made in step 3.
5. Open the `sass/bootstrap.scss` file and press *Ctrl + H*. Type `@import` into the first input field (this is the find input).
6. Click on the second input field (this is the replace input).

   Type in the following into the second input field:

   ```
   @import "../lib/bootstrap/scss/
   ```

7. Press *Alt + A* to replace all. Once Visual Studio completes the command, it will inform you of it by showing a popup with the **36 occurence(s) replaced** text inside.
8. Save the `sass/bootstrap.scss` file.
9. Open `sass/variablesoverride.scss`, erase all the contents of the file, and add the following code:

   ```
   $white: mistyrose;
   ```

10. Open the `sass/bootstrap.scss` file, and change the beginning of the file so that it looks as follows:

```
/*!
 * Bootstrap v4.0.0-alpha.6 (https://getbootstrap.com)
 * Copyright 2011-2017 The Bootstrap Authors
 * Copyright 2011-2017 Twitter, Inc.
 * Licensed under MIT
(https://github.com/twbs/bootstrap/blob/master/LICENSE)
 */

@import "variablesoverride.scss"; // $white = mistyrose; !!!!

// Core variables and mixins
@import "../lib/bootstrap/scss/variables";
@import "../lib/bootstrap/scss/mixins";
@import "../lib/bootstrap/scss/custom";
```

11. Add the new item to your Solution Explorer, using *Ctrl* + *Shift* + *A*. Choose NPM `configuration file`, as follows:

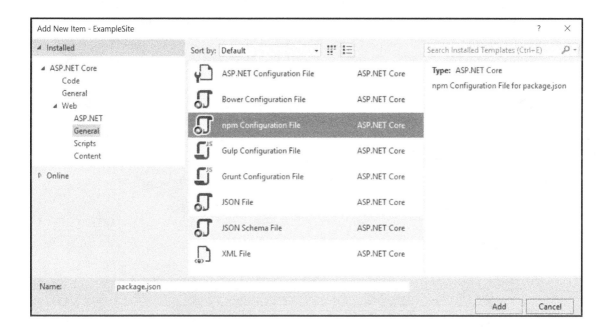

Adding npm configuration file to ASP.NET Core

12. Click on the **Add** button. The `package.json` file will open. Type `"grunt"`: inside the `devDependencies` JS object. This will trigger `Intellisense`. The latest stable version will be highlighted; double-click on it to select it.

13. Similar to the preceding step, add the `grunt-contrib-sass` plugin. Your `package.json` should now look like this:

```
{
    "version": "1.0.0",
    "name": "asp.net",
    "private": true,
    "devDependencies":
    {
        "grunt": "1.0.1",
        "grunt-contrib-sass": "1.0.0"
    }
}
```

14. Add another new item to your Solution Explorer, by clicking on the project in Solution Explorer, and pressing the *Ctrl* + *Shift* + *A* shortcut keys. This time we will add the Grunt config file, by selecting it in the pop-up window, and clicking on the Add button. This will add a new file, called `Gruntfile.js`, to the root of our `ExampleSite` project, as well as open the file in Visual Studio.

15. To make Grunt compile Sass to CSS, we will add it to the `sass` task options inside the `initConfig()` method. To begin, let's just add the example config, as seen at `https://github.com/gruntjs/grunt-contrib-sass`:

```
module.exports = function (grunt) {
    grunt.initConfig({
        sass: { // Task
            dist: { // Target
                options: { // Target options
                    style: 'expanded'
                },
                files: { // Dictionary of files
                    'main.css': 'main.scss', // 'destination':
                        'source'
                }
            }
        }
    });

    grunt.loadNpmTasks('grunt-contrib-sass');

    grunt.registerTask('default', ['sass']);
```

```
};
```

16. Adjust the line with the `'destination': 'source'` comment so that it looks like this:

    ```
    'wwwroot/css/site.css': 'wwwroot/sass/bootstrap.scss', //
    'destination': 'source'
    ```

17. Save `Gruntfile.js`, then right-click on it in the Solution Explorer and click on **Taskrunner Explorer**. It should open in the bottom-left corner of the Visual Studio workspace. Double-click on the `sass:dist` task (inside **Tasks > sass**), to run it. Once it is complete, Visual Studio will complain that the `site.css` file has been changed by an external program. That means Grunt is compiling our Sass to CSS. Click on **OK** to close the notification window.

 If your Taskrunner Explorer fails, you might need to install the NPM Task Runner extension, available at `https://marketplace.visualstudio.com/it ems?itemName=MadsKristensen.NPMTaskRunner`.

18. To install it straight from Visual Studio, click on **Tools | Extensions | Updates** on the main menu. Click on the **Online** section in the left sidebar of the **Extensions and Updates** pop-up window.

19. In the top-right corner of the **Extensions and Updates** window, there is a search bar. Type the following search term: `npm task runner`. Click the first result (NPM Task Runner) to install it, as can be seen in the following screenshot:

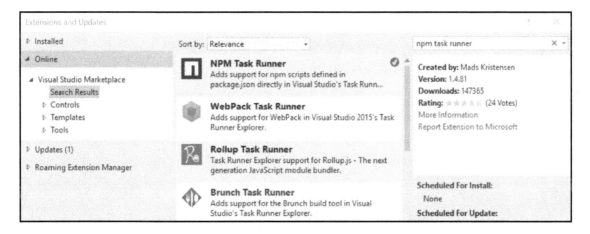

Adding NPM Task Runner extension

20. Once the SCSS has compiled to CSS, in order to preview the website with the *Shift* + *Ctrl* + *W* shortcut key, you first need to stop `Output`. To do that, go to the second tab in the lower-left section of the Visual Studio workspace, titled `Output` (just next to the `Task Runner Explorer` tab), click inside, and press *Ctrl* + *C* to stop it.

21. Finally, preview the website with *Shift* + *Ctrl* + *W*. The result will be the change of the previously white color of the website's background, to a shade of pink, that is, to HTML's color of mistyrose.

How it works...

In this recipe, you learned how to integrate NPM and Bower into our .NET Core workflow. You also learned how to set up Visual Studio to compile CSS from Sass, and how to tweak the result of compilation by adding custom variables, and thus tweaking the standard Bootstrap 4 styles.

Although there is a lot of complexity in setting up Visual Studio itself, the general process should be quite familiar, as we have gone through a similar workflow in a number of recipes in this book.

12
Integrating Bootstrap 4 with React and Angular

In this chapter, we will cover the following topics:

- Integrating Bootstrap 4 with React
- Replacing the default styles in Angular 4 QuickStart with Bootstrap 4 CDN CSS
- Integrating Angular 4 and Bootstrap 4 with the help of ng-bootstrap

Introduction

In this chapter, we will take a look at how to get started with using Bootstrap 4 in React and Angular. The assumption here is that you have not used these frameworks before. In this chapter, we are trying to achieve two goals. The first goal is to get started with React and Angular without getting bogged down with their technical details (which can be quite overwhelming if you have not used these frameworks before). The second goal is to show the easiest possible ways to combine Bootstrap 4 with React and Angular. Once you understand the basics that this chapter covers, you should be able to build on top of that knowledge and explore these two wonderful frontend frameworks further.

Integrating Bootstrap 4 with React

In this recipe, we will integrate Bootstrap 4 with React. To do this, we will use the `create-react-app` repository, available at `https://github.com/facebookincubator`.

We will also use the `reactstrap` project, as it has been built to use Bootstrap 4 as React components today. You can check out the project at `https://reactstrap.github.io`.

Getting ready

To preview the completed recipe, go to `chapter12/complete/recipe1` and open the `index.html` file in your browser. In order to get to this finished result, we need to use the `create-react-app` repository.

Navigate to `https://github.com/facebookincubator/create-react-app`. The reason to use this repository is simple, as explained in the repository description: *Create React apps with no build configuration*. Working with React this way removes a layout of complexity, which allows us to achieve the goal of using Bootstrap 4 with this framework that much simpler.

Go to the *Getting Started* section at `https://github.com/facebookincubator/create-react-app#getting-started`.

Note that most of the code in this recipe is compiled from these sources:

- `https://reactstrap.github.io/`
- `https://github.com/facebookincubator/create-react-app#getting-started`
- `https://gist.github.com/eddywashere/e13033c0e655ab7cda995f8bc77ce40d`

However, there are quite a few additional explanations and in-between steps added, and the example from the third referenced link has been extended and built upon to reinforce learning.

How to do it...

1. Open the `chapter12/start/recipe1` folder in your console.
2. Install the `npm` package globally:

   ```
   npm install -g create-react-app
   ```

3. Create a new app by typing the following command in your console:

   ```
   create-react-app
   ```

The preceding command will create the initial project in the current directory (`chapter12/start/recipe1`).

Note the following helpful message in the console: **Installing packages. This might take a couple minutes**, followed by **Installing react, react-dom, and react-scripts...** on the next row of our console.

4. Run the `npm start` command in your console. A few lines will be logged to the console, with the general information about the folder it is being served from. You will also get a few other notifications in the console:

   ```
   Starting the development server...
   Compiled successfully!
   You can now view recipe1 in the browser.
   Local: http://localhost:3000/
   On Your Network: http://192.168.1.141:3000/
   Note that the development build is not optimized.
   To create a production build, use npm run build.
   ```

   Once compiled and served, your project will open in your browser by itself.

5. View the minimalist web page in your browser; it will have the following text:

   ```
   Welcome to React.
   To get started, edit src/App.js and save to reload.
   ```

6. Press *Ctrl* + *C* in the console to stop the development server, as in the next step we need to add more npm packages.

7. Now, we will add Bootstrap 4 Alpha 6 via npm:

```
npm install bootstrap@4.0.0-alpha.6 --save
```

8. Follow it up with the installation of reactstrap and its related packages:

```
npm install --save reactstrap react-addons-transition-group react-
addons-css-transition-group react react-dom
```

9. Add Bootstrap 4 CSS to the `src/index.js` file:

```
import 'bootstrap/dist/css/bootstrap.css';
```

10. Your `src/index.js` file should now look like this:

```
import React from 'react';
import ReactDOM from 'react-dom';
import App from './App';
import registerServiceWorker from './registerServiceWorker';
//import './index.css';
import 'bootstrap/dist/css/bootstrap.css';

ReactDOM.render(<App />, document.getElementById('root'));
registerServiceWorker();
```

11. Delete all the code from `src/App.js`, and in its place, add the following code:

```
import React, { Component } from 'react';
import {
  Collapse,
  Navbar,
  NavbarToggler,
  NavbarBrand,
  Nav,
  NavItem,
  NavLink,
  Container,
  Row,
  Col,
  Jumbotron,
  Button
} from 'reactstrap';

class App extends Component {
  constructor(props) {
    super(props);
```

```
    this.toggle = this.toggle.bind(this);
      this.state = {
        isOpen: false
      };
  }
  toggle() {
    this.setState({
      isOpen: !this.state.isOpen
    });
  }
  render() {
    return (
      <div>
        <Navbar color="inverse" inverse toggleable>
          <NavbarToggler right onClick={this.toggle} />
          <NavbarBrand href="/">reactstrap</NavbarBrand>
          <Collapse isOpen={this.state.isOpen} navbar>
            <Nav className="ml-auto" navbar>
              <NavItem>
                <NavLink href="/components/">Components</NavLink>
              </NavItem>
              <NavItem>
                <NavLink
                href="https://github.com/reactstrap/reactstrap">
                Github</NavLink>
              </NavItem>
            </Nav>
          </Collapse>
        </Navbar>
        <Jumbotron>
          <Container>
            <Row>
              <Col>
                <h1>Welcome to React</h1>
                <p>
                  <Button
                    tag="a"
                    color="success"
                    size="large"
                    href="http://reactstrap.github.io"
                    target="_blank"
                  >
                    View Reactstrap Docs
                  </Button>
                </p>
              </Col>
            </Row>
          </Container>
```

```
        </Jumbotron>
      </div>
    );
  }
}

export default App;
```

12. While still in `src/App.js`, replace the contents of the import (starting at line 2 of the preceding file), with the following:

```
import {
  Button,
  Card,
  CardText,
  CardTitle,
  Col,
  Collapse,
  Container,
  Jumbotron,
  Nav,
  Navbar,
  NavbarBrand,
  NavbarToggler,
  NavItem,
  NavLink,
  Row
}
```

13. Add a simple card under the jumbotron section, by inserting the following code just under the closing `</Jumbotron>` tag in `src/App.js`:

```
      </Jumbotron>
      <Container>
      <Row>
        <Col>
          <Card block>
            <CardTitle>This is some text within a card block.
            </CardTitle>
            <CardText>With supporting text below as a natural lead-
            in...</CardText>
          </Card>
        </Col>
      </Row>
      </Container>
  </div>
    );
```

```
    }
}
export default App;
```

 For a complete list of examples of components to use, make sure that you check out the reactstrap examples at `https://reactstrap.github.io/co mponents/`.

How it works...

In this recipe, we have used Facebook's own create-react-app, a repository that has been starred almost 29,000 times on GitHub. At the time of writing this book, there were 1,060 commits on the project with 311 contributors.

We follow the *Getting started* guide up to the section that deals with Bootstrap integration. Unfortunately, it only caters for the integration with version 3 of the framework (which will stay that way until the official Bootstrap 4 release).

We easily went around that issue by integrating Bootstrap 4 components with the help of the excellent reactstrap npm package.

 There are a lot of complexities that have been avoided in this recipe, in order to make it work without having to introduce too many unfamiliar concepts. If you are interested in learning more about integrating React and Bootstrap, check out the following title from the Packt website: `Learning Web Development with React and Bootstrap`

Replacing the Default Styles in Angular 2 QuickStart with Bootstrap 4 CDN CSS

While React is the V in MVC, Angular is a full-blown framework. In this recipe, we will first take a look at how to install Angular 2 on our system using npm, and then we'll take a look at how to incorporate Bootstrap 4 CDN styles.

Getting ready

To get ready, we will visit the QuickStart guide, from the official documentation, which can be found at `https://angular.io/guide/quickstart`. There are a couple of prerequisites that we need to satisfy, namely that we use Node version 6.9.x or greater and NPM version 3.x.x.

To check the versions we are using, we need to run the following commands in our console:

```
node -v;
npm -v
```

 If you need to have multiple versions of Node installed on your machine, you may look into **Node Version Manager** (**NVM**). For more information, visit `https://github.com/creationix/nvm`.

How to do it...

1. First, we will install Angular CLI. Note that the command that follows will install a lot of npm packages, so you may need to wait some time for it to complete. To install Angular CLI, run the following command in your console:

    ```
    npm install -g @angular/cli
    ```

2. Now, we can install a new Angular project. This will also take quite some time, so be prepared to wait. Type the following command and wait for it to complete its installation:

    ```
    ng new recipe2
    ```

3. Once the preceding command is finished, you can cd into your recipe2 Angular app and run it:

    ```
    cd recipe2;
    ng serve --open
    ```

4. The preceding command will open your browser automatically, at `http://localhost:4200/`. Preview the app being served; it should have the **Welcome to app!!** heading with a big Angular logo under it.

5. Among other things that the Angular CLI made is an example component, available at `recipe2/src/app/app.component.ts`. Open this file in your editor, and you will see the following code:

```
import { Component } from '@angular/core';
@Component({
  selector: 'app-root',
  templateUrl: './app.component.html',
  styleUrls: ['./app.component.css']
})
export class AppComponent {
  title = 'app';
}
```

6. Looking at the `@Component` section of the code, note the `templateUrl: './app.component.html'`. Open the file referenced there, erase its contents, and replace it with this code:

```
<div class="container">
  <div class="jumbotron">
    <h1>
      Welcome to {{title}}!!
    </h1>
    <hr>
    <p>Lorem ipsum dolor sit amet, consectetur adipisicing.</p>
  </div>
</div>
```

What is this `@Component` thing? It is a decorator. Here is a quote from the official Angular documentation:

Component decorator allows you to mark a class as an Angular component and provide additional metadata that determines how the component should be processed, instantiated and used at runtime.

Components are the most basic building block of an UI in an Angular application.

To find out more, check out `https://angular.io/api/core/Component`.

7. At the @Component section of the code, note the styleUrls: ['./app.component.css'] line of code. Open the referenced CSS file, and note that it is empty. That's why the initial web page of our Angular app did not have any styles. We will change that, not by adding styles to the app.component.css, but rather by adding global styles to our app. To do that, open the styles.css file at the root of the src folder, and paste in the following code under the comment so that it looks like this:

```
/* You can add global styles to this file, and also import other
style files */
@import
"https://maxcdn.bootstrapcdn.com/bootstrap/4.0.0-alpha.6/css/bootst
rap.min.css";
```

8. OK, now let's look at our browser. No change! Obviously, there is a bug here. Here is how to fix it. In your console, press CTRL + C to stop ng serve. Run ng build and then run ng serve --open again.

9. Your browser page serving the Angular app should now have a simple jumbotron with an h1 heading, an hr, and a paragraph.

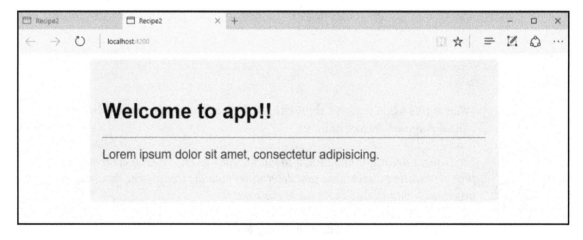

How it works...

In step 1, we installed the Angular CLI. In step 2, upon running the `ng new recipe2` command, we could see the following logging in our console:

```
installing ng
  create .editorconfig
  create README.md
  create src\app\app.component.css
  create src\app\app.component.html
  create src\app\app.component.spec.ts
  create src\app\app.component.ts
  create src\app\app.module.ts
  create src\assets\.gitkeep
  create src\environments\environment.prod.ts
  create src\environments\environment.ts
  create src\favicon.ico
  create src\index.html
  create src\main.ts
  create src\polyfills.ts
  create src\styles.css
  create src\test.ts
  create src\tsconfig.app.json
  create src\tsconfig.spec.json
  create src\typings.d.ts
  create .angular-cli.json
  create e2e\app.e2e-spec.ts
  create e2e\app.po.ts
  create e2e\tsconfig.e2e.json
  create .gitignore
  create karma.conf.js
  create package.json
  create protractor.conf.js
  create tsconfig.json
  create tslint.json
Successfully initialized git.
Installing packages for tooling via npm.
```

The command starts off by creating project files, then follows it up by initializing a Git repository, and finally it installs the necessary NMP packages.

In steps 3 and 4, we serve the default QuickStart App. In steps 5-7, we look at the `@Component` directive and change our `app-root` component, by altering its `app.component.html` and `src/styles.css`.

We changed the CSS in the `src/styles.css` file simply using the `@import` statement to call a minified version of Bootstrap 4 CSS from a CDN. We could have even just pasted in the complete CSS code directly this way. Although that would work, it would not be too efficient.

In the next recipe, we will look at improving our setup.

Integrating Angular 4 and Bootstrap 4 with the help of ng-bootstrap

In this recipe, we will build from the knowledge gained from the preceding recipe. Now that we understand just a bit about decorators and how components work, we can build a simple home page using Angular 4 and Bootstrap 4. However, in this recipe, we will take it a step further, by including `ng-bootstrap` into our project.

To find out more about `ng-bootstrap`, visit the project website at `https://ng-bootstrap.github.io/#/home`.

Getting ready

We will go through a similar scenario like in the preceding recipe. To get ready, verify that the installed version of Node on your system is at least 6.9, and that the version of npm you have is at least 3.x.x.

How to do it...

1. Open the console and `cd` to `chapter12/start`.
2. Run `ng new recipe3` to have Angular CLI start a new project called "recipe3".
3. Go to the new project, that is, `cd recipe3`.
4. Add Bootstrap 4 via NPM:

```
npm install bootstrap@4.0.0-alpha.6 --save
```

5. Add `ng-bootstrap` by running the following command in your console:

```
npm install @ng-bootstrap/ng-bootstrap --save
```

6. In the preceding recipe, we worked with the default component. Now, let's add a custom component:

```
ng generate component jumbotron
```

7. Go to `src/app/app.component.html`, delete everything, and add the following code:

```
<app-jumbotron></app-jumbotron>
```

8. In `app/jumbotron/jumbotron.component.html`, add the following code:

```
<div class="jumbotron jumbotron-fluid">
 <div class="container">
 <h1 class="display-3">Fluid jumbotron</h1>
 <p class="lead">This is a modified jumbotron that occupies the
entire horizontal space of its parent.</p>
 </div>
</div>
```

9. In `src/styles.css`, add the following code:

```
/* You can add global styles to this file, and also import other
style files */
@import "~bootstrap/dist/css/bootstrap.min.css";
```

10. Stop the `ng serve` command in your console by pressing CTRL C.
11. Generate the `navbar` component in the console:

```
ng generate component navbar
```

12. Copy the code for the navbar on the official docs at `https://v4-alpha.getboots trap.com/components/navbar/#supported-content`.
13. Open the `src/app/navbar/navbar.component.html` and paste in the code copied in the preceding step:

```
<nav class="navbar navbar-toggleable-md navbar-light bg-faded">
 <button class="navbar-toggler navbar-toggler-right" type="button"
data-toggle="collapse" data-target="#navbarSupportedContent" aria-
controls="navbarSupportedContent" aria-expanded="false" aria-
label="Toggle navigation">
 <span class="navbar-toggler-icon"></span>
```

```
    </button>
    <a class="navbar-brand" href="#">Navbar</a>

    <div class="collapse navbar-collapse" id="navbarSupportedContent">
    <ul class="navbar-nav mr-auto">
    <li class="nav-item active">
    <a class="nav-link" href="#">Home <span class="sr-
only">(current)</span></a>
    </li>
    <li class="nav-item">
    <a class="nav-link" href="#">Link</a>
    </li>
    <li class="nav-item">
    <a class="nav-link disabled" href="#">Disabled</a>
    </li>
    </ul>
    <form class="form-inline my-2 my-lg-0">
    <input class="form-control mr-sm-2" type="text"
placeholder="Search">
    <button class="btn btn-outline-success my-2 my-sm-0"
type="submit">Search</button>
    </form>
    </div>
    </nav>
```

14. Go to `src/app/app.component.html`, and add a new line to the very top of the
    file:

    ```
    <app-navbar></app-navbar>
    ```

15. Save all the files, and run `ng build`.

16. Serve your Angular app with a couple additional options, `ng serve --port
    8080 --open`, and view the result in the browser at `localhost:8080`.

How it works...

In steps 1 through 4, we set up our new Angular app. In step 5, we added the `ng-
bootstrap` package.

To generate a new component using Angular CLI, we have the following command:

```
ng generate component name-of-component
```

In step 6, we used the preceding command, naming our component "jumbotron". This command generated four additional files related to the component, and updated the `src/app/app.module.ts` file.

In step 7, we called the jumbotron component. In step 8, we added the code to our jumbotron component.

In step 9, we specified the styles to include. Steps 11 through 14 involve the creation of the navbar component.

In steps 15 and 16, we build and serve our Angular app.

Conclusion

Congratulations! You just went through quite a journey with Bootstrap 4. We have covered a lot of different topics and technologies in this book. There is always more to cover, and it is always possible to go into greater depth with any of the topics covered in this book's chapters. Now that you have gone through these recipes, you should be able to build wonderful custom-made sites with Bootstrap 4.

Next Steps

Hopefully, going through this book was a positive learning experience for you. If you are interested in learning even more about Bootstrap 4, make sure that you check out the Packt website, using the search term of Bootstrap 4, or simply go to the following link: `https://www.packtpub.com/all?search=bootstrap%204`.

Also, you can never go wrong with going back to basics and reading the official Bootstrap documentation, currently available at `https://v4-alpha.getbootstrap.com/getting-started/introduction/`.

Index

.
.display-*
  text classes, displaying 69
.NET Core project
  .NET Core project 293
  Bower, working with 291, 293, 294
  Grunt, working with 292, 294, 296
  Sass, working with 292, 293, 295, 296

A

Angular 2 QuickStart
  default styles, replacing with Bootstrap 4 CDN
    CSS 303, 304, 307
Angular 4
  Bootstrap 4 integration, ng-bootstrap used 308
animatedModal.js
  references 196
  used, for integrating fancy modal 195

B

blockquote element
  customizing, with CSS 81
blockquote styles
  extending, with Sass 84
blog
  deploying to web, with GitHub 278, 279, 280,
    281
Bootgrid
  plain tables, converting to sophisticated data
    tables 186
  references 186
Bootstrap 4 docs
  styles, customizing 17
Bootstrap 4
  custom Grunt tasks, creating 20
  installing, to Cloud9 IDE via git 12

  installing, to Cloud9 IDE with Bower 27
  installing, to Cloud9 IDE with npm 8
  integrating with Angular 4, ng-bootstrap used
    308, 309
  integrating, with React 298, 299, 302, 303
  Jekyll, making work with 261
  used, for setting up static server 30
  versions, comparing with Bower 24
Bootstrap builds
  customizing, by cherry-picking Sass partials 251,
    252, 253, 255
Bootstrap docs
  references 61
Bootstrap repo
  URL 13
Bootstrap Select plugin
  references 174
  Select Elements, functionality extending 174
Bootstrap Toggle plugin
  checkboxes, converting into Toggles 164
Bootstrap Tour plugin
  users, onboarding 167
Bootstrap
  reference link 95
  typography classes, text content enriching 78
  URL 8, 258
Bower
  Bootstrap 4 versions, comparing 24
  Bootstrap 4, installing 27
Bundler 14
button add-ons
  reference link 170
button groups
  rounding of corners, adjusting 113
buttons
  rounding of corners, adjusting 113
buttons component

references 110

C

c9.io
  reference link 7
card decks
  reference link 120
card layouts
  working with, flexbox grid used 232, 233, 234,
    236, 237, 238, 239
card-columns component
  number, controlling with SCSS on different
    breakpoints 116
  reference link 117
cards responsive
  making 120
cards
  center-aligning, on wider viewport only 239, 240,
    241, 242, 243
  taking up space, with .flex-wrap and .col classes
    223, 224, 225, 226
Cheatsheet
  reference link 170
checkboxes
  converting, into Toggles with Bootstrap Toggle
    plugin 164
clearfix
  reference link 87
CLI (command line interface) 31
Cloud9 IDE
  Bootstrap 4, installing with Bower 27
Cloud9 IDE
  Bootstrap 4, installing via git 12
  Bootstrap 4, installing with npm 8
col-* classes
  working 53
columns
  adding, in row 51
  adding, with flexbox 226, 227, 228, 229
comment section
  creating, media objects used 74
components
  reference link 98
  references 113
constraint options 107

containers
  data-* HTML5 attributes 48
  main.scss, renaming 49
  using, with margin class 46
  using, with padding class 46
CSS comments
  removing, with grunt-strip-CSS-comments plugin
    259, 260
CSS shaped polyfill
  reference link 91
CSS shapes
  references 91
CSS
  blockquote element, customizing 81
  unused, cleaning with Grunt 256
  unused, cleaning with UnCSS 256
custom alerts
  creating 97
  positioning, in viewport 97
custom buttons
  creating, Sass mixins used 110
custom Grunt tasks
  creating, in Bootstrap 4 20
custom jQuery code
  password fields, visibility Toggle 170
custom plugin
  creating, with extend() and each() methods 211,
    212
  working 213, 215
customizable notifications
  adding, with Notifyjs 193
Cygwin 13

D

default buttons
  reference link 110
default grid
  page, building 55
  real-life web page example, building 60
default styles, Angular 2 QuickStart
  replacing, with Bootstrap 4 CDN CSS 304
default table classes
  used, for pricing section styling 91
default web page, of .NET Core project
  migrating, from Bootstrap 3 to Bootstrap 4 287,

288
Document Object Model (DOM) 101
drop-down component
  reference link 146, 152, 157

E

Embedded JS (EJS)
  about 44
  reference link 44

F

fancy modal
  integrating, animatedModal.js used 195
flex direction, on card components
  breakpoint-dependent switching 220, 221
  working 221, 222
flex property
  reference link 134
Flexbox
  navbar, creating 141
Font Awesome icon font
  reference link 61
Font Awesome
  adding, to navbar 127
forms
  validating, with svalidate.js 202
full-page modals
  creating 101

G

Git Bash 13
git
  Bootstrap 4, installing to Cloud9 IDE 12
GitHub
  used, for deploying blog to web 278, 279, 280,
  281
grunt-sass plugin
  reference link 256
grunt-strip-CSS-comments plugin
  used, for removing CSS comments 259
Grunt
  used for cleaning unused CSS 256
  used, for setting up static server 30

H

Harp project
  reference link 44
  splitting, into partials 44
Harp
  URL 30, 66
  used, for setting up static server 30
hover effects
  adding, with Hover.css 69
Hover.css
  references 70
  used, for adding hover effects 69

I

Icons
  navbar, creating 141
Immediately-Invoked Function Expressionan (IIFE)
  210
inline forms
  positioning 122
input fields
  dates, adding with jQuery UI datepicker 182
Input Sliders
  adding, with Rangeslider.js 179

J

Jekyll blog-aware
  creating 271, 272, 273, 275, 276, 277, 278
Jekyll
  about 14
  files, splitting into partials 266, 267, 268, 270,
  271
  installing 15
  making work, with Bootstrap 4 261, 262, 263,
  264, 265, 266
jQuery Bar Rating plugin
  references 205
  used, for adding rating system 204
jQuery Pagination plugin
  pagination, making dynamic 199
jQuery plugins
  creating 207
jQuery simple-sidebar plugin
  reference link 189

utilizing 189
jQuery UI datepicker
  dates, adding to input fields 182
  reference link 182

L

layout, Bootstrap 4
  reference link 46

M

margin class
  containers, used 46
media objects
  used, for creating comment sections 74
modal component
  reference link 101, 104

N

nav-tabs
  positioning, with flexbox 243, 244, 246, 247, 248
navbar component
  reference link 146, 152, 157
navbar dropdown
  Yamm3 Megamenu images, adding 152
  Yamm3 Megamenu list of links, adding to 157
navbar
  creating, with Flexbox 141
  creating, with Icons 141
  dropdown, placing to right 131
  Font Awesome, adding to 127
  links, centering 134
  reference link 128, 131
  row of links, adding 146
ng-bootstrap
  used, for Angular 4 and Bootstrap 4 integration 309
Node Package Manager (NPM) 291
Notifyjs
  customizable notifications, adding 193
  reference link 193
numbered .col classes
  combining, with plain .col classes 230, 231

O

offset options 107

P

padding class
  containers, used 46
page
  building, with default grid 55
pagination
  making, dynamic with jQuery Pagination plugin 199
  making, dynamic with simplePagination.js 199
  references 199
password fields
  visibility, with custom jQuery code 170
pixels, for image
  reference link 61
plain tables
  converting, to sophisticated data tables with Bootgrid 186
plugins
  reference 22
popover component
  references 105
popups
  behavior, altering tether options used 105
pricing section
  styling, default table classes used 91
project
  starting in ASP.NET Core and Bootstrap 4, Visual Studio 2017 used 283, 285, 286

R

Rangeslider.js
  Input Sliders, adding 179
  references 179
rating system
  adding, jQuery Bar Rating plugin used 204
React
  Bootstrap 4, integrating with 298
real-life web page example
  building, with default grid 60
reboot
  reference link 96

responsive breakpoints
  reference link 88
rounded images
  text, wrapping 88
row of links
  adding, to navbar 146
row
  columns, adding 51

S

Sass mixins
  used, for creating custom buttons 110
Sass partials
  cherry-picking, for customizing Bootstrap builds
   251
Sass variables
  used, for controlling color of ToolTips 108
  used, for controlling opacity of ToolTips 108
Sass
  blockquote styles, extending 84
SCSS
  number of card-columns component, controlling
   with breakpoints 116
Select Boxes
  customizing, with Select2 plugin 177
Select Elements
  functionality, extending with Bootstrap Select
   plugin 174
Select2 plugin
  references 177
  Select Boxes, customizing 177
shape-outside property
  reference link 88
simple CSS Class Replacement plugin
  integrating, with Bootstrap 4 216, 217
  working 218
simplePagination.js
  pagination, making dynamic 199
simplest possible jQuery plugin
  creating 207, 208
  working 210, 211
static server
  setting up, with Bootstrap 4 30
  setting up, with Grunt 30
  setting up, with Harp 30

Surge
  reference link 41
  web project, deploying 41
svalidate.js
  forms, validating 202
  references 202

T

tether options
  reference link 105
  used, for adding behavior of popups 105
text around images
  aligning 85
text classes
  extending, of .display-* 69
text content
  enriching, with Bootstrap typography classes 78
text
  wrapping, around rounded images 88
Toggle
  checkboxes, converting with Bootstrap Toggle
   plugin 164
  references 164
ToolTip component
  color, controlling Sass variables used 108
  opacity, controlling Sass variables used 108
  references 108
transparent navbar
  creating, on darker background 137

U

UnCSS
  used, for cleaning unused CSS 256
users
  onboarding, with Bootstrap Tour plugin 167

V

viewport
  custom alerts, positioning 98
Visual Studio 2017
  used, for starting project in ASP.NET Core and
   Bootstrap 4 283, 285, 286

W

web project
  deploying, with Surge 41

Y

Yamm3 Megamenu images
  adding, to navbar dropdown 152
  reference link 152, 157
Yamm3 Megamenu list
  of links, adding to navbar dropdown 157
Yamm3
  reference link 157

www.ingramcontent.com/pod-product-compliance
Lightning Source LLC
Chambersburg PA
CBHW062059050326

40690CB00016B/3144